For Vivienne
Enjoy reading
Regards Warren 6/5/17

CW01551692

BEYOND BELIEF
LIVING A FEARLESS LIFE

DR. WARREN STANTON

BALBOA. PRESS
A DIVISION OF HAY HOUSE

Domain name: warrenstanton.com
Email: dr.warrenstanton@gmail.com

Copyright © 2015 Warren R Stanton.

All rights reserved. No part of this book may be used or reproduced by any means, graphic, electronic, or mechanical, including photocopying, recording, taping or by any information storage retrieval system without the written permission of the publisher except in the case of brief quotations embodied in critical articles and reviews.

Graphics design of diagrams and cover by Michelle Sonter, Masarnie Creative
Cover concept of Meeting with Warren by Greg Jorss, Upside Creative
Back cover photo by Hillary Green [hill@stillsbyhill.com.au]

Balboa Press books may be ordered through booksellers or by contacting:

Balboa Press
A Division of Hay House
1663 Liberty Drive
Bloomington, IN 47403
www.balboapress.com.au
1 (877) 407-4847

Because of the dynamic nature of the Internet, any web addresses or links contained in this book may have changed since publication and may no longer be valid. The views expressed in this work are solely those of the author and do not necessarily reflect the views of the publisher, and the publisher hereby disclaims any responsibility for them.

The author of this book does not dispense medical advice or prescribe the use of any technique as a form of treatment for physical, emotional, or medical problems without the advice of a physician, either directly or indirectly. The intent of the author is only to offer information of a general nature to help you in your quest for emotional and spiritual well-being. In the event you use any of the information in this book for yourself, which is your constitutional right, the author and the publisher assume no responsibility for your actions.

Print information available on the last page.

ISBN: 978-1-4525-2618-8 (sc)
ISBN: 978-1-4525-2619-5 (e)

Balboa Press rev. date: 06/11/2015

Acknowledgements

Thanks to the many people who read earlier drafts of this book and provided valuable comments for editing, in particular Michele Stanton, Jacob Stanton, Kara Stanton, Gail Libman, the extended time of Marianne Cameron, and the professional editing skills of Helena Bond. I also recognize the contribution of the many people who have attended the discussion sessions over the past 15 years where a lot of the ideas were tested and refined, in particular those who 'lasted the longest' including Crissi Schmidt, Gail Libman, Angela Culhane, Sue Goodwin, Ric Raymond, Maya Rusch, Jurgen Rusch, and Dietrich Lasa. Special thanks to the tenacity of my wife Michele - still lasting! Thanks also to Jost Sauer for helping me get back on track on my return to Australia in 1998. Many others have listened to me, challenged me, given their insights, and supported my efforts; too many to mention, though I do remember you and appreciate your contributions.

Dedication

To life and all who sail upon her

Contents

Foreword xi
Preface xiii
Introduction 1
The Story of a Lifetime 1
    Summary 4
One 5
You Know 5
    Instinctive Knowing 8
    The Limit to Thinking 11
    Subjective Impressions and Objective Thought ... 16
    A New Approach 20
    Summary 22
Two 24
Our Dilemma 24
    Why do We Care? 26
    Beliefs versus Instinct 27
    Creative Capacity of Our Mind 36
    Summary 38
Three 42
Good Use and Misuse of Our Minds 42
    Being in Two Minds 43
    Our Minds in Discord 51
    Misunderstanding the Output of Our Minds 55

  The Bottom Line...60
 Summary...61
Four...63
Beliefs...63
  Beliefs, from Simple to Abstract 64
  Belief versus Experience..69
  Misuse of Attention..71
  Pain versus Suffering..74
  Intelligent Cooperation of Our Minds.........................76
 Summary...80
Five..82
Unpleasant Experiences 82
  Making Problems..83
  Learning to See Life as a Horrible Experience............87
 Summary...96
Six..98
Belief in Fear...98
  The Nature of Fear...99
  The Difference between Fright and Fear 100
  Fright without Fear 102
  A Culture of Fear 107
  Why use Fear?... 110
  The Extremities of Fear... 113
  The Consequences of Controlling Fear...................... 116
 Summary... 119
Seven... 121
Belief in Control 121
  In Control versus In Charge... 124
  The Harm Done by Choosing Control...................... 127
  Thinking without Control 131
 Summary... 137

Eight	140
Choice of Belief or Instinct	140
Challenging our Belief in Discipline	141
Want versus Need	144
The Prisoner's Dilemma	150
Positive Thinking	157
Life Wasn't Meant to be Easy	161
Listening to the Objective or Subjective Mind	163
Summary	167
Nine	170
Living the Natural Solution	170
Creating Ill-health	170
Deposing Fear from the Throne	172
The Nature of the Beast	172
Freeing Our Mind of Fear	174
The Solution to Release Fear and Control	176
Instilling the Input from Instinct	179
Free Choice to Express the Solution with Beliefs	179
Goodwill versus Control	183
Summary	188
Ten	190
Knowing Your Will	190
Instinct without Fear	191
The Direction of Instinct	193
An End to Suffering	195
Listening to Instinct	200
The Source of Instinct	207
Summary	211
Eleven	214
Well-being Beyond Belief	214
Choosing Wisely	215
Mindfulness-based Positive Psychology	219

  Mindfulness Viewed as Giving Attention 221
  A New Direction for Mindfulness 224
  Mindfulness Existence (ME) 229
  ME in Practice 236
 Summary 245
Twelve 249
Finding the Meaning of Life 249
  No Idea 250
  Asking the Question 254
  Guided Self-exploration 256
  Philosophy of the Meaning of Life 259
  Getting Answers that Satisfy 261
  Still No Idea? 267
 Summary 273
Appendix 277
Introducing ME to Clients – A Health Practitioner's Guide 277
  An Introduction to MBEA 279
Index 289

Foreword

Thirty five years ago my interest in anything to do with consciousness resulted in my meeting Warren. When I first experienced the early stages of what would later become my preferred way of living, never would I have thought that I would become a part of the final recording of the development of this, his brainchild.

Imagine for a moment that a mindful act which allows you to live a more meaningful and self-determining life could be understood simply and effectively by reading about it in a book such as this.

Such is the journey you are about to embark on. After having read this book, I have noticed the extent to which the ideas contained in it have given me a much greater understanding of how my mind can and does work in a positive and life affirming way, or to the contrary depending on what I choose to believe.

Journeying through the chapters, the concepts and ideas presented for your consideration subtly show the foundation for living simply, effectively and mindfully in the present, where the worries of the past, or anxiety about the future, need no longer be part of day to day life. This too can be your reality for the choosing.

When I asked Warren why he had written the book in the first place, his response was "to set the record straight. It is a story that has to be told about the power of our minds. The mess that we as a species have got ourselves into needs to be resolved". Who better to demonstrate how, than someone who has lived the majority of his life experimenting, developing and refining this process, and in the course of this becoming an example of what is possible.

An exemplary 'thought experiment', expressed in such a way as to take you on a journey that culminates beautifully and almost magically in the closing chapters. It left me feeling I can apply what I read, and be equipped with an uncomplicated and effective means to live happily ever-after. You too are able to sail over life's stormy seas riding the peak of the wave, instead of losing one's self in the murky depths, which is where I'm sure many would agree, most of us find ourselves.

If you wish to discover how to use the abilities you already have to move forward and live a more rewarding life, carefully read and study the thoughts set out in this book. As for Warren, some say he is a genius, others say a saint. He says we all are both, and more. He also has been called all sorts of horrible names, but not one of us is truly any of these. If you can make an opportunity to study this person or interact with him, do not pass it up!

Marianne Cameron

PREFACE

Can we know the meaning of life? We can if our minds answer every question we ask, and we know the truth when we think it. Can we live happily without suffering? We can if we have a mind that can conceive of anything, and we choose wisely. This book was written to reveal what I found out about my mind; how to live a fearless life, and get a meaningful answer to any question about life. Along the way I would like to explain how a pleasant life experience happens, and how you can have one now, and each moment that follows.

What you are about to read has not been told before—not like this. This is a story about the human mind; how we use it and how we abuse it. The good news is we have a choice to have pleasant experiences or unpleasant ones. We are the architects of our own suffering, and it is in our hands to do the unthinkable; to create an enjoyable life and not suffer.

The contents of this book are a result of my lifetime of self-exploration and self-encounter. This is an account of how I moved from a life of hell to one hell of a life. But more importantly, my experiences can be verified in yours.

This story is about each and every one of us. It is the story of life. Not the physical events, but the main part of our life; the experience created in our minds. We are all on a journey to know what life is about, and one of the things we can come to know is, we do not have to suffer unpleasant experiences. This seems an outrageous statement because we have suffered for so long, and so many have sought to address this undesirable event. So what have we overlooked in our efforts to resolve this dilemma?

My contribution to our journey is to describe what I have discovered about how our minds work, and how they can be used to benefit us. The misuse of our minds causes us to have unpleasant experiences in life. This is my definition of suffering. The question is, would you like to know why we make ourselves suffer? And would you then prefer to use your mind to have a life full of pleasant experiences? The path to this has implications for those who want to heal their pain and those willing to assist others to do the same, but most of all for those who simply want to know themselves.

Could there be a solution right in front of our noses which we have not understood? Yes, and the solution I found that works for me, is delivered in this book. It truly is beyond belief. The solution is simple, though a good part of the story is in the detail. This is important if we want to clean up the unpleasant mess we have created.

While you are settling in to read this book, consider this example. If you let go and let yourself be still, what do you sense? In the first instant is it a pleasant sensation, for example calm, relaxed or happy? If so, can you accept you did not produce it with pleasant thoughts? This is evidence of your true nature. **You are not dependent on thinking, to be calm and happy. Then, if you give this pleasant sense more attention, does it start to increase or have a greater effect?** Read on for how to experience a life of pleasantness. I start with an introduction on how beliefs are created, to set the scene for your self-exploration.

Study this story and I promise you a description of how to end your suffering and live happily ever after. This you can create for a moment in time or for the rest of your life . It's in your hands!

Introduction
The Story of a Lifetime

My goal in writing this book is to explain the human experience of life—our experience. It was prompted by my personal experiences of the highs and lows of life, and my wish to resolve what I thought was wrong with me. The path I take is a little unorthodox, but the implications of a life without suffering are far reaching by any measure.

I have placed the discussion of everyday experiences in the context of the loftiest question I could think to ask; what is the meaning of life? Such a question provides an opportunity to explore most people's experience of life events. Along the way, I want to identify our main issues with life and offer some practical solutions to deal with them. So the nuts and bolts content of the book is a down-to-earth examination of how your minds work and what you are capable of doing with them. This includes discussion of what we do that is harmful to us, and how to change it.

In this book I'll explore four of the most sought-after explanations of the human experience:

1. How do our minds work?
2. How can we live a pleasant life without suffering?

3. How do we get a satisfying answer to any question we ask?
4. How can we live a fearless life?

When all is said and done I return to the question about the meaning of life, to test whether even lofty questions have a practical, satisfying answer. In general, people do not get satisfying answers to such questions. This does not mean these answers do not exist, and I will explain why and how you can get them. In exploring this, I also reveal why we have unpleasant experiences in life, and how we can choose to have pleasant ones. The end of our suffering is at hand! I demonstrate how our mind can create pleasant experiences, and explain just how good life can be, if we want to live that way.

This story is based on five basic human experiences. These can be described simply as follows:

1. Each of us has an instinctive sense of knowing, which is the essence of intelligence.
2. As a consequence, we have an instinctive appetite to want to know ourselves.
3. Our natural condition or true nature is a sense of harmony and pleasantness, despite appearances.
4. We are creators; everything we think and do is like an artist creating the story of a life.
5. We often use our thinking, based in the objective mind, to create unpleasant experiences in life which are not in accord with our true nature.

These five experiences can be used to reframe how we look at life, and how we guide others to look at their life events. They represent the means to move from a life of suffering to one of freedom.

These five statements describe repeatable and verifiable experiences in life. They are not derived from beliefs, and I do not present them as my beliefs. They are not statements I want you to believe in. Rather, they are experiences I invite you to explore; to consider their significance and application. Throughout the book I will show how they gave me a way out of the hell that was going on in my life. I trust you can relate them to your life, and by the end of the book you can regard the practical end to your suffering as something well within your grasp.

As you read this book, I hope you come to understand why I regard these experiences as self-evident truths which apply to all of us, and why I do not hold them up as beliefs. I have no affiliation with any school of thinking, and the ideas presented here do not represent any organization or institution. These ideas and insights are offered by me as an independent thinker for your consideration. If by the end of this book you have a glimpse of where you could go with these ideas, my goal is accomplished.

In my role as a counselor, I have talked to many people about their experiences of life. Most of them have no objection to the above description of our potential and our plight. The majority of people seem aware of these basic human experiences, or they find them to be acceptable ideas. In this case, enjoy your reading. If you think you have not had these experiences, nor accept them as a possibility, reading this book may be more challenging. If you accept the challenge, you are likely to gain a great deal from it, so read on. In any event I think you will find this book both challenging and enjoyable.

Summary

My goal for this book is to explain the human experience:

- There are practical solutions for all of our issues with life.
- Why do we have unpleasant experiences in life? How do we resolve them?
- How can we get satisfying answers to questions like "what is the meaning of life?"
- How do our minds work? What harm do we do to ourselves with our thinking?
- How can our minds create pleasant experiences?
- Can we live a fearless life?

Five basic human experiences can be used to reframe how we look at life and move from a life of suffering to one of delight:

- Each of us has an instinctive sense of knowing, which is the essence of intelligence.
- We have an instinctive appetite to know ourselves.
- Our natural condition is a sense of harmony or pleasantness.
- We are creating the story of our lives.
- We often use our thinking minds to go against our nature and create unpleasant experiences.

Everything I claim in this book can and should be verified in your own experience.

ONE

YOU KNOW

I have always had an intense sense I *knew*. This was very much a subjective feeling, not made up of learned opinions or facts. At an early age there seemed to be nothing I could identify as *what* I knew. Yet the sense I knew persisted, as though it were a core part of me. It felt like a source, or primary urge to find meaning in my life. For much of my life through to adulthood, I sought confirmation of this sense of knowing, which I likened to being aware. At the time, it seemed the only way to proceed was by asking questions.

Since I first became aware of my own thoughts, I have been asking questions about myself and others, and exploring the answers. Why did that classmate ridicule others, while I didn't want to? What ability allowed him to reduce other classmates to tears in less than five minutes? How was I to escape this fate? I also recognized, I had been asking such questions from a very early age, perhaps as young as five. If you are inclined to interpret my introspection in a negative way, bear with me; being centered in self in this way is vastly different from being self-centered. I will return to the distinction shortly.

How did I arrive at the conclusions I'm about to reveal? Quite simply, I have spent my life studying myself! The context for this includes my mind and body, as well as my relationships with people and the world around me. However, this is true for all of us; we have a natural instinct to explore. In my case, I was most interested in the mind delivering this sense of knowing. Other people's use of their minds was the perfect mirror for my exploration, though I didn't understand this at the start.

I listened intently to what others said, and pondered what I read about every facet of life. Information came readily from many sources, including the thoughts of my elders and religious interpretations of life. During my upbringing, all sorts of things were said about me; ranging from what a good boy I was, to being a disgusting little creature. Much of it just didn't sit well with me. It neither felt right nor made any sense. It confused me no end, but somehow I did not think this was my fault.

In my childhood years, it was very difficult to make sense of what I saw going on around me. Adults were acting in unpleasant ways which seemed strange, even crazy. Did you notice this when you were a child? Why would anyone choose to be unpleasant when they could be pleasant? As a child this didn't make sense to me because, with only a few exceptions, those adults around me were not making sense of life, particularly the ones who believed they were. My conclusion was; there was something about life we didn't understand.

At this stage of my life, very little felt good to me, and I knew I was very unhappy. It seemed the only good feeling I had was coming from the sense I **knew**. So the approach which served me best was to move along, only with the ideas which made sense to me.

Later in life, I realized this sense of knowing was not related to things of the world. Rather, it was an attribute of me which

I brought to the world. It gave me a greater appreciation of life experiences, in particular, knowing I had a place in the world. So when anything made sense to me, it was because it came from an internal, subjective knowing. Coming to know myself is a process of turning my instinctive impressions into conscious understanding. How simple is that? The implication is startling; I do know the truth about myself when I hear it, or more specifically, when I conceive it. I still ask questions, but now I also have answers.

Over decades of exploration, by following the signals of my instinct, I gradually pieced together explanations which made sense. I didn't realize it at the time, but there was a sign I had been using from an early age. If something did not seem right, based on my instinctive impressions of life, then I did not accept it was true. I didn't just believe what I was told. The things I didn't understand were not discarded though. I tucked them away for consideration at a later time, in case some new evidence came to light.

So I'll set the scene with a bold question. Can you and I find the answer to any question about our life experience? What follows in this book are my answers.

If I could give you a mission in reading this book, it is to explore your sense of knowing to see if these answers are true for you. In advocating people explore their own minds, I have made a difficult choice not to cite references—though a couple of recommended readings are included. I hope by the end of the book you will understand the reason behind this decision. In essence, this book is about your sense of knowing, and I am suggesting the only reference you can use to access this is your instinctive impressions of life.

Dr. Warren Stanton

Instinctive Knowing

How could you or I possibly know anything to be true beyond doubt? Having an answer to this question is a major stumbling block for some, so I will say it plainly. The answer is threefold:

1. We have an instinctive sense which recognizes the truth about ourselves. Most people aren't taking notice of this because they have been taught not to listen to it.
2. Our true nature is the instinct felt as a range of pleasant impressions or appetites, which collectively we could call goodwill. This term doesn't seem to have a good name in some circles, but I do not mean some moral code of conduct. I use this term to refer to our natural sense that it is good to be alive—acknowledging some people have lost touch with it. Goodwill supports our continued existence, in the same way hunger supports the continued existence of the body. When we listen to it, there is no doubt in our mind.
3. Most important, we do know what is good for us because we get confirmation. Yes, there is a feedback loop! As most people aren't listening though, they miss this crucial signal.

So what is the nature of this confirmation? It is this; we know if what we have in mind is true by the effect it has on us. Every thought and action carries a pleasant or unpleasant feeling. I think of it as my gift. In other words, confirmation of what we have in mind is provided by the natural effect the thought or action has on our experience of life. In my day this was called instant karma. Note I am talking about consequences here, not conscience. Our intelligence system comes with built-in support for our instinct. **You and I can know if what we have in mind**

is in accord with our true nature, by the effect it has on us mentally, emotionally and physically. This may well be the most important point in this book.

This is true justice. What we have in mind at every point in time, determines whether we are having a pleasant or unpleasant experience in that moment. Even if unpleasant things are going on around us, our attitude and thoughts about the event determine which way we experience it. For instance, consider the situation of being a customer in a shop, when the attendant speaks unpleasantly to you. Your personal experience of unpleasantness only begins when you follow suit and have unpleasant thoughts. Alternatively, what happens if you don't follow suit? Have you ever stayed with a pleasant feeling in a situation such as this? If so, you have confirmed it is possible to stay feeling good. You can even make a comment to the attendant about their unpleasant expression—preferably with a smile.

The eye-opener for me came as the following insight. When I express my instinctive impressions of what feels genuinely good to me, I have a pleasant experience of life! Closer examination of this experience gave me the answer; I am free to choose whether or not to use my mind to create a pleasant experience of life. Listening to my will feels good because it manifests as goodwill; impressions of being happy, friendly, assured, and contented, which I can then give expression. If I do this when the shopkeeper is unpleasant to me, I am not affected. When I don't do this, I leave myself open to the unpleasantness expressed by other people.

Through observation and study, I identified an important fact about life. The things I conceived with my conscious mind became my reality. Created realities, also called belief structures, consist of patterns of thoughts, vivid images, feelings, and body sensations. These realities are the creations of my mind which make up the content of my experiences, be they pleasant or unpleasant ones. So my personal experience shows me what I am creating with my mind. There you have it!

In any and every moment, the choice not to live from a sense of goodwill is the worst choice we can ever make, and as close to a definition of insanity as you can get. Yet this is what we continue to do. We take on board what we are shown and told. As children, we were taught to replace instinct with beliefs, many of which were based in fear. The worst of these is the denial of our personal sense of knowing, which is the main reason we can't make sense of our lives.

As a child, I was told I didn't know anything. With respect to the objective world out there this may have been true, but with respect to my personal, subjective sense of life, it was never true. I do know, as do you.

At some point, the proverbial penny dropped. We do know instinctively what is beneficial. Our will has a way of showing what is true and good for us. This sense of innocence is how we behaved as children before the grown-ups spoiled it. The good news is that the innocence within is always waiting to be heard. In a child we see innocence as naivety, but in an adult mind it is empowering.

Somewhere along the way I came to the following realization; things only made sense when I was listening to **me**. My innocent sense of knowing gave answers! These answers proved I knew, and I applied this to my thoughts as well as the things other people said to me.

I also noticed along the way, everyone is in this same position, and little makes sense to begin with. Our journey is the same. How far each of us has traveled, or how much we have used our sense of knowing, varies among people. It depends on the direction taken, how much encouragement we were given, what was encountered along the way, and how we were taught to deal with it. No matter what differences there are between us, we are fundamentally the same. We all have the same sort of mind and body, the same instinct, the same primary sense of existence, and the same capacity to get answers. What differs is the content of our realities.

The basis for our equality is our instinctive sense of knowing. This is the presenting feature of our intelligence. Our sense of knowing has nothing to do with information learned. It is not about what you know or even who you know, but more simply about realizing you know. This sense of knowing is not learned, but is an instinct felt by us as an appetite to create. You can find it in your sense of wanting to know yourself.

I am using the term instinct to mean the event happening naturally to us, rather than the product of what we think. Instinct is an innate impulse or appetite happening without prior thought. Bear in mind, the act of thinking itself is based in instinct. We do not learn to think any more than we learn to blink. Some people use terms such as intuition or gut feeling as synonyms for instinct. Intuition may be an aspect of instinct, but I am using the term instinct much more broadly. Instinct is best viewed as our natural inclination. Can you think of some appetites not related to your body? Wanting to feel happy, be heard, get ahead in life, and have intimate relationships are all examples. Wanting answers to questions about life is a big one for me.

The Limit to Thinking

In addition to my self-exploration as a philosopher, I have spent my career years as a research academic, learning and applying the scientific approach. The approach presented in this book is consistent with this, but adding instinct to the mix might make the end result look quite different. The disciplines of philosophy and science have both served me well, but something is missing; something more than thinking and experimentation. That something can be found in the instinct, of which both philosophy and science say little. I can only hope the scientific community will someday be pleased with my meticulous observations and study, tested and reproduced with myself as the subject, somewhat like the newly adopted thought experiments of theoretical physicists.

The discipline of philosophy is based on thought structures and reasoning. One poses and ponders questions, seeking solutions in the form of other ideas. Essentially, philosophy means enquiry into any idea entering our mind. Have you ever wondered where this inclination to ask questions comes from? For me, enquiry is one of the most elementary aspects of instinct. It is directly linked to our survival, or in the bigger picture, coming to know about ourselves. Nevertheless, from my endeavors in philosophy I found no evidence of my instinctive sense of knowing, or my subjective sense of existence. In philosophical terminology; I concluded this is because instinct is beyond the realm of reason.

I'll give you a teaser about a philosophical issue I take up later. At school were you taught that our instinct is all about survival, or staying alive? Calling our primary instinct a survival instinct is very, very limiting. Our primary instinct is much more about thriving than surviving. An instinct to thrive is more pro-life than just staying alive. Instead of looking over our shoulder to stay alive, our instinct prompts us to look forward to and enjoy life. This is an entirely different concept to the view we are driven by instinct. In the scenario I present, instinct is not fear-based.

The discipline of science is based on experimental, reproducible proof. One asks questions with the objective mind and seeks evidence in the physical environment to provide answers. Using the scientific approach, I again found no evidence of my subjective knowing or self-evident sense of existing. No matter how much information science provides, like the body being two-thirds water or we usually have 70,000 thoughts a day, it doesn't show the link to the significance of my experience of life. In fact, this subjective sense has traditionally been heavily discouraged in science. Science is objective in its endeavors, and proud of it. For example, understanding the nature of our bodies, other species, and the planet, is based on observable re-producible evidence. The admission of a subjective sense of anything is its antithesis. Science places questions about the meaning of life outside its realm.

However, there is a danger in exclusive use of objective thinking which science does not acknowledge. Objectivity, by definition, means to be impartial or detached. Thus, objective reasoning is supposed to be devoid of any sense of self. We have an objective sense of self developed from thought and images, as well as a subjective, direct experience of self. Objective thinking discards both so as not to contaminate what is being studied. This seems reasonable, as you might expect because it is based on reasoning. The majority of people in western cultures cannot see any problem with placing emphasis squarely on objective reasoning. We apply this paradigm of thinking to life in general, but it comes at a price.

The danger with exclusive use of objective reasoning is the development of information and beliefs which have no bearing on our actual subjective sense of life. In particular, this applies to our senses of self. People relying on objective thinking usually have a sense of self based on individuality—separation from others. Thus a purely objective view of self is at odds with our subjective experience of self, which is based on inclusiveness—totality. This leads to a misconception about our place in the world when we are faced with scientific facts. For example, from the point of view of science we are specks of dust in the universe. Arguably, this view may help when it comes to understanding the laws of physical nature. However, it has adverse implications when it comes to questions about our existence, and the meaningfulness of our lives.

In contrast, our subjective sense does not originate in the objective mind. Alongside the objective mind with its capacity to reason, we have another mind with a capacity to know without reason. A prominent feature of subjectivity is a sense of an inner self independent of thoughts and beliefs. By this I mean an instinctive sense of core self, not the perceived sense of self made up of images and beliefs. This is the realm of subjectivity. Our instinct is part of that mind. It is the same mind which instigates pleasant experiences, and answers questions about our life. In this realm the limits of thinking do not apply.

The subjective event is often referred to as occurring in the subconscious mind. However, in this book I propose a realignment of these terms for the following reasons. The term "subjectivity" means our personal *impressions* of life. Subjectivity is commonly referred to as a source of bias or prejudice in our comprehension of events. This is a belief which should be challenged. Bias in our thinking is due to the beliefs and values we hold. These beliefs and values are our *expressions* about life, developed by the conscious mind. In other words they are a result of our objective reasoning. Even superstitious thinking is the product of faulty objective reasoning, for example thinking that walking under a ladder will result in seven years bad luck. On the other hand, subjectivity is simply and purely the sense of existence experienced as the core or inner self. It is the self-evident sense you exist. As subjectivity is not based on reasoning, it has no capacity to think or affect our thinking. Subjectivity allows us to be impressed by instinct. When instinct is allowed to fuel our thoughts and deeds, a whole brave new world opens which does not interfere with our reasoning.

Throughout the following discussion, the difference in these minds and the experiences they deliver is central to my case. I avoid the term "subconscious mind," for this includes the storehouse of memory; yet memories are produced by the thinking mind. So I refer to the location of our instinct as the subjective mind. Production of information in the form of thoughts and memories enables us to interpret our subjective impressions, and interact with the world. This expression is a creative operation of the conscious mind or thinking mind. I will refer to this as our objective mind for consistency in terminology.

Having said they are different, to me it seems obvious the subjective and objective minds work together. It doesn't make sense to think they are designed by nature to work against each other. If they don't cooperate, we have little chance of living happily or answering any questions about the meaning of life. Yet for most people, this cooperation of the minds doesn't seem to be happening. So what is going on?

Exploration of my minds has led me to see an imbalance in how we use our minds. Use of objectivity, in the absence of subjectivity, causes problems. Most of our objective thinking about our existence is based on a fundamental belief; unpleasantness is a valid experience of life. Do you agree or disagree with this? If that statement is not true, which I aim to demonstrate is the case, then the current basis of our thinking is flawed, and little of what we think and believe about ourselves is in fact true. Ironically, if we believe the errors to be true, then the ideas we have the strongest reactions against are the ones more likely to be true. One of those ideas is that subjectivity is as important, if not more important, than objectivity. It is an idea permeating much of my thought, and one which greatly helped me reinstate a pleasant experience of life.

Dr. Warren Stanton

Subjective Impressions and Objective Thought

Each mind comes with a sense of self, and the idea our subjective self is less useful to us than our objective self needs to be reconsidered. A person centered in their objective mind may dismiss me as being too subjective, but I am looking for balance between these two minds. Our use of objective reasoning to believe the source of bias is coming from the subjective mind is not a balanced viewpoint. Rather, it is a case of our belief in the superiority of the objective mind leading us to blame its shortcomings on whatever we can find as a scapegoat.

As demonstrated with the following example, our beliefs produced by the objective mind and stored in memory, are at the center of our dilemma. Not so long ago, the majority of people believed the earth was the center of the solar system. People believed the sun and planets revolved around the earth. This belief was based on observation of the heavenly bodies moving across our sky. The sun was seen to come up on one side of the earth, and go back down on the other. Relative to the objective self or ego, this was perceived to be movement of the sun. It seemed logical to conclude that on earth, nature revolved around people. People projected this idea of self onto the physical realm, as a belief in our place at the center of the physical universe.

The misunderstanding here, is that the subjective sense of self led people to believe everything revolved around humans. Rather, perception is based in the objective mind, and this ego-centered self is developed by objective reasoning. So the belief in heavenly bodies revolving around the earth was derived from objective thinking, based on incomplete evidence. Historically, this belief was then taken for a fact and caused a huge amount of resistance to the new scientific explanation of how the earth, sun, and other planets interact. However, the laws of physics provided a provable explanation of how and why the planets in our solar system revolved around the sun, and eventually the old idea was overturned.

In many respects, the beliefs developed from new ideas can be just as resistant to change as the old beliefs. As an example, ideas coming from scientific investigation of the solar system, have taken us to the other extreme. The view of us being at the center of the universe has been replaced with the view of us as specks of dust in the universe. From the perspective of this new belief, the old view is seen as egocentric. Anything remotely smelling of an egocentric view is now dismissed from consideration, in a similarly narrow-minded manner to those who believed in the old set of beliefs.

What has happened is a new belief has replaced the old one. If I suggested each of us is the center of the universe, it would meet with much resistance in some quarters. But have we "thrown the baby out with the bath water?" Are we in a time when all such ideas should be reviewed? For me the answer is "yes", otherwise we are stuck with a life of suffering. At this point I want to touch briefly on some metaphysical philosophy. I promise not to get carried away!

What if we are both central *and* insignificant in the universe? From the point of view of the objective mind we are a speck of dust, and from the point of view of the subjective mind we are the center of the universe. But here is the spin—both are true. Our mistake is in thinking these seemingly opposing views are in opposition. The way I see it, they are perfectly complementary to each other; one could not exist without the other. It is a paradox. But why do we think a paradox cannot be an explanation of everything? As I understand it, quantum physics and superstring theory now explain how this can be the case and I recommend reading on this topic.[1]

---

[1] For an excellent overview of quantum physics and superstring theory, see Brian Greene's book *The Elegant Universe*, 2nd edition, 2003.

In the absence of beliefs, it is easy to consider the possibility we are both. In terms of our objective individual self, it seems evident we are of little significance in the grand scheme of the universe. On the other hand, have you examined your subjective self? Most of those who look deeply, say we sense the universe in our own being and we experience it as one being. It seems evident each of us is capable of sensing ourselves as the center of the universe, the point at which the un-manifested manifests.

For me, this duality is a wonderful paradox. Yet we seem to think they cannot both be true. The main reason for this is because it is not logical for them both to be true. From a logical point of view this duality is a contradiction, in which only one or the other can be true. Therefore most people feel obliged to identify with one view or the other, or to try and integrate them. But what if they are both true and both have a place in us coming to know ourselves?

How could they both be true? My understanding came as an insight that astounded me. The wording of it which formed in my mind some years ago was; "each cell is contained in every other cell." I admit this is a pretty weird idea, and one you can't easily wrap your objective mind around. But as I conceived it, for a moment everything made sense. The concept could also mean; everything folds back on itself, or is contained in every part of itself, like the concept of a hologram. This is a basic idea in quantum physics and metaphysics, and reading on these topics may give you a fuller understanding. It is also an experience which can be gained from self-exploration.

Historically, the practice of science has considered only objective information and objective thought to be valid. However, this is under question in some quarters of science. Advocates of the explanatory power of quantum physics, acknowledge that events are changed by the presence of an observer. This is one hell of an idea for any traditional scientist! Again, this may not matter too much to a physical science based on reproducible objective proof. But when we enquire into the events of our own lives, it makes a difference; in the case of our thinking, we shouldn't just be objective. As implied by the principles of quantum physics, the reasoning itself is influenced by the person interpreting the event.

This effect of the observer is not yet a formal part of string theory, at least from what I have read to date. Under the banner of string theory, theoretical physicists have combined the laws of relativity theory—macro-universe—with those of quantum physics—micro-universe—in order to better understand the functioning of the universe; but are they any closer to understanding our role in it? Some questions I would love to ask a theoretical physicist include; could our subjective self be a black hole? Are we an added dimension not yet specified in string theory? Could "change" be the missing, unifying pre-dimension? Could all the concepts of string theory, such as folded dimensions, be evident in the human experience or human psyche? It seems to me they have to be, otherwise quantum physics and string theory will need a separate theory just for the human experience. Still, quantum physics has its links to the physical sciences, and the prospect of a "string theory of everything" being related to the subjective self as well as an objective self, seems some way off.

Fortunately, we don't need to wait for theoretical physics to develop a whole new approach to life. Ironically, most of the ideas are already around and just need a little tweaking to develop a completely different view of the world; one built on the old ideas but in many ways vastly different. If we did this, it could be much like the scientific revolution in physics. New theoretical concepts have tweaked general relativity theory and quantum mechanics under the name of string theory. This has opened a whole new world of explanations, based on ideas once regarded as plainly absurd—and in some quarters still are. The conclusions and solutions found in my enquiry may, I suspect, initially seem as absurd to some people. However, before you dismiss any of these ideas, ask yourself this question. If I have a choice between dismissing absurd ideas and living without suffering, which would I prefer?

A New Approach

An approach not based on beliefs, disciplines or a set of rules, is required for us to find our way home; back to a sense of knowing from which we can get answers and create pleasant experiences. The answers to the following questions set the scene:

1. What would this new approach be if it were not a discipline? The answer to this question is, of course, our instinct. The appetites of our instinct are not a discipline.
2. Can we live without disciplines? If our will is in fact goodwill then we could live without imposing self-discipline and rules.
3. Would we use disciplines if we can live without them? We would still use the objective mind to interface with the world, but in accord with our instinct.
4. Can something that is not a discipline be useful or helpful for our endeavors? Use of our instinctive goodwill is the way for each individual to live without fear and suffering.

Just as string theory represented a new approach to physics, a new approach is required for us to stop suffering. Using our instinct to guide us it can be done, drawing on our subjective and objective minds and our will. This is based on an old approach, for instance the concept of goodwill, redefined by an examination of how our minds work. In this way, we can get back to the most natural approach of all; a way not based in fear, meeting the conditions of living in today's world.

As you proceed, I encourage you to suspend your beliefs, in order to be more comfortable with what you read. As an example, consider the belief it is bad to be self-centered. If you hold this belief, then the more I talk about myself, the more you may become convinced my results cannot be valid because the process seems egocentric. However, as is often the case with beliefs, the issue is a matter of definition based on another belief. In this case it would be based on the definition of the word "self." If the definition of self is related to the ego, then I would agree it is an egocentric approach and not a valid way to go. However, if the word "self" is used in the context of our subjective sense of existence, true self or perhaps un-manifested self, or some meaning not based on the ego or self-concept, then it means something entirely different. In this context, being self-centered does not mean the same as being egoistic, or egotistical. As a way around this particular clash of beliefs, a different way of expressing my concept would be helpful, so I use the term "centered in self" rather than "self-centered."

Not all the concepts presented in the book are broken down in this way, so I urge you to suspend your beliefs as best you can. Considering other ideas will not betray your own beliefs, or make you susceptible to brainwashing. These commonly held views are based on fear and are not true. Let the ideas circulate in your mind and see what other ideas occur to you. Ideas are not dangerous. It is the beliefs about ideas that pose a danger. And even then, it's not all beliefs—just the ones substituting for our subjective impressions.

Dr. Warren Stanton

Summary

What we have in mind at any point in time, is the primary determinant of whether we have a pleasant or unpleasant experience:

- Even if unpleasant things are going on around us, our attitude toward the event determines how we experience it.
- If we express our instinctive impression of what feels genuinely good, we have a pleasant experience of life.

We have an instinctive sense of knowing—true intelligence—that recognizes our true nature as goodwill:

- Our sense of knowing confirms the truth when we conceive it.
- We know if what we have in mind is true by the positive effect it has on us mentally, emotionally and physically. This is the feedback loop for showing when our instinct is met.
- If what you have in mind doesn't feel genuinely good, then it is not meeting your instinct and therefore not supporting your continued existence.
- Getting satisfying answers to the questions about our lives is the proof that we know.

Our will has a way of showing what is good and true for us personally. This "way" is our instinct:

- We have free choice as to whether or not we use our minds to listen to our will and instinct.
- Instinct prompts us to look forward to life, not fear it.

- Instinct is best viewed as our natural inclination or appetites.
- As children, we learn to replace our instinct with beliefs based on fear.
- Most people aren't listening to their instinct, and therefore aren't living from their sense of goodwill, instead believing unpleasantness is a valid experience of life.

Thinking and knowing are complementary abilities:

- The objective mind gives us the conception we are specks of dust in a vast universe.
- The subjective mind gives us the conception we are the center of the universe.
- The subjective and objective minds are both valid and naturally work together.
- Subjectivity allows us to be impressed by instinct—to know without reason.
- Subjectivity contains a sense of self, independent of thoughts and beliefs.
- Our subjective sense of self is formed from our instinct and goodwill.

Beliefs developed only from reasoning have no bearing on our subjective life event:

- The ego-centered self is a product of the objective mind, not the subjective mind.

Explore your experience of life by being subjectively centered in self and drawing on your sense of knowing. There is more information about how to do this, later in the book.

TWO

OUR DILEMMA

What is the meaning of life? This question poses one of the biggest challenges to our mind. How many people have asked this question, and how many have found an answer? I would say almost everyone has asked it in some form, and few have reached an answer that satisfies. This is our dilemma; generally we don't use our minds to create pleasant experiences or answer the meaningful questions about life, yet we have an instinct to do so. In finding a resolution to our dilemma, having satisfying answers and pleasant experiences go hand in hand, because the means for doing them is the same.

Would it surprise you if you already know the meaning of life? The irony is, everyone knows the real answer, but most aren't taking notice. We aren't listening to the part of our mind which provides solutions, because we have been taught to distrust our instinctive knowing or intelligence. I would love to tell you the meaning of life in one word, right now, but at the moment I suspect few would agree with me. Some would regard my answer as a source of amusement, most would scoff at the idea, some would respond with disdain and a few would be enraged. So I will start at the beginning of the story, and trust by the end the answer I got will be welcomed and confirmed by you.

Do you think your life has meaning? We could start with the possibility of the answer being "no", life does not have meaning. However there is no real proof of this. Sometimes when I look at my life it can appear meaningless, but this is a perception, not proof. The question can be asked more scientifically by rephrasing it; "is there any evidence showing life does *not* have meaning?" But still, any evidence introduced to support this case, such as meaningless acts of violence, seems to prove nothing. They too, can be interpreted as necessary for our survival or growth, or part of our punishment.

Yet something in me says it doesn't make sense to live with unpleasantness and without meaning. This is a dilemma, but is there a way to move forward if you don't have answers? During the course of my life I found an alternative; if something doesn't make sense, the question is ill-conceived. Does it help if you ask the question this way; "is living meaningful?"

Often we think we don't know or don't care, but the truth is we just don't accept the consequences of knowing. We have learned to ignore the part of our mind which answers such questions. The answers come as an instinctive prompting deep within our mind, which occurs prior to becoming a concept or thought. We learned to cut off this most natural occurrence, so it seems we don't know because it does not reach the full conscious level of thought. Even if we sense life is meaningful, our thinking mind is likely to dismiss it as something we "want" to hear, and therefore not necessarily true. When we ask is living meaningful and the instinctive answer reaches the surface, it *is* something we want to hear, but it will also feel true.

Try reframing the statement from "life has meaning" to "life is meaning." If the definition of life with meaning is considered broadly, most people concede living can, or could, have meaning under certain circumstances. So my starting point is to rework the question; "is living meaningful?" We can make life meaningful, can't we? If so, under certain circumstances it can be meaningful. And if we can make life meaningful, it's not reasonable to say life has no meaning. Equally, if we can make life meaningful, we can choose to make life meaningless. Our capacity to make it either way is what gives life meaning. So if life can be meaningful, why do we struggle with the meaning of life? This chapter outlines the basic ideas from which I will build my case for the solution to our dilemma; how to live a meaningful, pleasant, and fearless life.

Why do We Care?

What prompts us to explore the meaning of life, or anything else? The most common response seems to be that life is a mystery, and we explore it because we want to know why we are here. But why do we want to know this? There is no apparent reason. We can provide a rationale—a justification after the event—but this is no more satisfying than believing life has no meaning. Rather, it seems to be an appetite, widely felt as a sense of curiosity. For us to acknowledge this is to admit we have an instinctive sense of enquiry about life. A primary instinct urges us to know ourselves. This is one of the premises on which this book is based.

Yet our exploration of the meaning of life seems to leave most people feeling short-changed, denied answers that satisfy. One common reaction to this apparent failure is to fold it back into the idea life is a mystery, and thus the question is inherently unanswerable. Some people choose a religious interpretation. Others challenge the validity of questioning the meaning of life at all, and usually give up looking. It seems the lack of a satisfying answer has led a lot of people to stop asking questions, or to stop listening for answers. Many believe we are not capable of knowing the answers to such questions.

I dispute this view of life. In my experience, we *do* get answers to every question we ask. That is if we ask genuine, well-defined questions, and answer them by calling on our instinct as well as our thoughts. I know this is a bold statement, but consider the implications for a moment. What would it mean to you if the lack of satisfying answers was of your own making? What would it mean if we make—if *you* make—not just a difference, but *the* difference to the meaning of life? Life would be completely different. It could be incredible. It could be deeply fulfilling. I am suggesting we each as individuals, stand poised between a life of misery and one of joy. So if you find yourself disagreeing with what I am suggesting, give me a chance. If I am mistaken, you have nothing to lose. But if I am not mistaken, imagine the possibilities!

Beliefs versus Instinct

People have various reasons for not accepting instinctive answers to questions about life. These reasons include:

1. Listening to instinct as a source of knowing is not acceptable.
2. Believing instinct will lead us astray.
3. Beliefs we hold are contradicted by what instinct seems to be saying.
4. Believing instinctive answers are too good to be true, or too simple for our complex lives.

What these reasons have in common is they stem from ideas people hold as beliefs. A common example from my upbringing is "ours is not to question why, ours is but to do or die". Given some of our beliefs about the meaning of life, you could be forgiven for thinking we do not really know. Alternatively, the way we are using the thinking mind denies us good answers. Our beliefs are an important part of life, but misuse of them is a major part of our dilemma.

So why don't we get answers that satisfy? Simply, we put our beliefs in the way. Our beliefs can then lead us to reject answers which would otherwise receive support from our instinct. This is the cause of our dilemma; we have rejected our instinctive knowing in favor of beliefs. This sounds too simple, but to give you an example, if you rejected this idea from the belief it is too simple, then ironically you have your proof. If you trust in any belief, you risk creating a state of self-delusion.

Having rejected our instinct, we replaced our source of answers with beliefs. These are concepts developed by the objective mind using thoughts, and stored in memory. Variously known as scripts, schemas, programs, values, and belief structures, beliefs are largely learned from those entrusted with our upbringing. They are interpretations of life's events, which are taught by example and by direct instruction. Beliefs cover all facets of our experience, from our view of the world as a safe or unsafe place, to a perception of life as pleasant or unpleasant, including our self-concept as a good or bad person. The fundamental error in our thinking is to regard thoughts as better than instinct because we can control them—or so we believe.

You might ask when it was we began rejecting our instinct. It probably goes back to when we first started thinking about why we are here. According to anthropologists, this may have been when we discovered how to produce fire. From this point on, life became a lot easier; our time was no longer totally consumed with survival. Many hours spent looking into the fire at night, which most agree is a totally absorbing activity, led us to contemplate our own existence. At this time our thoughts may have been given prominence over instinct. Although the origins of this are of interest to me, I want to focus on the impact in our lifetime.

Why do we reject our instinct? I remember as a child I was told we are here to rise above the animal in us. This belief seemed to be based on the observation of animals doing horrible things, notably arising from their predatory nature and sexual instinct. Reflecting on our self as an animal species, at some point must have been conceived with disgust; one of those thoughts which are uncomfortable to hold. Thus, if we allowed our instinct to prevail it would lead us to do all manner of despicable things. It was reasoned our basic nature is animalistic, and this was in turn conceived as bad; in terms of human thought full of greed, avarice, and willingness to do wrong.

Having created a dilemma, we then had to fix it. We identified the ability to reason as a uniquely human ability. So we elevated it to a position of great importance, invested in it, and commanded it to control the instinct. Since then, some disciplines such as psychology, have figured out that trying to repress sexual instinct can result in even deeper perversion. In some quarters, this has led to a new approach to work with this aspect of instinct in some sort of healthy alliance. But we seem not to have figured out that this principle applies to every area of life in which we try to exercise control, in the sense of permitting only what we think should be the case. In this way we have undermined the input of our instinct. In particular we have abandoned the natural authority of our instinctive sense of knowing. This is an error of thinking for several reasons.

Belief 1: Instinct Controls Us

Over-riding our instinct is often justified on the grounds that when these appetites are felt, all else—including morality—goes out the window. Therefore, instinct needs to be controlled. It was most strikingly expressed to me by a man of my parents' generation who used to openly say; "there is no morality in a stiff dick." At first this seemed self-evident, and while I didn't like the idea, I couldn't find grounds to refute the statement. Yet I wouldn't accept this could be the whole truth. Finally, I accepted some aspect of the statement was true, and then I was able to put it in perspective. After several years of questioning, the response which finally came to me was; yes, there is no morality in a stiff dick, but there is still morality in the person who owns it.

If our instinct controls us, in fact if anything controls us—rather than advising, guiding or urging us—then we may as well give up asking about the meaning of living. Believing our instinct controls us is ill-conceived, and results in us fighting against our nature. For instance, a belief we are being controlled leads to concepts such as fate. If our lives were pre-determined there would be no point showing any initiative. Fatalistic beliefs about life also prompt thoughts suggesting nothing matters, which can result in depression. The moral of this part of the story is to be very careful—full of care—about what you entertain in your conscious thinking mind; you are a creator of realities.

Choosing what you entertain in your mind is the key. Our appetites are based in instinct, and there is no doubt they can prompt us with strong impulses to eat, sleep, and procreate for example. However, such appetites do not over-ride our capacity to choose. Our choice remains intact, as shown by our demonstrated capacity to starve ourselves to death, restrain ourselves from blinking or excreting—with much difficulty—stop breathing to the point of losing consciousness, or abstain from expressing our sexuality.

Consider the view we are not forced to do anything by nature. Our appetites are an expression of our will, manifested as "want". We always have choices about how we express want in action. Naturally, it is in our best interests to cooperate with our instinct to eat, blink, and breathe. They are after all, expressions from an intelligent system ensuring our continued health and existence.

If our true nature is goodwill, our natural expression of these urges cannot be harmful to others. We are, as has been repeatedly demonstrated throughout history, capable of expressing goodwill in our sexual behavior and other biological appetites. Nevertheless, at some point a belief was developed whereby there was a problem with natural appetites—they seemed to control us—and we had to fix the problem. The belief there is something inherently wrong with us, is one of the underlying flawed beliefs we have adopted and passed down through our culture, with devastating consequences. Its negative effects are compounded, if we believe we will or should be punished for this.

Belief 2: We Should Deny Knowing

There are several reasons why over-riding our instinct is an error of judgment. In particular, the primary part of our instinct is a sense of knowing. It is this instinctive knowing or intelligence which prompts and guides us truthfully, not our conscience based on guilt. If you think instinct would lead us astray, consider the likelihood of this statement; the higher order instinct of knowing —the human psyche—prevails over the lower order physical expressions of appetites. If you confirm this in your experience, then you can accept it is okay to listen to instinct.

Getting back in touch with our higher instinct provides the solution to our dilemma. This is where the answers come from. Questions we pose can be likened to a sonar signal bouncing back from the sense of knowing with a signature pulse. This signal is interpreted by the conscious mind to form answers. Unfortunately, we deny ourselves this pathway when we accept a belief in the concept of self-control. Having decided to control ourselves, we couldn't really continue to believe we truly know anything.

Subsequently, our cultural values have developed with the aim of achieving control and self-denial; though people instinctively do not like being controlled. Consider this example of authoritarian parenting. When I was a child, most attempts to express my opinion were met with the tirade "Don't tell me what to do son. You do what I tell you." Often it would have the addendum, "I have lived for 50 years and been through a depression. What would you know?" This can be very damaging to a child! These days I can laugh about it and say my father was still in the depression—depressed—because he had accepted control as a meaningful principle of living.

As children, we were taught we knew nothing of importance. Yet accepting this teaching means learning to overlook and distrust our core sense of self. Children who reject their own knowing tend also to reject other people's knowing. As a result, I have come to a life-changing conclusion. Trying to get children to over-ride this sense of knowing is the real, unrecognized cause of most behavioral problems. Our sense of knowing is central to whom we instinctively feel we are. It is like giving up the only real truth we have, to be replaced by empty beliefs and rules of behavior. Why wouldn't kids become delinquents? Without this sense of knowing we feel lost and alienated, and wonder why the hell we experience life as an empty existence. The result is a huge conflict within us.

However, all this is done with good intent—to keep the child safe. As such, authoritarian parenting is based on the belief the caregiver knows best. In order to look after the children it is important they do as they are told. This means unquestioning obedience to the parent, denial of self-determination and often the right to an opinion.

Further discussion of our belief in control involves the concept of fear. This is a huge topic I will cover in detail in a later chapter, but let me indicate where I am heading. I see the concept of control, and its associated denial of self, as the second most damaging construct conceived by human kind—second only to our belief in fear. And, in case you are wondering, lack of control does not mean anarchy rules, because we instinctively prefer harmony to chaos. Why: **because harmony supports our continued existence.** Isn't this what our instinct is on about? If we use our conscious mind to think in accord with our will—goodwill—our subsequent actions will not be harmful to ourselves or others. At a personal level, once I started listening to instinct, my mind started giving me good, consistent, life affirming answers.

What could be so terrible about knowing the answer anyway? I can think of one instance; our fear the true answer is "there isn't any meaning." Without the fear though, even this wouldn't be so bad. This leads to a fascinating idea, namely fear blocks the answers or turns them into terrible ideas. In this event, fear is the cause of our dilemma.

Belief 3: Rely on Thinking

Essentially we have replaced listening to our instinctive sense of knowing with reliance on our thinking. What's the matter with that, you might ask? Well, I can suggest several things:

1. Reliance on thinking leads us to become too dependent on the thought processes. If we use the thinking mind to go against the instinctive, subjective mind, we isolate ourselves. Without ready access to other faculties, we have created a degree of dependence on the thinking mind to provide answers. Although at times we might use this mind just to think about something, when it matters we should be accessing every resource available to us, particularly instinct. Typically, people are only conscious of instinct in an emergency, for instance when someone close-by is seriously injured. My point is it matters all the time, because listening to instinct means the difference between a life of confusion and one with meaning.
2. Our instinct is expressed as an appetite to know. We can ask any and every question, including "what is the meaning of life," because we want to know. Arguably then, the instinct should prevail, with the thinking mind serving the instinct.
3. Our nature is governed by our will, and that nature is goodwill. If you use your awareness to listen to the guidance of your will, for instance in meditation, it feels genuinely good. Not "goody, goody" but an authentic sense of harmony, pleasantness, completeness, and enjoyment which feels right. Hence, if you want to be genuinely happy, it is critical to listen to your instinct ahead of thought. It is not our will urging us to do wrong,

to rape and pillage, or control; the beliefs we live by cause this, which are products of the thinking mind.

Relying on thinking goes against our true nature. By ignoring our instinct or trying to shut it up, we are following a recipe for disaster. Using the thinking mind to combat our instinctive knowing is an act of self-denial. It has led us so far astray it is in essence self-abuse. As a child, little did I realize my life of suffering began by accepting the view I knew nothing, from those supposedly "in the know".

Having rejected our sense of knowing, we replaced it with something else to guide us through life. Enter the beliefs! We have used the thinking mind to deduce a system of rules, principles, ethics, values and concepts to replace instinctive knowing. Now don't get me wrong. I don't mean all conceptions from the conscious, thinking mind are bad or injurious to us. Many of our beliefs are consistent with our will, and to the extent they are based on and subservient to it, they do not cause us problems.

Beliefs become a problem when they are elevated above instinct, specifically our goodwill. Once this is done with the conscious mind, we are in deep trouble. From this point on we are, as the saying goes, an accident waiting to happen. We have created an error of thinking, which will be borne out in our experience of life. Life events, be they pleasant or unpleasant ones, are our mirror. Have you ever wondered how a pleasant feeling can suddenly become an unpleasant one, like all of a sudden feeling resentful? When experiencing or expressing resentment, we are using a belief not grounded in instinct.

Under the banner of control we have accepted the legitimacy of placing beliefs above all else. Those beliefs which contain any concept of unpleasantness, such as fearfulness, result in us feeling discomfort. Once elevated—enshrined—they then have the status of a law which must be adhered to, irrespective of the consequences. When you and I did this with our thinking mind we created unpleasant realities. As we grew up, continued use of these beliefs made them resistant to change. Once beliefs are a law in our mind we become inflexible, and sooner or later this leads to behavior that is inconsiderate, ill-advised or non-empathetic. Even simple, positive beliefs like "control" lead us astray if elevated above goodwill, and can result in arrogance, narrow-mindedness, and self-righteousness to mention a few. Isn't it blatantly obvious, beliefs not based in goodwill are the cause of the inhumane acts we see and hear about in the news?

The point is simply this; when we do not have a reference to something other than a belief, we become totally absorbed with thinking. We become dependent on thoughts, and as a consequence place ourselves in subservience to our objective mind. As an example, our self-concept can become dependent on images. From this point on, if we do not create our reality in accord with our true will, we are vulnerable to thinking things which cause unpleasant experiences. This is especially true in our reaction to unpleasantness produced by others, for instance, having horrible thoughts about someone who is resentful toward you.

Creative Capacity of Our Mind

For me, the source of our predicament is captured in a simple statement about our capacity to create. Whenever I say this, people seem to understand it. Yet my sense is they do not understand the enormity of it, or comprehend the significance of the implications. It is important you make an effort to come to terms with this statement, because it is the single most useful idea to explain the predicament in which we find ourselves.

You have a mind capable of conceiving anything! Stop and contemplate this for a minute. There are no restrictions, no rules, no guidelines, and no manual. It is amazing; we can conceive anything. It is in fact a testament to our capacity as creators. We can conceive anything, and we do. We have used our conscious mind, with its ability to image—imagination—to create all manner of realities in our mind. Some of these creations are to our detriment, and this is a misuse of our minds.

There is one logical conclusion from this with major ramifications for us. The implication of this misuse of our minds is that ***we are the architects of our own suffering.*** We do not have to suffer. Not even at the level of minor inconvenience. Once you comprehend the significance of having a mind which can conceive of anything, you will reconsider your choice to suffer all manner of unpleasant things like stress, contempt, hate, despair—the list is endless. In my mind, I can barely conceive what manner of ignorance, arrogance, fearfulness, or superstitious thinking is represented in a life of unpleasantness. We are not yet quite out of the dark ages!

Any use of our mind which is not consistent with our will, causes an unpleasant experience. If we use our conscious mind to conceive horrible things, especially if we also act on them, we experience discomfort. It is a natural function of our mind to be able to create in this way. However, we misuse our minds by not choosing to create thoughts and actions consistent with our true nature. If we make the better choice, we do not suffer. The key ingredient is, we have free choice; we can do what we damn well please with our minds—irony intended.

But don't take my word for it. Try it. If you choose to think of things that feel genuinely good, and you keep doing this, you start to feel good. That is, the thoughts affect your emotions and mood. Notably, if you feel pretty bad, this can take quite a while.

As a small test, stop reading for a moment and think of the thing you most enjoy seeing or doing. What effect does it have on you?

This type of positive thinking is not a satisfactory solution though. A lot of people initially get good results with positive thinking, but this is difficult to sustain. Initially, we choose to allow these thoughts to resonate with our will. As we repeat this action with the thoughts, we develop it as a technique; a set of rules constituting a script or program. During the process of doing it again and again, our conscious choice becomes less and less involved and we get a decreasing amount of resonance or confirmation from our will. Often we come to see the technique as a trick of the mind and lose confidence. Sometimes, spurred on by our initial success, we bring our mind to bear and make it a belief. From here on, getting a pleasant experience is hard work. An alternative approach is presented later in this book.

We seem to have a dilemma in life and no acceptable way out of it. Nevertheless, we have created the problems ourselves. Having no acceptable solution tells us something. It is a conclusion which the methods of philosophy and science converge on. Namely, if we did not continue to prop up the old ways of thinking, we would arrive at the conclusion we were not thinking correctly. We have made some errors in our conclusions that need to be undone. Having summarized the dilemma, I will present the case at a more leisurely pace.

Summary

So what is the essence of our dilemma?

- Everyone has thought about the meaning of life; few have an answer that satisfies.
- Everyone knows the answer, but most aren't listening.

- We have an instinctive knowing or intelligence which we have been taught to distrust.
- If we can make life meaningful, it is not reasonable to say it has no meaning.

Misuse of beliefs is a major part of our dilemma:

- People's reasons for not accepting the answers are based in beliefs.
- A commonly held belief is; we are not capable of knowing the answers.
- If it were possible to not know, this would make us pawns in the game of life.
- My sense is we get answers to every question we ask.
- This makes us designers in the game of life.
- We each as individuals stand between a life of misery or joy.
- We have rejected our instinct in favor of beliefs developed with the thinking mind.
- Beliefs containing fear-based concepts cause us to feel unpleasant.
- With no reference to something other than a belief, we do things which cause us to suffer.
- It was reasoned, if we allowed our instinct to prevail, it would lead us to do despicable things.

Reason is not the answer:

- We elevated reasoning to a position of importance and invested in it to control instinct.
- An error in thinking is to regard beliefs as preferable to instinct because we can control them.

- We seem to have figured out that controlling the sexual instinct results in perversion. It seems we have not figured out this applies in every area we try to exercise control.

Instinct is okay:

- Instinct does not over-ride the will; it is an expression of our will.
- We are urged by our instinctive appetites, but have a choice in how we manifest them.
- If our true nature is goodwill, our natural expression of these urges is not harmful.
- We are capable of exercising goodwill in our sexual behavior and other appetites.
- Our instinctive sense of knowing guides us—this is where the answers come from.
- As children we have been taught to overlook this core sense of self.
- Lack of control does not mean anarchy rules.
- We instinctively prefer harmony to chaos because it supports our continued existence.
- If we conceive in accord with our will, our subsequent actions support our existence.
- Over-riding instinct with beliefs or ignoring it, is a recipe for disaster.
- We are misusing our mind, causing harm, and suffering.
- If we use awareness to listen to the guidance of the will, it feels genuinely good to us.
- Our will does not urge us to do wrong, to rape and pillage, to control or to live by beliefs.
- You have a mind capable of conceiving anything—no rules, no instruction manual.

- If we understood the significance of this, we would know we do not have to suffer.
- We are the architects of our own suffering.
- We experience unpleasantness if we don't create thoughts aligned with our will.
- The key ingredient is, we have a choice; we can do what is to our liking.

THREE

GOOD USE AND MISUSE OF OUR MINDS

While exploring the meaning of life, we can find ourselves facing a seemingly infinite number of questions; any answer we come up with can also have a question asked about it. If we are seeking answers, how can continued questioning be satisfying to us?

Let's deal with this one straight up. We are creators. That is what we do; we create. The capacity to continually ask questions and get answers is part of how we use our minds. The fact we can go on asking questions is the evidence of our true nature as creators. It isn't an obstacle. We make it a problem only if we believe a satisfying answer should end the process of asking questions. In fact, we benefit by continuing to ask questions. Asking every question you could imagine can lead us to more definitive answers—if it is done well.

Everything we do is an act of creation. The movement of our arms and legs, our thoughts, constructing memories and activating them, our development of language and its use to communicate, are all creations. Posing a question about the answer to your previous question is a creative thought experiment to find the solution to all manner of things.

Continually asking questions can be enjoyable if we are prepared to listen to the answers. If your mind gave you a simple and completely honest answer to every question you asked— which it does— it would be desirable to ask questions, because getting answers would be as enjoyable as asking questions. You will always get answers to your questions, so there is no dilemma; provided you can accept that no answer means there is something the matter with the question.

Needless to say, as a child I plagued my parents with questions. My mother often said it drove her crazy. Her frustration with my enquiry into life was obvious; partly because it was not considered a desirable thing to do, and partly because she believed she didn't have the answers. This was very discouraging, but I wouldn't stop.

As every good educationalist knows, enquiry is the essence of growth and learning. It is behind every human endeavor resulting in our advancement, and is the basis of science and technology. Any tendency to discourage enquiry would lead to great cultural loss. So where is it, in an education system based on rote learning? Can you remember how many teachers promoted true enquiry when you were at school? At a personal level, enquiry is crucial to finding answers that satisfy.

Being in Two Minds

In pursuit of answers to questions about life, understanding the functioning of our minds is invaluable. Most people, however reluctantly, accept the existence of two minds, which are usually referred to as the "conscious mind" and the "subconscious mind." The subconscious mind is commonly associated with the primitive brain in humans—the animal in us—while the conscious mind is commonly seen as a superior system—our saving grace. However, I propose this is not the case.

There is more debate about the faculties associated with these minds than I care to go into here. The subconscious mind is more mysterious and unfathomable, and this feeds our suspicions about what is in there. For reasons such as these, we mostly focus on the more obvious conscious mind, and almost exclusively on the part seen as its main attribute; the faculty of reasoning, our ability to think.

Notably, the faculty of reasoning is not the intellect. The intellect **uses** reasoning to pose a question or obtain information, and is the part of us which understands the product of reasoning. In the terms mentioned above, the intellect is our instinctive sense of knowing, housed in the subjective mind. There is also debate as to whether the subconscious mind is our memory store. Based on my self-exploration, I am of the view that the memory store is an unconscious part of the conscious mind and not the so-called subconscious mind.

There is also debate about whether mind and brain are one and the same. Anatomically, current understanding is that we have 3 brains: the primitive brain at the top of the spinal cord (medulla oblongata), the mid-brain (cerebellum), and the forebrain (neo-cortex or cerebrum). These physical structures may equate to our minds, but if they do not, science would have difficulty describing the concept of a mind. An alternative view is a single mind divided into frequency bands, polarities, or qualitatively different systems, such as mind and brain. Any of these may be further subdivided, for example the forebrain clearly has different functions based in its left and right hemispheres, as demonstrated by scientific exploration. However, there is no definitive scientific evidence about where faculties such as intellect, consciousness, attention, and memories reside in the brain.

Let us put these issues to one side, and use the following definitions based on observation of how these minds function. I will refer to the conscious, thinking mind as the *objective mind*, which includes our memory stores. Our other mind, which houses our sense of knowing, expressions of goodwill, and instinct, I refer to as the *subjective mind*. It may also be possible to separate the source of goodwill from the subjective mind and identify it as a third mind, which I call the *will*. Some may find it helpful to think of the source of goodwill as "goodwill minus an o."

The objective and subjective minds each have their own attributes. More importantly, they have different natures and modes of operating. There are other important differences between the two minds which we tend to overlook. One of these is the distinction between the sense of "I" experienced in the objective mind and the sense of "myself" delivered by the subjective mind. This is one of the ways to tell which of the two minds you are listening to; the subjective mind delivers a stronger, deeper sense of self.

Generally we speak about conscious awareness as if these are one attribute, as if both belong to the objective mind. However, from my self-exploration I came to make an important distinction between being conscious and aware. I am happy to agree, consciousness is an attribute of the objective mind, but in my experience awareness is an attribute of the subjective mind. For me, awareness is a quality of my instinctive sense of knowing.

On close examination, I found awareness sits behind my thinking. In particular, it is still there when I sleep, though it is hard to tell when I am not conscious. Awareness monitors the function of my objective mind and provides a deeper level of knowing, beyond the information produced by the objective mind. It became obvious to me, awareness is unaffected by the functioning of the objective mind, for instance when I woke at night from a bad dream. In my early adult years this quality enabled me to examine these fearful dreams. The significance of this distinction between being conscious and being aware will be made clearer in later discussion of mindfulness meditation.

The objective mind has some incredible qualities. Consciousness is one of its primary attributes accompanying the act of living. Another attribute of the objective mind, and arguably the most amazing, is our capacity to think. I regard our imagination as the essence of thinking, of our ability to conceive, but some would debate this. Imagination is the capacity which allows us to form images in our mind; thought could be described as our ability to add words to what we image, or imagine. When I examine my process of thinking, the basic output of my objective mind is ideas, or concepts. These seem to arise first in my mind as precepts; vague, shadowy, amorphous shapes on a screen-like part of my mind which can be called the stream of consciousness. Precepts appear to be primitive thinking, produced in the brain prior to conscious thinking. They are the building blocks for the concepts. So concepts are fully fledged thoughts, developed from precepts and represented as images.

In terms of our dilemma, most of our concerns relate to the objective mind, because we grossly misuse it. We use it to construct beliefs which are not based on our true nature. An example of such beliefs is that the faculty of reasoning is superior to all other faculties of our mind. This focus we have placed on the objective mind, fails to acknowledge the two minds are perfect companions; they operate in synchrony, and they work beautifully together—until we interfere.

A brief description of the cooperative functioning of our minds could be useful at this point in time. The subjective mind consists of instinct, awareness, and a sense of existence—actuality—beyond the concepts of the objective, thinking mind.

The objective mind is required to translate the impulses from the subjective mind into thought and action. For instance, the feeling of hunger is turned into how, when, and where to look for food. Awareness of our instinctive impulses and impressions enables us to use the faculties of the objective mind to see things consciously; which produces a trace of the event in memory. The objective mind also receives input from the senses, which is translated into images, then used to construct concepts and beliefs. In turn, the objective mind provides feedback to the subjective mind about whether the instinctive inclinations or appetites are met. The function of the objective mind is to provide a chronicle of events—reality.

There is another piece of information mentioned above, which could be represented in a model of the minds. Having studied the activity of the subjective mind on a daily basis for more than 50 years, I have found no evidence the will is contained in that mind. It seems to be beyond the subjective mind. I think of the minds as a hierarchy of will, providing input to the subjective mind, while the subjective mind provides input to the objective mind. The objective mind has its connection to physical existence through the senses. The system also has a feedback loop, flowing from physical existence, through the objective mind, to the subjective, ending with the will—see Figure 1.

Physical existence affords the opportunity for us to know ourselves as creators. It does this by enabling us to conceive of anything, by providing a means to act on our environment, and by showing a reflection of what we have created—in the form of a pleasant or unpleasant experience.

FIGURE 1

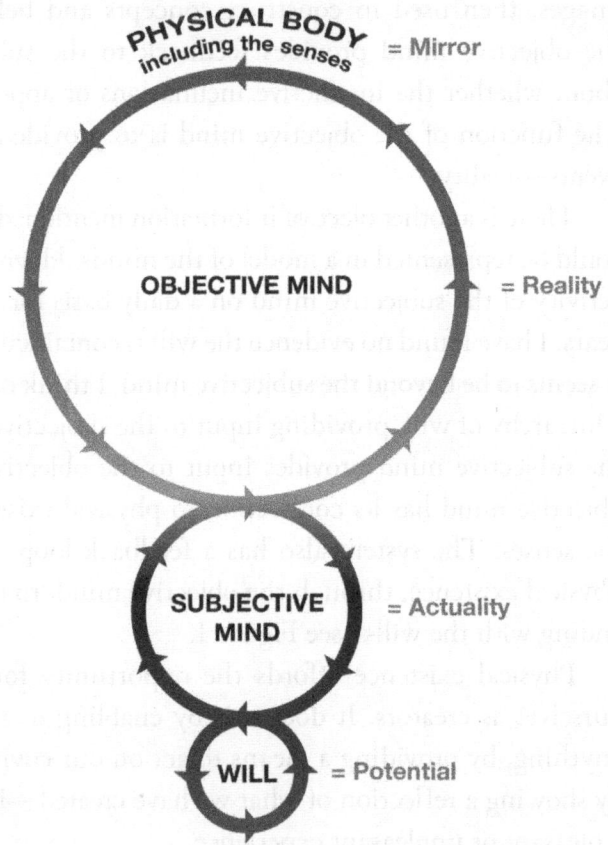

Figure 1. Model of intelligent cooperation of our minds

The output of the will is in the form of instinct. So much so, it often seems there is a direct pathway from instinct to action, with no thought. However, I don't think this is true. We do become conscious of the instinctive impulse, which is a function of the objective mind, and we can choose to observe this process more closely. I think this path naturally has minimal thought governing it, rather than no thought. This might consist of a simple recognition of the importance of an instinct, so this impulse is allowed through the objective mind unimpeded, to enable immediate action. Such recognition is a key to our minds working in harmony. If instinct truly passed directly to action, it would mean we don't have free choice. This is surely one of the ideas which led us to believe we are controlled by our instinct. Believing we lack conscious control, has led us to fight against being at the mercy of these impulses. This misconception is a large part of the predicament we have created.

Let me give you an example using the startle response. When humans experience a sudden unexpected event, such as a loud noise, our instinct prompts us to act urgently, as if our lives depended on it—which on occasion it does. The startle response seems to be involuntary, which looks like support for the idea we are controlled by such impulses. However, when this happens to me I see my agreement for the objective mind to listen and go along with instinct, because it may be important to my continued existence. My minds are therefore acting cooperatively. People can, however, teach themselves not to react to loud noises; choosing to over-ride their instinct. The startle response still exists, but the conscious mind can over-ride it. If you work or live around loud noises you can even get used to them, to a point where you effectively no longer notice the sounds. This is referred to as habituating to the noise, which means developing a script in the conscious mind which defines sudden loud noises as normal. This turns a non-response to loud noise into habitual behavior. Note this is not the objective mind controlling the subjective mind, but the objective mind putting a screen in place to filter out noises one doesn't want to respond to. Unfortunately, we have used this capacity to develop screens— beliefs and scripts—to great disadvantage.

Look again at Figure 1. One feature of the model is that the objective mind is not self-directed; it does not have a direction of its own. The faculties of the objective mind are there to serve you, in particular, to serve your subjective mind. In this hierarchy, the subjective mind directs the objective mind, and the objective mind directs the physical senses. In turn, the physical senses provide the objective mind with feedback, to be interpreted and provided as feedback to the subjective mind about the experience we are having. The implications of this concept make it contentious; if the objective mind cannot direct the subjective mind, what have we done to ourselves by elevating the objective mind to its current position of primary importance?

A more memorable way of saying it is, "the objective mind does not have a mind of its own." It can think, but it is not the source of intelligence. We have elevated the objective mind to its current position of power in an attempt to control ourselves. That's because we believe the "bad" in us resides in the subjective mind; mixed together in the concept of the subconscious mind, identified with the primitive brain. As a consequence, we use thoughts to over-ride the instinct, and find ourselves being controlled by our thoughts. This is a strange reversal on having our minds work together.

If this idea about the role of the objective mind bothers you, it may be of consolation to note the subjective mind is there to serve your will. How this all becomes corrupted will be explored in the chapters about beliefs, fear, and control, but the workings of it are outlined above. In the later chapters about the solution, I will make a case in which the source of the "bad" is actually the objective mind. Thus, using the objective mind to try and control the subjective mind, or cut ourselves off from it, is the worst choice we could ever make. The extent of corruption it has caused in our minds and lives is beyond comprehension.

Our Minds in Discord

Let's get back to the question of why we don't get answers that satisfy. Just as we don't understand *what* the objective mind should be used for, we also don't understand *how* to operate it. We are like children in charge of bulldozers; no wonder it spells disaster! Because we don't understand the relationship of the objective mind to the subjective mind, we distrust our minds and seek to control them. In the case of the objective mind, many people think it deceives us and leads us astray. They observe it acts erroneously and can lead to weird behavior. We are even fearful we can lose our minds. None of these beliefs are true in the way most people think of them. So what is going on?

If we are not using our objective mind correctly in how we pose questions, how can we expect to get a sensible, satisfying answer about anything? People ask questions in all sorts of places, looking mainly to other people for the answers. Most people don't accept they know much at all, and the idea of having an instinctive sense of knowing is not a part of their belief system. Consequently, they would not think any questions posed by their objective minds can be answered and made sense of by their own instinctive intelligence. Some people use methods such as a horoscope to try to access some insight or intelligence at a different level. If they could accept this other level existing in their own mind, they could consult it directly, not via the stars.

Dr. Warren Stanton

There is, of course, a distinction to be made between questions relating to objective, known information and those relating to subjective impressions. In the former case the question is directed to the rational part of the objective mind, which answers questions about, for example, how a piece of equipment works, known facts about history or business, or the application of a mathematical formula. The intellect is involved in order to understand the details, and the answers relate to other details stored in the person's memory or in external form, such as books. These "what" and "how" sorts of questions are answered with information. This is not knowledge in the sense of referring to your subjective mind's instinctive knowing.

Questions relating to life experience, directed to the subjective mind, receive answers usually referred to as wisdom. These answers come from our instinctive sense of knowing, refined by feedback from our life experiences. This type of knowledge is about "why." However, "why" questions asked of the objective mind, for example "why did the plane crash?" are really about "how," for example mechanical failure, pilot error, or unanticipated weather conditions. The "why" questions I'm talking about here are philosophical in nature. If you ask, "why did the chicken cross the road" the objective mind can provide answers from observation, like; it was looking for food, because a big, black dog was chasing it, or a cute, functional answer such as, to get to the other side. You don't get rational answers about the intent of chickens from your subjective mind; if it seems you do, it is a projection of your own thoughts or beliefs. In the case of our chicken, a response from the objective mind in accord with the instinct would be something like "because it wanted to," which contains no reason. This is a non-specific, functional subjective answer not based in reasoning or logic. If we believe only in logic this will seem an unacceptable motivation.

Nevertheless, I would like to assure you, when you ask a question of your subjective mind you always get an initiative delivered to your objective mind. This comes from our instinctive sense of knowing, which is fed by the will, in whatever capacity you prefer to think of it: the will to live, the will to thrive, the will to exist, but in all cases goodwill.

Often we think we didn't get an answer, or the answer we got doesn't seem to make sense. So what goes wrong? Basically, we are not careful enough with how we use our mind or with how we interpret its output.

There are at least six fundamental flaws in the way we use our minds, and they combine to cause one almighty mess:

1. We are not conscious of the fact we get answers from our subjective minds every time we ask a question. Let me say it again; it always gives an answer when we ask. When I became conscious of this, the course of my life changed irrevocably. For the first time in my life, all my questioning had meaning.
2. We believe it is our mind's fault when we do not get an answer, rather than our misuse of it. Such a derogatory view of our mind is asking for trouble.
3. We fail to appreciate, the question and answer are directly related; if you ask a poor question you get a poor answer. The responses we get are a mirror image of the question. If the answer lacks specificity, so did the question. This was the most important point for me in understanding why I wasn't getting satisfying answers.
4. Sometimes we mistakenly think we have asked a question when we have actually made a statement. Inside our minds, a question has a genuine sense of inquiry and willingness to know, not just a question mark! If we only

half formulate the idea, for whatever reason, it may not be submitted to our mind as a question. For example, if we get anxious half way through a question, because we believe the implications might be unacceptable, we often do not complete the question or genuinely seek an answer. Generally speaking, a null response happens because we have not actually asked a genuine, complete question.

Our minds are precise, and we have to use the objective mind precisely to narrow down the possible interpretations of the answers we receive. As an example we might ask "what is the meaning of life?" and not receive any response or insight in return. On the basis of this experience, most of us have reached one of the following conclusions; there isn't a meaning to life, it is not comprehensible, it's a mystery, my mind is not working as it should, or I am not very smart. Relatively few people think there is something wrong with how they are asking the question, or challenge whether their beliefs about the answer could be wrong.

5. We are not precisely aware of the actual question we are asking. This is probably the most misleading flaw. Often, there is a hidden part to a question. The question may seem fully formulated, but if we are not aware of the complete question, we risk misinterpreting the answer. If I have asked what I think is an open question, though it really has a boundary or limitation to it, then I will misunderstand the answer. For instance, if I think I have asked myself "what is the meaning of life" but my real question was "what is the meaning of life that doesn't threaten my beliefs", it is hardly surprising if the answer seems to be nil response or at best "there isn't any meaning." In this event I think the question I asked was

"what is the meaning of life?" and the answer I got was "there isn't any," but I am being led astray, because I wasn't aware enough or honest enough to see the full question. In this context you can appreciate the value of increased use of awareness, with its attribute of sensitivity, as part of the solution presented in Chapter 9.

6. The most common reason we discard an answer is because it goes against our beliefs or pre-conceived ideas. It is the most dangerous of the flaws in how we use our minds, because it is deliberate. We commonly substitute beliefs for answers when we seemingly get no response to our question. Beliefs don't have to be a problem, but we have made them one by elevating them to a place of importance above our own experiential sense of self. Beliefs are there to serve our impressions of life, not to create it, just as reporters are there to report the news not to make it.

If we do not understand or accept the capacity of our subjective mind to always give a true answer representing the instinct, we are the proverbial ship without a rudder. All that is left is to follow what others have said should be done. We have learned to dismiss the truth in the blink of an eye, almost imperceptibly, hardly even interrupting the flow of our thoughts. But if you use your awareness to watch intently, the signs are there. What a beautiful mind it is, but our abuse of it is very scary and rather ugly.

Misunderstanding the Output of Our Minds

A common and deeply damaging misunderstanding, resulting from our flawed thinking, is the belief there is something wrong with our minds. If I accepted the prevailing social and medical views about the high prevalence of mental health illness, rather than being the most successful species on the planet, I would consider us the most maladapted species in existence. I have a shocking viewpoint; for the most part there is nothing wrong with the functioning of our minds. Basically the problem is in the rubbish we feed our minds and the ways we misuse them. If we cleaned up the input and used them properly, in the majority of cases all would be well.

The objective mind operates from our instruction. If we use it to conceive horrible things and store these in memory as beliefs, life will mostly seem horrible. Develop a concept of "I have to", meaning forced against your will, or "I should", from a sense of duty, and you will experience stress or pressure throughout your life for as long as you hold this belief to be true. Interpret life as miserable and guess what you will experience in your life? Even if you go against such beliefs in thought and action, they will still affect you because they surround you.

Our objective mind is the most amazing thing in existence. Its powers of creation are incredible. In effect we create our own realities, or perhaps we should call them idealities. Let me restate the key point here; we have minds that can conceive of ***anything***.

It is tempting to blame stupidity for this predicament, but that would be falling for a belief. Calling it a misunderstanding seems too simple and too low-key, but is effectively what it is. Ironically, misguided thinking causes us to use our objective mind to conceive of things which are unpleasant to us. All the horrible things going on in the world are ***not*** evidence against this explanation. Most of them are the result of people thinking from fear; conceiving of horrible things, believing them, and acting on them. We create our realities—including the horrible ones.

To make matters worse, we interpret life events to maintain consistency with our beliefs, in this case "horribleness". For example, many people think one animal killing another to survive is cruel and horrible, mostly because we fear it happening to us. But I suspect the animal does not conceive it is killing something in the way we think of it. Science maintains only primates are capable of abstract thought, though it seems only the human mind is capable of conceiving of things as horrible? An animal does not think it is doing wrong. Similarly, we use beliefs to make other acts of nature seem cruel. If I choose to live on a river's flood plain, how can I blame a flood for causing massive disruption to my life?

Does it seem odd to you that we do such horrible things with our objective mind? So why do we do it? Because it is what we have been taught to do. This is what was done to our parents, and what our parents did to us. It is what they showed us to do, and what they themselves did. We looked around us and saw almost everyone doing the same thing, with only a few exceptions. These damaging beliefs are even endorsed and supported by our culture and most institutions in it. The classic example of this is the widespread use of fear-based beliefs underlying the social, legal, political, and educational systems. Can you see how we use fear to create our own suffering?

As a child you knew the horribleness was wrong, didn't you? We instinctively know this because it feels horrible, but as small children we had to make a choice. Before being able to think for ourselves at about age 10, how could we accept or argue our parents might be wrong, or most of what people told us and did to us was wrong. As children, we sensed we could not do well without our caregivers, and knew they cared for us just as we cared for them.

Strange as it may seem, it was our caring for them which led us to put down our sense of knowing and accept what they were showing us. To do this we had to ignore or over-ride the part of us sensing what was right for us, and most of us were encouraged to do exactly that. So, out of love for our parents we ignored our instinctive sense of knowing, with varying degrees of success. Our sense of knowing could be avoided, our parents showed us that, but it couldn't be totally shut down or controlled. This put us in a position of conflict within ourselves, with no easy way out.

We have learned to deny responsibility for what we think. We tend to believe the thoughts of others, presented to us as the truth. Some hearty souls dare to go against this body of knowledge, but they do so at great peril to their mental health and well-being, because it results in criticism or being socially ostracized by the keepers of the belief systems.

This is not about parent bashing, or blaming someone. First, our parents themselves did exactly the same when they were children; through example, they learned to ignore their sense of knowing and abdicate to the errors in their parents' thinking. When they became parents they taught us as they had been taught, so the problem is handed down from generation to generation. By analogy, it is like a social disease. However, everyone does it in good faith because they are convinced by their belief it is the right thing to do. Second, despite being passed down, for the most part it gets watered down from generation to generation. Each generation knows it is wrong and everyone is doing the best they can with what they have to work with. Each generation does something to change the problem.

Let me give an example to illustrate this. In my parents' generation, handing down the lessons of life was strongly enforced with physical punishment. In the time of my childhood much was said about physical punishment, and my father often said it had done him good. In other words, he rationalized his parents were right to punish him in this way. But he didn't inflict physical punishment on me. Why not? If he thought it did him good, why didn't he hit me as a matter of routine—even if it was against my mother's wishes? From my current perspective, I can see he instinctively knew it had the potential to do harm. On the other hand he still supported or justified physical punishment as a helpful thing to do; otherwise he had to accept his parents were wrong in doing it to him. This would have been a major source of conflict for him.

Another story illustrating this principle, relates to my generations' supposed rebellion against our parents. In the 1960s and 70s, people my age rebelled against the hypocrisy we could plainly see in our parents' lives, captured by the common saying, "do as I say not as I do." This was the hippy era, in which we were encouraged by our peers to turn our backs on the values of our parents. It was rarely said but implicitly understood, this was us standing up against what we thought was wrong and doing something radical about it; going against many of the things our parents valued. In its extreme this included money, success and power. The irony of those hearty days of sex, drugs, and rock-and-roll is the belief it was our idea. We rebelled against our parents' generation and their values, supposedly because we knew something had to be done; we should not let ourselves be controlled by them or society. At least, that is my take on the philosophy behind it at the time.

At a later age I realized our parents were either behind it or party to it. During the course of investigating how my mind worked, I had this shock realization my parents themselves had taught me to rebel. Rebelling against goodwill was a set of beliefs my grandparents held, which they demonstrated to their children with the use of physical punishment. Out of their care for my grandparents, my parents took on the rebelliousness they were shown, but expressed it in their own way. Their instinctive goodwill had not been totally eclipsed by the unpleasant scripts; which is why my parents did not use physical punishment to the degree it was inflicted on them. In turn, instinctive caring for my parents guided me to do what they did, to rebel. In other words their disdain and contempt led me to hold disdain and contempt for them. This is how the goodwill gets corrupted in our expression.

We demonstrated the rebellion more overtly than they did. But underneath all they said, about what we were doing wrong and "whatever is the world coming to," they supported our rebellion. It was their rebellion against their parents borne out in our rebellion.

Dysfunctional scripts are handed on to us, like a social disease. Strange as it might seem though, it was the love of our parents which led us to take up the rebellion. It had much less to do with our contempt for what they represented. The contempt was the script handed on to us. Rebellion was how it was expressed. We thought we had fixed the problem by going against our parents' values, but really the unpleasantness just got transmitted in a shrewder capsule. Rebelliousness is now a popular, supported part of our cultural beliefs. But let's not mistakenly believe it fixed the problem of contempt. Contempt is still a common reality for most people.

The Bottom Line

After all this bad news, the bit of good news may be worth repeating. The good news is, our instinctive sense of knowing, our goodwill, cannot be totally eclipsed by the unpleasant scripts we take on. I think most of us sense this, for example when we are prepared to look for a shred of decency in even the most unpleasant person. All is not lost. We still manage to make changes in our lives, and in the balance of things, goodwill prevails. In the context of the example above, I don't think too many people from my era live by the saying "do as I say, not as I do."

The reason instinct cannot be totally eclipsed is because the scripts are in the objective mind, whereas instinct is in the subjective mind. The hierarchy of our minds means the objective mind does not have control over the subjective mind. Lucky for us, in my opinion! This prevents us from being the most dysfunctional species in existence, even though it sometimes looks as if we are. If we had our way, we would control our instinct. As it is, persistent effort to control ourselves causes a sense of futility. With few exceptions, many people ignore this sign, adopting a belief that futility is one of those cruel experiences life inflicts on us. How wrong they are, I will go on to explain.

Much of the following discussion hinges on understanding that the nature of our will is based in harmony, and corruption occurs by misuse of the objective mind. Using fear to keep a child safe is a classic example of how we have created ideas which are inconsistent with our will. Yet we see so many people acting unpleasantly or in some cases doing horrific things! If our true nature is goodwill, an explanation of where it all goes wrong is sorely needed.

Summary

There are three parts to our mind, which work as a hierarchy—summarized visually in Figure 1:

- Our will is the fundamental element.
- The subjective mind is there to serve your will.
- The primary input from the will to the subjective mind is sensed as instinct.
- The subjective mind requires use of the objective mind for these impulses to be interpreted in thought and action.
- The objective mind is there to serve your subjective mind.

- Consciousness is part of the objective mind and awareness is part of the subjective mind.

Our minds naturally operate in synchrony, and they work fine—until we interfere:

- We misuse our objective mind when we give it priority over the subjective mind.
- We construct and inherit beliefs which are not based on our true nature.
- Using the objective mind to over-ride the subjective mind causes us harm beyond comprehension.

When you ask a question relevant to your subjective mind you always get a response in your objective mind:

- If we are not using our objective mind correctly we cannot expect to get a sensible, satisfying answer about anything.
- If we do not understand or accept the capacity of our mind to always give a true answer, we are the proverbial ship without a rudder.

For most people there is nothing wrong with the functioning of their mind. Basically the problem is in the rubbish we feed it:

- The objective mind operates from our instruction. If we use it to conceive horrible things and store these in memory as beliefs, life will seem distorted and horrible.
- Beliefs that cause harm are handed on from generation to generation like a social disease.

It is important to understand, we have a mind which can conceive of anything.

FOUR

BELIEFS

To recap, I'm exploring why we don't seem to know the meaning of life or get satisfying answers to our questions. I chose the question "what is the meaning of life," because it is the loftiest I could think to ask. However, we struggle just as much with answers to basic questions like "why bother doing anything?" Apart from the necessities of sustaining life, for a lot of people there doesn't seem to be many answers. They seem to live mundane, ordinary lives, devoid of inspiration and satisfaction, full of fear and unpleasant experiences.

Some believe this is just the human condition, but I think not! Misusing our objective mind is the source of our problems, and that is a choice. You may say you have no choice, but it is simply choosing to believe you have no choice. This means the problems are of our own creation, and we can use our mind to overturn them. Have you ever wondered if you could make life pleasant and free of fear?

Bear in mind, moving in this direction requires use of the same faculties of our mind, the capacity to create, which we use to make our current mess. In line with a positive psychology approach, I am more interested in what we can do to right it, than where we have gone wrong. However, in order to start setting things right, it would be useful to understand how we create the problem in the first place. So let's tackle the topic of beliefs!

Beliefs, from Simple to Abstract

The topic of beliefs is a complex one, so I'll start with a brief overview. There is a basic error in how we look at life, and it stems from our misuse of belief systems. Beliefs of all shapes and sizes are being misused, from the big systems of beliefs concerning the meaning of life, to the day to day ones such as manners. In saying this, I do not mean it is inappropriate to have beliefs. We just need to use them differently.

Beliefs of many types seem to have crept in and taken over our objective minds, presiding at the core of most people's lives. If they cause unpleasantness, even at the expense of instinct like the expression of goodwill, people still adhere to these beliefs as if their lives depended on it—which it does not. The damage caused by placing beliefs above all else is immense.

Reflecting on the big picture, I trust the following comments will be in accord with your experience. First, I think it is obvious to most people that strongly held beliefs are behind the strife we see in the world. Second, it is obvious we cannot live without beliefs. Third, it is also obvious that trying to live primarily from beliefs, disregarding our natural instinct, is also totally unsustainable. However, solving the world's problems will have to wait until tomorrow. For now, I want to look at the impact of misusing beliefs in everyday life, because this same scenario is behind the conflict we experience in every aspect of our lives, including work, personal interactions and family relations.

Beliefs are a product of thinking. Belief structures are thought forms we create with concepts and reasoning. I don't think anyone has ventured to say exactly what a thought is made of, but it seems to be a primary type of energy. Thought enables us to develop ideas and concepts using our capacity to image things. We then use reasoning to structure an understanding of the events we are experiencing in life. When given attention, these thought structures leave traces in memory, which become reinforced with continued use. This enables us to recall thoughts, particularly ones we have used to navigate situations with success. Thought structures are also grouped together to form beliefs. Our beliefs are also represented in memory, enabling us to respond in a learned and comprehensive way to the events of daily living. These belief structures are also called scripts, schemas or programs, though these terms may represent different levels of beliefs.

There are different types of beliefs and I can't say I've categorized all of them. However, for the purpose of discussing our misuse of beliefs, there are two types I will compare: simple beliefs and abstract beliefs. In seeking to understand a belief, a very useful question to ask is "what is it in reference to?" One of the dimensions in which beliefs differ is the extent to which they refer to one's own experience. Simple beliefs have a personal experience as their reference point. For example, I have a belief that when I turn the tap handle water will come out, and when my finger is cut it will hurt. These beliefs are based on two things: first, personal experiences of these things happening, though clearly they may not happen every time, and second, development of thoughts about these experiences, which are developed into the belief.

At the other end of this dimension are beliefs which are very abstract in nature. Abstract beliefs have a reference to ideas and concepts not grounded in personal experience; they are essentially made up, for example, rules of social behavior. This is where we can get into trouble. In using abstract beliefs we have to be careful not to lose sight of the fact they are an arbitrary product of a human mind. That is, abstract beliefs are made by a human mind, and are only as good as the use people make of them. We can easily introduce flawed perceptions of our life events, because we have this capacity to create beliefs that are not based on a direct, personal experience.

The concept of manners is a great example of an abstract belief structure. Manners are guidelines for appropriate behavior in particular circumstances, made up of a complex interlocking web of concepts. Beliefs about manners are based on perceptions of appropriateness, which differ from one culture to the next, or even for different people within the same culture. As a simple example, European cultures believe it is appropriate to look people in the eye when speaking to them. Failure to do so is frequently interpreted as dishonest, disrespectful, or both. However, some Asian cultures believe it is appropriate for people to lower their eyes when speaking to those they respect. Nevertheless manners can be useful, to the extent they help facilitate social interaction.

The concept of manners also illustrates how things can go wrong with abstract beliefs. As a child I was fairly well mannered, though I did not like how it made me feel—sort of empty. My enquiry as an adolescent led me to see manners as "putting on an act", or pretending to be somebody important. I saw others display manners, but it was never really explained why. Yet I was shown what happened if I failed to tow-the-line; a very unpleasant experience.

Most beliefs work to our advantage if we keep in mind the reference point for their use. In the case of manners, this is to create something from goodwill which facilitates social interaction. If we say manners are important, but don't say why, the reason for them is lost. This may happen innocently. For example, when trying to streamline communication with a child, parents and teachers may say "good boys have good manners". In this situation they have dropped off the connection; "boys want to have friends and good manners help this."

The inherent danger with all abstract beliefs is, sooner or later, the belief will become disassociated from the reason for its inception. When we don't know why we should use manners, we end up believing it is the manners which are important. When this happens, manners will be pursued for manners' sake. These kinds of miscommunications are how beliefs corrupt our experience of life.

Once manners have lost the connection to their original purpose, they achieve an arbitrary elevated status—no reason necessary and resistant to change. When this happens, a person who believes manners are important, without knowing the reason for these rules, will be upset or offended if the rules are not followed. Can you see the irony in this? The manners created to facilitate pleasant social interaction, have become the cause of unpleasant interaction. This basic principle is involved in the development of all concepts and scripts related to unpleasant experiences. When beliefs take over in this way we become narrow-minded, judgmental, arrogant, self-righteous, and so on.

The misuse of beliefs eventuates from getting further and further away from beliefs based on direct, personal experience. Abstract beliefs make it easy for us to lose touch with our natural sense of honesty. As the basis for the belief becomes more and more arbitrary, it can only be justified or supported by more beliefs. These beliefs about beliefs become even more abstract and even less related to experience. We end up with systems of beliefs which basically no-one understands as it bears no relation to their own experience. All too often they become enshrined in the culture and resistant to change, on the grounds that people who do not know where they came from are not worthy to question them.

It is like the fable about the emperor's clothes, made of the finest linen. According to the con-man designer, people unworthy of their position could not see the clothes. No-one could see them of course, including the emperor. But they couldn't say so, for fear of being exposed as unworthy. Only an innocent child who had no position to lose eventually asked why the emperor had no clothes on.

The danger in holding beliefs is they end up taking over if not related to a natural, subjective sense of life. By analogy, developing beliefs is like programming a computer. The program is an objective creation by the programmer, who in this analogy is the subjective source. Once the program is activated, it operates independently of the programmer. We program the objective mind to take control, and it will then appear to resist any and all efforts to change; like HAL, the computer in the film *2001 A Space Odyssey*.

When the objective mind is in control, it will also corrupt the interpretation of subjective impressions which would see it deposed. For instance, our subjective experience is one of harmony and understanding, yet many readily take offence when someone doesn't do as expected. Have you ever thought this to be a bit odd? A person who is offended by what someone else says or does, will most likely believe the offending party is in the wrong, rather than asking themselves why they are offended by such behavior. This is especially inappropriate when the supposed offender is acting with good intent. Returning to my earlier example, a person offended by someone else not following the rules of good manners, is likely to blame and accuse the other person of an indiscretion.

The end result is that we listen to the products of the objective mind—our beliefs—and rarely listen to our subjective mind—instinct. In asking any question we want answered, such as the meaning of life, most people substitute an answer from their belief structures. In the extreme it becomes unacceptable to listen to our own mind—the one with the goodwill—and this is pretty much how most people live their lives.

Belief versus Experience

A belief is not a direct, personal experience. Nor do beliefs generate natural experiences. The appropriate place for beliefs is as a descriptive representation of our experiences. Beliefs are our responses to life, which colors our experience via a feedback loop. When the representations take over, watch out! We are then an accident waiting to happen.

Many people know of the wonderfully simple exercise known as Chinese whispers, designed to demonstrate how a message gets changed when it is passed from one person to another. Sit a group of people in a circle, give one person a message and ask them to whisper it to the person beside them, quickly passing it around the circle until it returns to the initiator. The message may only be said once each time, with no questions allowed. Inevitably, the message bears little or no resemblance to the original by the time it comes back to the first person. Yet each person has tried to pass on the message said to them. Some know they did not fully understand the message and may have changed it. Others believe they have passed on exactly what they heard, or at least the sense of what they heard. This is a chilling example of how people's interpretations can corrupt the transfer of information.

In this exercise, there are two mechanisms by which the message changes. One is simply mishearing the message, and the other is interpreting what was said with the objective mind, filling in the gaps based on beliefs. When information does not refer to a direct, personal experience in our own life, it is guaranteed a misunderstanding will occur sooner or later. The unsupported development of abstract beliefs is how we are led away from other natural experiences. This is a main danger in exclusive use of the objective mind.

The objective, rational mind cannot operate effectively in isolation. We need a reference point as a basis from which to conceive. This applies to the development of both simple and abstract beliefs. However, when we provide internalized beliefs as the reference point, the objective mind effectively spins on itself. We can't get past the belief. This is how we have created the conditions known as the "vicious cycle" and "catch 22". At this point, the thinking mind has become a legend in its own mind. For the objective mind to operate effectively and remain objective, its reference point has to be outside the realm of the objective mind.

So where is the source of personal experiences, if not in the objective mind or the physical sensory input to the objective mind? My answer is the impressions happening in the subjective mind, the realm of awareness, instinct and knowing. After all, every one of our natural senses is instinctive, including all manner of pleasantness— known as goodwill.

We are misusing our capacity for abstract reasoning to discard the pleasant impressions in our instinctive, subjective awareness. When our natural sense of life is no longer seen as valid, to paraphrase the saying; you have a misunderstanding waiting for a place to happen. If the objective mind is used as its own reference point, anything is justifiable. This is how we instigate, and put up with, being unpleasant to each other.

The subjective mind and objective rational mind are clearly designed to operate collaboratively. Use of beliefs to elevate the role of either mind is a mistake. Living only by the products of either mind is folly! Let me say again, our error in thinking starts with using beliefs which have no direct experience in our life.

Separation of beliefs from our instinctive senses, is our point of divergence; the elementary error in our thinking. Who knows where this started? Maybe it began back as far as the evolution of reasoning goes. What I can confidently say is most cultures today are "full of it."

Consider the implications of running our lives by beliefs. The end result is we no longer listen to the wisdom in ourselves. No wonder we don't get answers that satisfy. Our source of authority has become other people; what they think, what they say, and what they write. In many respects, it has become unacceptable to acknowledge our own sense of knowing.

Misuse of Attention

A classic example of how our beliefs corrupt our realities can be seen with our attitudes toward the concept of attention. Although it is slowly changing, society's prevailing view still seems to be that attention must be withheld so children do not get spoilt. Somewhere down the track in English culture, a norm was established whereby attention was a bad thing to have or to give—this belief was very prevalent in the era of my upbringing. It probably relates to a belief linking attention to ego, which needs to be controlled. This might be a good construct to break down to its components.

Let me start with an alternative view about attention; attention is the single most significant thing we have to give. Consider the possibility that other qualities, such as caring, are already built into the system. In other words, all our good qualities such as kindness, nurturing, and consideration, are part of our nature or will which is impressed upon the subjective mind. Attention to these subjective impressions enables us to express them, thus making these pleasant qualities our direct experience. If attention to our subjective impressions does this for us, what benefit does it have to give it to others?

Attentiveness, our conscious choice to attend to an event, is the only quality which is one hundred percent at our disposal to give or withhold. As such, it wields great power. Receiving attention is the key to feeling validated as a person. Not receiving attention, at a deep level means not existing—annihilation—which is one of our greatest and darkest learned fears. Therefore, withholding attention is something we must be very careful with. I have seen many young children devastated from an accidental oversight by a parent. How much more damage happens if attention is deliberately withheld? **Giving attention is the single most important gift we give to anyone, in particular our children**. It is the very basis of our relationship with them, because this simple act of acceptance gives a sense of belonging and meaningfulness to their life, and promotes willingness for them to give you their attention. In this connectedness they feel loving acceptance from others and for others. In the world of the objective mind, giving generously of attention is the greatest of all things humans have to give, and therefore the most valuable.

We have dirtied and corrupted the concept of attention, evident in our language when we talk about it. We talk about *seeking* attention, *demanding* attention, *paying* attention ... even about attention deficit disorder. Attention seeking behavior is perceived as very negative, in both children and adults. As kids, most of us were made to feel bad about wanting attention.

The commonly cited example related to attention is the "attention seeking" behavior of children. Many parents are very uncomfortable with giving their child attention. They observe children liking attention and doing whatever it takes to get it, so they believe giving attention to the child rewards attention-seeking behavior. In essence this is the psychological principle of reinforcement, though a better application of it for parents is to be discerning about which aspects of the child's behavior receives attention. Pleasant behavior should be rewarded with attention. Unpleasant behavior should be carefully redirected, by asking for the child's attention and showing your attention being given to pleasant behavior—yours and theirs. Also, many parents do not understand that yelling at the child or ridiculing them is giving them attention, and in the list of human "wants" attention rates very highly, so for the child negative attention is better than no attention. In this instance the parent is showing their attention is given to unpleasant behavior.

Sometimes the child has been given attention only when they seek it. Some parents huff and puff about giving attention, as if it is a total inconvenience to relate to their child. This is incredibly damning to a child's self-image. The child can then develop an insatiable appetite for attention. In this situation the child has been taught only to seek attention, and has not been shown what it means to *give* attention. Attention given by the child to the parent most likely was overlooked or ignored by the parent; **yet responding to a child giving attention to you is crucial to having a balanced child**. In other words, the parent should accept and receive the child's attention. Hence one of my favorite pieces of simple advice to any parent is to treat your child as a friend and an equal.

At school we were told to "pay" attention. It was demanded of us as something expected and forcibly extracted from us, which is why most people begrudge giving it. But we instinctively know its power. It is the only thing we can withhold when all else is stripped from us, leading many children to introversion or non-communication as their protest. I knew well this approach as a child. We were rarely asked to give attention, and with few exceptions we were not freely given it ourselves, except when we did wrong. When we were not misbehaving we were left alone and not given attention. How wrong this is, I will leave you to ponder.

Another important aspect of giving attention is being able to give ourselves attention. Can you do this easily? If the parents can do this for themselves, the child will also learn to do this. The net result of this is the child will also be happy in their own company.

Pain versus Suffering

Another example worth examining is our beliefs about pain. A common challenge to counter the view of life, that all's well, is the experience of physical pain, which doesn't feel good to most people. This makes it a special case, because the pain itself is not a script or belief. However, beliefs are involved in how we handle pain, so this is a good opportunity to see if pain fits into the view that all is good with life.

I'll start by making a distinction between pain and suffering. Pain is a noxious stimulus delivered by the nervous system, which prompts the physical system to act in a particular way. Intense pain can send us into shock, but many people have also experienced intense pain which did not overwhelm their calm mental state. Have you ever had this experience?

Suffering is an emotion, which may or may not be triggered by physical pain. If we have learned to regard pain as unbearable, then we will suffer our pain, and it will overwhelm our calm—it will not feel good. In this situation a belief has been used to overlay the experience of pain. Whatever we allow into our objective minds affects our emotions. If we entertain the belief suggesting pain is unpleasant, then we get an unpleasant emotion about it. In effect we are then having an unpleasant experience of pain.

In this example of physical pain, the pain can also be considered life enhancing. For example, if you receive a cut to your arm it stings. This pain is a unique signal to the brain indicating the system has been compromised and action is required. It is also a hard-to-ignore signal from your body to your conscious mind, asking you to give attention to the body. In response to the pain signal, the brain initiates the release of coagulants into the blood, to go to the source of the injury and stem the blood flow. At a later time, endorphins are sent to reduce the pain and the corpuscles are stimulated to begin new tissue growth. The healing response is built into the system. Consciousness of the pain also enables you to render active assistance to your body, such as helping stop the blood-flow. Thus, when our system is compromised, it is good we feel pain, despite it being a noxious experience. If it were a pleasant experience we wouldn't mind bleeding to death!

I saw an interesting documentary which brought home this point about pain being life enhancing. It was about a young girl about seven years of age, who could not feel pain because of some rare medical condition. I remember a vivid scene of this girl running around the yard at home, with her leg badly broken and not in a cast. It was evident this was a life-threatening condition, because she did not know when her physical body was compromised and in need of attention.

We simulate this situation when we use beliefs to manage pain. Many people have developed—learned—a strong fear of pain, and want to avoid both physical and emotional pain at any cost. In this event, the resulting unpleasant experience is a function of the belief about pain. This is another dysfunctional script; not the avoidance, but the use of fear to avoid pain.

Dr. Warren Stanton

Intelligent Cooperation of Our Minds

Let me come back to why misuse of our minds to elevate beliefs is so damning. Clearly, I am advocating such use of beliefs is not based in instinct, and this is where things have gone wrong. Shutting off our instinct has been the main error. We have taken our instinctive initiatives for meeting life events, and tried to change them with our conscious, thinking mind. The following example highlights how this harms us.

Instinct is a blueprint of what works for us. For each of us, an instinctive expression when faced with unknown or unrecognized stimulation is to be startled. However, what happens if a child uses their objective mind to develop fear-based beliefs about being startled? For example, during my primary school years children used to make a loud noise to startle others, then ridicule them for being a "scaredy-cat". If fear is used to develop a generalized belief that being startled is followed by ridicule, the net result when the child gets alarmed will be to freak out—meaning get very anxious. Without a reference point to the instinct the child sees only the belief. In so doing, they are by definition in error.

There is an implication here I will now refute. Some of you may read into the above comments that I am taking the line of "don't meddle with nature." Such an implication would go against a whole lot of lines of scientific endeavor. This is definitely not what I am advocating. The response I talk about in the chapter on solutions is one of intelligent co-operation between our minds. We do pose questions, and we *do* get answers. Consequently, we should defer to our inherent intelligence rather than believe nature got it wrong.

The model I am presenting maintains instinct is an incentive for us to think and act. The mechanism by which this impulse reaches the objective mind is in the form of appetites or "likes", which the objective mind translates as want—Figure 2. This may seem over-simplified, but this is not critical to the case I am developing.

The point I wish to make is, from here on things can go wrong. The objective mind translates want into concepts by using the thought processes, for example wanting food. In turn, concepts are used to make up belief structures, which are the basis of further thinking and action, such as where to get food. However, we commonly misuse the objective mind to create beliefs which are not a true reflection of our natural appetites. An example would be to translate my hunger into a belief I am deprived of food. This belief will have a corrupting influence; it will cause me to suffer from hunger, and put me at risk of over-eating.

A primary mechanism behind this is fear, discussed further in Chapter 6. In the model shown in Figure 3, when the objective mind is running the show using fear, we turn against our instinct. In the case of hunger this might mean having no enthusiasm or excitement at the prospect of finding food, and no enjoyment in eating it. This represents a denial of our core sense of self.

So do I have a chance of exposing the misuse of beliefs? Who would believe me? Well, on this score I hope no-one, because an examination of beliefs is best based on your own experience. Ask yourself in honesty, what do beliefs do for you if they are not based on your own experience? That is one scary question I implore you to pursue relentlessly, because our misuse of beliefs is a central part of why we have unpleasant experiences. If you want not to suffer, going **beyond belief** is essential.

FIGURE 2

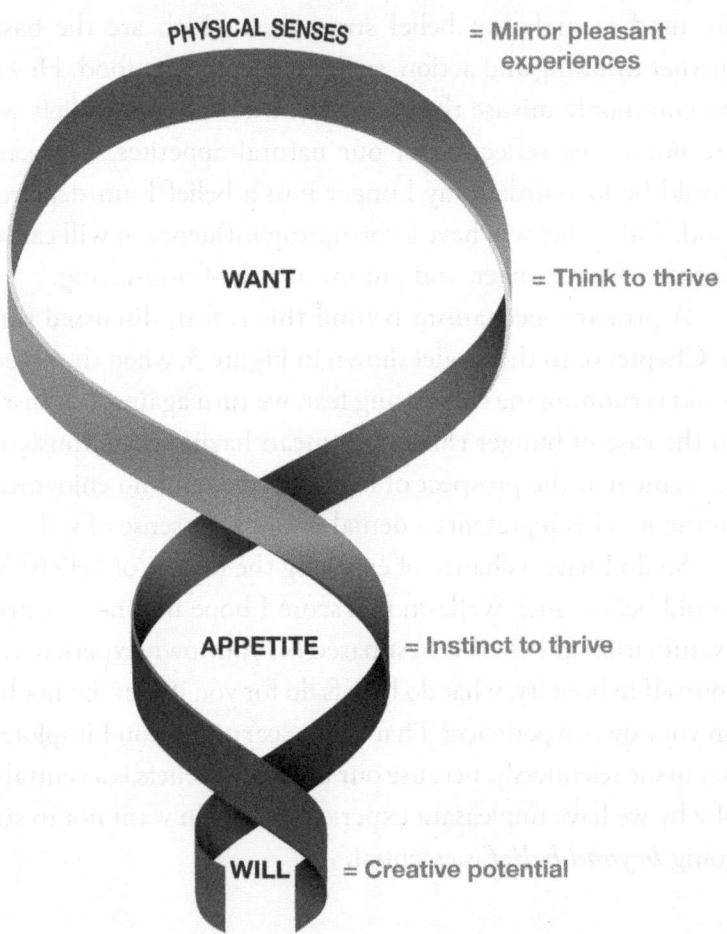

Figure 2. Model of our minds governed by will

FIGURE 3

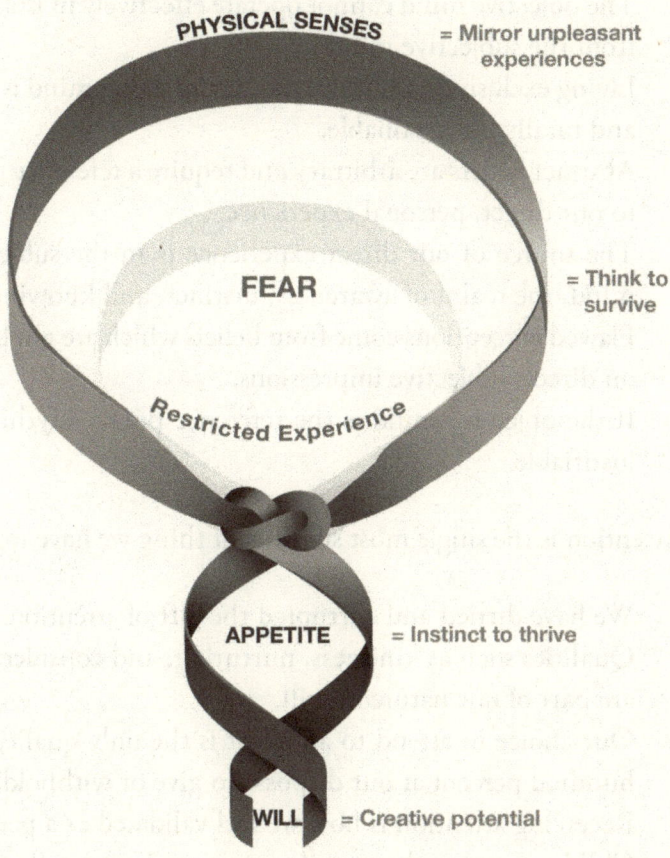

Figure 3. Model of our minds governed by beliefs from the objective mind rejecting the instinct

Summary

The subjective and objective minds are designed to operate in collaboration:

- What we conceive of becomes our reality.
- The objective mind cannot operate effectively in isolation from the subjective mind.
- Living exclusively from the product of either mind is folly and totally unsustainable.
- Abstract beliefs are arbitrary and require a reference point to our direct, personal experience.
- The source of our direct experience is in the subjective mind, the realm of awareness, instinct, and knowing.
- Flawed perceptions come from beliefs which are not based on direct, subjective impressions.
- If the objective mind is the reference point, anything is justifiable.

Attention is the single most significant thing we have to give:

- We have dirtied and corrupted the gift of attention.
- Qualities such as kindness, nurturing, and consideration are part of our nature or will.
- Our choice to attend to an event is the only quality one hundred percent at our disposal to give or withhold.
- Receiving attention is how we feel validated as a person.
- Children are taught to seek attention, but usually aren't taught to give attention.

The use of beliefs not based on our instinct is where things have gone wrong:

- Without our beliefs having a reference point to instinct, we are by definition in self-denial.
- The instinct is an impetus for us to think and act.
- If a belief is not a reflection of a natural appetite, it has a corrupting influence.
- Corrupted beliefs taint our wants.
- If we believe pain is unbearable, we will suffer our pain.
- Beliefs are often used as a substitute when we don't get satisfying answers from our mind.

For you not to suffer it is essential to go beyond belief.

FIVE

Unpleasant Experiences

When we experience pain in our body, has our system got it wrong or got it right? Is pain an indication the body is failing to do its job? I would say not; it is working fine, and giving us feedback. Similarly, if we experience unhappiness or suffering, are our minds letting us down or still doing their job? When the output of our mind is unpleasant, we see this as proof something is wrong with it. Does this seem logical to you? To me it is the most absurd conclusion we could come up with, yet this view is so widely accepted. Few believe, if their body is in pain it is malfunctioning, and doing the wrong thing by them. So why believe this about our mind? It is a rare event for our physical system to go wrong without us having a hand in it. This applies even more so to your mental system, because this is the one we are directly in charge of with the intellect.

The idea our minds get it wrong is a concept I wish to challenge. Rather, if the output of my mind is unpleasant, it is a signal I am misusing my mind at that moment. When I feel distressed I don't blame my mind. If my present moment experience is unpleasant, it means I am using a belief structure containing unpleasantness—a belief with no reference to my instinct.

Consider what we know about our bodies. Our entire system from head to toe, functions to sustain the existence of the body. When it is compromised it lets us know. Our mind is no exception. It gives us a signal. However, having invested so much in the thinking mind to solve the problems, we have lost sight of the instinct's signal.

Making Problems

The example I wish to take up here is the view life presents us with problems. When I use the term "problem" I mean "something wrong," associated with feeling unpleasant. The view of events as problems is a belief structure. This concept has lost its reference to intelligence exhibited as goodwill. When we perceive a problem, we are choosing to believe something has gone wrong. We discount the possibility that how we are thinking, makes it look like a problem. When we conceive of things as problems, we have created exactly that—a problem. We tend to ignore our role as creator of the problem, failing to see our point of view can distort what we are looking at.

Seeing life as a problem is a distortion, similar to "looking at life through rose-colored glasses." But "problem-colored glasses" give an unpleasant distortion, which, unlike roses, convince us life stinks. Once the problem is in front of our eyes, how we then think and act is distorted by the perception it really is a problem. Since others will agree with this point of view, it confirms your perception, so it must be true, mustn't it? Do you agree? I certainly do not!

This belief in a life of problems ensures we experience life as a burden. Having dispensed with our sense of goodwill, we readily find support for a life full of problems. We see plenty of examples of things going wrong in the world, all manner of trouble and strife, and we use this as confirmation for the idea life is problematic. In the big picture this includes expressions of cruelty and inhumanity. Conceiving of inhumane ideas and acting on them is born from fear, and shows ignorance about how our minds work. Those who participate in these events have lost touch with the signal of instinct felt as goodwill.

Allow me to challenge some common beliefs about the virtues of the "problem" view of life. People who adhere to this view tend to think if something is not seen as a problem, nothing will be done to change it. But I challenge whether seeing anything from an unpleasant point of view actually helps motivate us. I am suggesting most people are less likely to be motivated if unpleasantness is the established view of life.

For a number of reasons, seeing problems as a valid part of life reduces the likelihood of taking action to change them. First, life is full of problems—too many to deal with. Second, they are familiar—better the devil you know. Third, having problems feels bad to us—it is not natural for us to act from disharmony. We have to force ourselves to do this. Fourth, the concept of a problem is based in fear—our natural response is to avoid or resist it. Anything which is unpleasant is naturally abhorrent to us, so is unlikely to inspire us.

Other beliefs compound the problem. For example, rather than seeing avoidance of unpleasantness as part of our instinct, we believe it is a weakness. Having seen it this way, we then have to justify this weakness to ourselves. We do this by developing more beliefs, such as considering the resistance to be laziness, stubbornness, or other negative traits. This allows us to avoid or sidestep our natural revulsion to the unpleasant things we have conceived in our mind—the problems. The key to unraveling this mess is to understand why we force ourselves to do what is unpleasant to us. I will shortly discuss this in the context of learning to be unhappy.

The unpleasant feeling accompanying the "problem" view of life is the real indicator the mind is being misused. This self-evident statement was a bombshell for me; when there is unpleasantness in your experience, look no further than the belief being used in that moment. What is more, I saw unpleasant experiences such as the vicious cycle of negative thinking, sustained by me persisting with those beliefs.

For people caught in this loop, it can be hard to see that the way out of the loop is not rational or logical. We cannot find the solution with objective thinking alone. This is how over-reliance on objective reasoning imprisons us. As a result, we have come to fear our thinking mind because we do not understand how it works, and we defer to the explanation there is something wrong with it. If you want to live without suffering, this is a belief you must challenge.

On the other hand, if we choose not to believe life is a problem, the vicious cycle of a problematic life is not evident. Our minds are then open to solutions, or to moving on. Life is not actually a problem. Seeing it as a problem is what causes it to be a problem. If your attitude to life's challenges is "no problem", chances are they won't become one. Our mind can produce unpleasant experiences and the body can feel pain. These experiences indicate the system has been compromised. As a result the healing response is set in motion. Where is the problem?

Rather than think our mind is doing the wrong thing by us, consider this possibility; our fear and ignorance of how we use our minds causes most of our suffering. Using our mind at odds with our will can result in extreme effects. For those few who still think the mind doesn't affect the body, consider the effect of stress on the digestive system, which can alter the acidity level of the stomach, resulting in a range of physical symptoms including indigestion, heartburn, and reflux. I think most people now accept our mind does affect the functioning of the brain, emotions, and body, so why do many find it hard to accept it can have an extreme effect, like depression and other mental health conditions. This is not saying all imbalances are the result of misuse of our mind, just the greater majority. The point is, we are the ones who mostly cause the imbalance, not our mind doing something wrong by us.

Most people accept, at least in theory, that stress is predominantly a result of how we perceive life events. In other words, our experiences of stress are the effect of our belief structures. The most common belief structure causing stress relates to expectations. In this context, holding unrealistic expectations is an example of how misuse of the mind affects the body. Stress is a function of how we perceive life events, which is firmly at our discretion. Unfortunately, we tend to wait until the effects of stress manifest in the physical body before we try to reduce it, which in the case of a stroke, can be much too late.

There are other factors at work, including hereditary and environmental influences. Take care not to blame them either. Some people may be more disposed to feel stressed when these influences are present, but it is hard to argue our genetic make-up initially causes the stress. If it does, this would mean we have no choice about whether or not we get stressed, and this is obviously untrue. Environmental factors, such as a tendency to become more stressed when tired or hungry, are usually under our influence. If we had no such choice, this would make us a catastrophically unsuccessful species, especially if natural selection weeded out the ones not adapting to their environment.

Nothing has control over us in any absolute sense of the word. There are strong influences, but no control. Even our will does not control. The issue of whether or not the body is controlled by the will or instinct could be discussed at some length. However, the point I am making is this; even if instinct controls my body, it doesn't control "me." An intelligent system in which the will and subjective mind direct a co-operating vessel, the objective mind and body, does not fit the definition of control. I shall defer a full discussion of control to a later chapter.

Learning to See Life as a Horrible Experience

Let us look at some other examples of how beliefs affect our daily living. We all harbor an intriguing web of beliefs, most of which we believe are based on someone's experience. In content, these range from the simple to the absurd. However, most of them are not based on personal experience at all.

As a simple example, consider the situation of the shop assistant who believes life is horrible because he or she has to work. If they are serving me, odds are they will in some way be horrible to me. If my response is to feel horrible, and then in turn act horribly, isn't this proof I am horrible? Well, actually no! I would have adopted this behavior as a means of responding to the perceived horribleness. It is learned horribleness, not my true nature.

Here comes one of my potentially outrageous statements. The idea of being a horrible person never came, nor will ever come from, the instinctive sense of knowing. No child has ever thought they were horrible, without someone else seeding this idea. Personally speaking, I have felt horrible and had horrid thoughts, but I have never experienced or sensed a genuine source of horribleness in me. Have you? Someone else's interpretation of my actions may result in me being seen as a horrible person. It is just like the example of manners.

This statement then begs the following question. Where did the horribleness come from? It may sound ridiculous, but the answer is "I caught it from someone else," much like you catch a cold. I would only see myself as horrible if I were told and accepted this from a source whose opinion I trusted or valued. If I have not had my instinctive sense of knowing validated, being told I am horrible can over-ride the natural impression of my true nature as goodwill. Now I believe I am horrible, and I have an experience I interpret as backing up this belief.

A major influence on our misguided thinking comes from believing the horrible behavior is there against our choice. Again, this is far from the truth. This belief comes from misunderstanding the source of the horrible thoughts and behavior. For example, we have produced the erroneous belief our true nature is in part unsavory, or animal, and therefore undesirable. This seems to be confirmed when we choose to direct horrible behavior toward others. However, if you understand the following example of how we can learn to be unhappy, you may see how this is not the case and understand how and why we exhibit horribleness in our social interactions.

As discussed, the horrible beliefs and behaviors are not there without our choice in the matter. We have simply lost sight of why we put them there. These horrible effects are there because we still want them there. This sounds harsh, but it really isn't and I want to explain why. The best example I can think of to illustrate this is how we learn to be unhappy. Before I tell this story, let me give you the up-shot of it. The unhappiness, like manners, serves our purposes. The unpleasant beliefs and behavior work for us, but they have side effects. They make us feel awful. Why then would we choose horrible beliefs and experiences? As discussed, it is done out of love for the person who exhibited the horribleness to us in the first instance. The following example of learning to be unhappy, explains how this is functional in the context in which it is learned.

How does the horribleness work for us? When a horrible view of life is a common belief, using it to interact with others works better than other alternatives. If your parents think life is difficult, then relating to them from the perspective of having difficulty will more likely get a response from them, and from others who share the same view. So in this situation, being in difficulty supports the family interactions. It is the glue binding people together. Of course it has a downside. It means you will see more difficulty in your life; first of all because it gets a response, second because other people will present their life as difficult when they want a response, and third because if you go against it, you will be shown how much more difficult your life can become. This is probably why most people cannot accept the horribleness is there by choice. After all, who in their right mind would choose to feel unpleasant?

Consider why we would want to be unhappy. The simple answer is because it works for us. It has a payoff of helping us get what we want. The fact of the matter is, when we are unhappy, we have chosen this outlook. It is not a natural part of our nature. Even so, why would we keep holding on to constructs or beliefs which cause us discontent and disharmony? People continue to use these beliefs in other environments such as the workplace, and often find it works there as well. So a heavily reinforced belief will not necessarily be given up in situations where it is not working.

Let me relate a story to you to explain how we learn to be unhappy. It is an account of events most people seem to relate to in their own experience, and certainly applied to me. During my childhood, authoritarian parenting was considered both normal and desirable. Parents were expected to have control over their children. Children were expected to do as they were told and parents were expected to hand out punishment for transgressions. Of course this was believed to be necessary. Children had to be disciplined or they would give in to the unruly or unholy part of their nature, right? Yet forcing children to do things makes them give up their instinctive, innocent sense that all is good and well. This usually sows the seed of rebellion in children, as they express and transfer the natural anger produced by being forced to believe they are bad or do bad things.

The story goes as follows. Imagine a child, full of the joy of life, as all children are. This is most evident in an infant and is noticeably changing by about two years of age. In this joy the child instinctively feels life is good, and cannot yet conceive of it any other way. In joy, the child is happy to see it reflected in other people. This innocence is so beautiful to see. No-one really wants to see it corrupted do they? At least those listening to their instinct in the face of such innocence would not want this corrupted. This is especially the case for the mother of the child.

Above all, the parents want the child to be happy. Now imagine this sense of life being good has been corrupted in most of us. Imagine the mother being unhappy with her lot in life. She does not want to expose the child to the unhappiness she feels. Therefore, when she is unhappy she will turn away from the child and withhold her attention. At some point in time the child will sense this as rejection. This effectively gives the message the child is doing something wrong by being happy. The better alternative in this situation is for the mother to accept the child's joy in place of her unhappiness, but this is difficult if following an authoritarian path of parenting. Nevertheless, happiness is not lost yet because at other times when the mother is happy, there is significant pleasant interaction to counteract this rejection.

However, there is a second part to the story which changes things completely. Imagine the child going to school and one day gets pushed around by another child. The child comes home unhappy. When the mother sees the child unhappy, being the last thing in the world she wants for the child, what does she do? She showers the child with affection, attention, and concern. What has she taught the child? Unhappiness can overcome the mother's unhappiness. Previously, she taught the child that happiness was not enough to overcome her unhappiness. In sum, she has taught the child to be unhappy. Why? The child's sense of goodwill wants two things with their mother: to have significant attention and interaction with her ***and to see her happy***. For the child it is evident, being happy achieves the first outcome some of the time, but doesn't have any effect on the second one.

However, being unhappy achieves both very effectively. It is a double bonus! Adopting the unhappy view of life as a belief, achieves significant interaction with most people, particularly those who have adopted sympathy as a life script. Added to this, the child gets what he or she wants; to experience happiness, reflected in seeing the mother happy. What is the cost? The child is in total conflict about being happy by perceiving greater benefit from being unhappy. Sounds neurotic to me—and this would be evident in the child's behavior!

There are a number of points I want to clarify. First, I am not talking about pretending to be unhappy. I am talking about taking on a view of the world as an unhappy place. There will be plenty more experiences of bullying or control to back up this belief, many coming from the parents themselves. Second, belief structures tend to be combinations of beliefs. If the mother regards the happiness of the child as more important than her happiness, this also is transmitted to the child. The consequence of this is the child will take on having a happy mother as their own number one priority. In other words, the child has taken on board a belief in which the happiness of others is more important than their own. Truly, out of love for the mother, the child will take on unhappiness. Additionally, the child will take on putting self aside, as the proper means to care for others. This is a common belief called selfless caring. This script justifies the mother turning away from the child when unhappy, and hanging onto the unhappiness in the face of the child's happiness. Is this true caring? I certainly challenge this belief.

In this way, unhappiness is based on a belief and is learned. It is kept in place because it works. We choose to be unhappy. It is not there against our will. As we grow up, we retain and continue to use the same strategies and beliefs which worked for us in the past. In this way we actively hang on to the belief structures causing us disharmony and discontent. However, in later life, when we experience the unhappiness we are not usually aware of how it was created. Because it goes against our wishes to be unhappy, we tend to rationalize and develop incorrect beliefs about why it is there, usually blaming the factor which triggered the unhappiness, for example the parents or the mind. At least this is the case until we are willing to recognize and challenge our belief about whether we have to be unhappy.

The elements of this story reflect the very basis of an important psychological principle. In this example being unhappy is rewarded and over time repeatedly reinforced. This strengthens these particular learned responses to life events. They are stored in memory to be used whenever the opportunity arises. These beliefs are called dysfunctional schema or scripts, but in the context of the environment in which they are learned they are functional. Remember, there is good intent behind the transmission of these scripts, though it may not be evident if you look at the behavior alone.

Now, if we learn to conceive of unpleasant things and take them on as a way of life, the implications are huge. Imagine if all the experiences which originate with us and do not feel good to us, are of this nature. If this is true, and my instinct says it is, then it provides the evidence our true nature is not in any way undesirable, and our motivation is always seeded from goodwill—perverted as it is in our expression on many occasions. Our true intent is not based in some horrible, shady or undesirable part of our character or core nature.[2]

The point is, undesirable responses are learned, and we hang on to them even though they make us suffer. They are there because we want them there. They are not there against our will or our choice. In the example of learning to be unhappy, as applied to my upbringing, it seemed a small price to pay to get what I really wanted; to see my mother happy, or at least not feeling miserable. Had I known by doing this I allowed the transmission of unhappiness from my mother to me, perhaps things could have been different. Little did I realize at the time; this is also how she became unhappy in her childhood.

When I say to people, whatever doesn't feel good to us is of our own creation, it often invokes expressions of disbelief. In general, people justify their experience of not feeling good by citing a range of unpleasant beliefs or scripts. These can range from the simple belief "you can't be happy all the time" to the seemingly profound "life wasn't meant to be easy." In all such cases we

---

[2] Some people use the term "character" interchangeably with "personality," but I reserve "personality" for the sum of our learned behavior, residing in the memory system of the objective mind. Our personality is the modes of behavior we present to the world, based on belief structures which form our personas.

have chosen a view of life as a burden or some other unpleasant construct. However you look at life, your beliefs will turn out to be a self-fulfilling prophesy. If you wear unpleasant-colored glasses everything you see will be tainted by unpleasantness.

A key piece of evidence used to support this belief in "unpleasantness", is all the horrible things going on in the world. Every manner of unpleasant human behavior is held up as proof of humans' inhumanity to humans. It doesn't really matter which came first; the belief or the experience of unpleasantness. If we first experienced unpleasant behavior from others, we were told to be on guard against such behaviors in ourselves, for example greed, jealousy, hatred. If the beliefs about unpleasantness were presented to us first, human behavior provided the evidence, for example, stealing, violence, corruption. Can you see the error in taking this as proof? Once the interpretation of unpleasantness is put in place and upheld against any other interpretation, it is hard to see how it could not be true. This is how we deceive ourselves.

What is all this unpleasantness based on? Simply from experiencing other people perpetrate this unpleasantness, and believing it's the right way to interpret life events. Why do we do so? It is seen as the normal thing to do. It is how we are told the world works, and it seems to be confirmed by our experience of life. But it is not our natural experience. For evidence of this you need only look at the joy exuding from an infant. They show the natural experience of life to be joyful, before it gets corrupted. The issue for us is how to restore this experience back in an adult mind.

Our corruption occurs throughout early childhood, particularly in learning how to treat other people. For instance, people will say they like people, but often they are really thinking of just a few people they like. In general, people learn to put up with other people being unpleasant. This seems to be based on a learned idea of tolerance, or a wish to be socially acceptable, or part of how we get ahead in a world where we have to deal with people. If you listen closely, most people do not actually like a lot of what others do. How many genuinely pleasant people do you know—and I mean genuine from the core? Many people don't even see it as a desirable quality, instead embracing beliefs such as, "you have to be a bastard to succeed." It should not surprise you that many people do not like other people. It is not difficult to understand why.

Although there are a lot of exceptions, in general people are unpleasant to other people. Most often these unpleasantries are subtle to the point of not being noticed, usually in the form of not giving attention, or slight indifference—uncaring—or disregarding the presence of another person. At the other end of the spectrum our attitude to others can be veiled in contempt, disdain, disrespect, intimidation or some other equally unpleasant attitude. Why? Not because it is our true nature. Rather, unpleasantness has worked for us in the environment in which it was adopted. It is a belief structure or script we use to interact with our environment and get what we want. Remembering the story of learning to be unhappy, this exhibition of unpleasantness is the hypocrisy I saw as a child. As I look at it now it seems nothing short of criminal, a violation of the most basic of human rights.

So, in the next two chapters, I will move the discussion of corrupted beliefs on to the most significant beliefs governing our perception of life events as unpleasant. These are the most damaging constructs conceived by the human mind: beliefs based on fear and control. It is our belief in these two constructs which causes most of our troubles. They are the most damaging, because they are so embedded in how we think about life they are hardly recognizable as beliefs anymore.

Summary

Our will, mind and body form an intelligent system functioning to nurture our existence:

- When this system is compromised it lets us know.
- When the output of our mind is unpleasant, we are misusing it.
- Our natural response to fear or anything unpleasant is avoidance or resistance.
- It is not natural for us to act from disharmony.
- Anything unpleasant is naturally abhorrent to us.
- Nothing has control over us in the absolute sense of the word, not even our will.

This is a summary of the mess we have created with our beliefs:

- Development of beliefs in the absence of instinct has led to unpleasantness.
- The presence of unpleasantness in our experience is the real indicator of when our mind is being misused.
- We find fault with our mind rather than accept responsibility for creating the unpleasantness.
- Seeing life as a problem legitimizes the view that problems are naturally occurring events.
- To believe life is horrible is to induce a horrible, unpleasant experience.

Some challenges to our typical attempts to think our way out of unpleasantness are:

- No child has ever thought they are horrible without someone else seeding this idea.
- It is misguided to believe the horrible things in us are against our choice.
- We take on the unpleasantness out of love for the people showing the unpleasantness.
- Unpleasantness in any form is learned, it is not our direct impression of life.

The way out of the vicious cycle of unpleasantness is not logical or rational, but instinctive.

SIX

BELIEF IN FEAR

The issue of fear isn't central to my explanation of how we set things right, but it is central to how we got it wrong. The explanation I present, says fear is the centerpiece of our misunderstanding about life. For me this "shoe fits the best", because it explains so much about why we suffer. The case I am going to make is that fear is the primary horrible "dis-ease" infecting and corrupting us, and it is not our natural response to life. Our experience of fear is the reason we think there is a problem with life. However, if we can undermine fear, this is one piece of evidence that a solution to our suffering is at hand; a sizeable piece I would say.

Again, I ask you to please suspend your beliefs as much as you can while you read, this chapter in particular. Suspending your beliefs allows you to gain a broader, more open view of my perspective, without your beliefs lending an interpretation which may not be the meaning I intend. You can compare these ideas with your beliefs later on, and see what you think.

The Nature of Fear

I ask you to consider this idea; fear is the basis of all the unpleasantness we experience. If this is so, fear is the worst experience we have in life. You may believe fear is unavoidable, unwelcome, and a part of our instinct we should have under control. I want to make a head-on challenge to these beliefs.

My main comments about fear are sometimes met with disbelief, so now is a good time to look beyond your beliefs. ***Fear is not part of our instinct. Our use of fear is learned***. Of course instinct supports our survival, but does fear do this? I would say not. At least, not the experience we usually refer to as fear. We use the word "fear" to mean two vastly different experiences. One is based in instinct and the other in belief. I will tease them apart and explain why this distinction matters.

What does the word "fear" mean? We lump lots of different meanings and a lot of power onto this word. In everyday use, the word fear can mean: terror, horror, doom, dread, panic, trepidation, feeling afraid, worry, apprehension, alarm, and fright. I have ordered these synonyms of fear as I perceive them, roughly along a continuum from greater to lesser intensity.

However, to me these terms do not represent a singular dimension of our experience of life. ***Dread*** is not just a more intense version of ***alarm***. The experiences described by these words differ in terms of whether they are functional or dysfunctional. Dread and alarm are completely different experiences, yet we commonly use the term fear to refer to both.

As an example, consider how we address potential danger. An unusual sound triggers a startle response—alarm—which allows us to give greater attention to, and be prepared for a possible threat. This is an instinctive sense for coping with danger. Interpretation of the unusual sound by the thinking mind, gives us options for action. Some of these are constructive, such as "get out of the way in a hurry", and some dysfunctional, such as panic, which sometimes results in us going nowhere. In this case, the panic is an interpretation of the consequences, unrelated to the initial startle response. The point I wish to make here, is that the instinctive, functional initiative occurs in the subjective mind. The learned response, which may be functional or dysfunctional, occurs in the objective mind.

In sum, we use the term "fear" loosely, to refer not only to the instinctive component, but also to the experiences of horror and dread, which are very unpleasant and disempowering. For this discussion, we should call the instinctive initiative something different from the mental response. It seems reasonable to retain the terms fright—frightened—for the instinct, and fear—fearful—for the dysfunctional thoughts and emotions.

The Difference between Fright and Fear

I observe the experiences of being frightened and fearful, coming from different places in me; that is, different minds. Fright is a subjective sense linked to my awareness; an initiative of instinct. Fear is a morbidly unpleasant experience always involving my objective mind; a response of the thinking mind. Scrutiny of my feelings and thoughts shows me other important differences between being frightened and fearful:

1. They affect my mind differently. When frightened, my objective mind remains clear; when fearful, my objective mind becomes clouded and confused.
2. They have different pathways. Fright precedes and initiates clear thoughts. Fear appears as an image in my mind, usually a type of blackness. This image is an

interpretation of the event I am facing, for example my possible death, which adversely affects my emotions.

These important distinctions between fright and fear can be summed up in the terms "proactive" and "reactive" respectively. Let's look at these terms in more detail. When I watched the experience of fear closely, I noticed it was a response, or reaction, to a stimulus in the world. The stimulus happens, my mind interprets it, and the fear follows. The unpleasantness of fear is not there before an event triggers it. In this sense fear is reactive. This is not to say you can't feel fear all the time if the trigger is generalized to all life events.

You might ask "isn't getting a fright also a reaction to an event?" I think not, and this is why; my instinctive system is always on, so I am alert all the time. In other words, my instinct is active before the event. I can find no evidence of instinct reacting to the environment. It is proactively looking for the cues which signal harmony. When the harmony is interrupted by a loud sound, my system increases my arousal level dramatically to cause a fright. The fright is an intense magnification of a normal level of ongoing alertness. For example, a magnification of my normal alertness is often experienced as excitement or alarm. But if I have fear running as a belief at the time of the fright, my thoughts and feelings get further intensified as anxiety. It is reasonable to conclude, ***anxiety is excitement corrupted by fear***.

Instinct is already in place and acting upon the environment. By this I mean I am always ready to act in one way or another, including thinking. In this sense, instinct initiates all our actions and interactions with the environment. For me this is a most important detail when discussing solutions to our dilemma. So let me say it again. Instinct is already prompting us to do proactive things to the environment to continue our existence. Not just to survive but to *thrive*. Instinct is sensed as an appetite to act on or change the environment, like physical hunger, but not so slow in the case of a fright!

There is also a time difference in the occurrence of fright, compared to fear. A clean instinctive vital urge always precedes the morbid experience of fear. It all happens pretty quickly, so you need to be on the ball to notice it. When I hear a loud noise, my normal sense of alertness becomes fright. This causes a sense of readiness to take action. Then a split second later I may start to get the morbid experience of fear. Whenever I feel fear, it comes just after I start to interpret the events. In other words, fear comes just after I call upon my scripts and beliefs to make sense of the unfolding event. That is why I refer to the fear as an "add on." The proactive instinct has already met the loud noise prompting a fright, before the reactive fear sets in. The instinct and fear thus have different mechanisms of operation.

The key to understanding the difference is in the nature of the experience. My normal sense of alertness is a pleasant experience, and when the fright occurs it retains the sense of harmony. It does not always turn into an unpleasant feeling, depending on whether or not the fear gets triggered in the objective mind. On the other hand, pleasant experiences don't have to be triggered. My goodwill is always acting upon the world via my instinct, in this case causing me to be alert. This is my appetite for life. It's just that sometimes the signals of my will are obscured by the product of my objective mind.

Fright without Fear

Eventually, I understood the significance of these differences between fright and fear. They are characteristics of how the subjective and the objective minds operate. All purely subjective impressions contain a pleasant feeling, such as feeling assured I can cope, whereas purely objective thinking takes me away from feeling and toward emotion, such as being unsure.

You may already be aware of the difference between feeling and emotion, but we usually do not make anything of it. It took me most of my life to figure out that they are completely different types of experiences. The objective mind is linked to emotion, the subjective mind is not. A low-level harmonious feeling is always there as a subjective impression of life, whereas emotions come and go. Feelings act upon the environment like a sense, whereas emotions are a response to an event, usually a reaction to something said, done or expected. Feelings are proactive, emotions reactive, which is of no surprise if they are coming from different minds.

Notably, emotions can be unpleasant, indicating fear is an emotion. A feeling of alarm will often trigger fear, making it seem they are related. However, we usually fail to notice that something happens in the thinking mind, before we respond emotionally with fear. The fact that the fear only starts when we begin to interpret the event, including use of memory, indicates emotion is the result of images created with the thinking mind. So fear is an experience of fright that has been corrupted by a belief not based in goodwill. It is a chosen means of dealing with life events. Therefore, fear must be optional.

Feelings, in contrast, are based in instinct. I will venture to say everyone at some time has experienced a fright or alarm which felt functional. That is, it stimulated them or filled them with an energy and readiness to take action and deal with an event. This is referred to as the fight or flight response, a surge of adrenalin which is startling but not unpleasant, and definitely not disabling. In fact most people like it, unless the event also triggers fear.

To illustrate, I shall relate a personal experience of a relatively recent event, which was a very lucid experience of fright without fear. It was summer and I was driving to the coast for a self-exploration workshop. There were four other people in the car with me. I was getting low on petrol, so pulled into a petrol station. As I returned the nozzle to the petrol bowser after filling the tank, I felt a strange sensation around the lower part of my left leg. The hairs on my leg were responding strongly and there was a clammy sensation as if there was something on my leg.

Needless to say it alarmed me, as I had no idea what it was. I instinctively knew it was out of the ordinary. I felt my attention shift from the task at hand to the situation of standing by my car with a petrol pump in my hand. My mind sharpened, and I chose to shift my attention back to the strange sensation coming from my leg. I recognized it had the potential for disaster. My left foot had been set alight when I was about eight years of age, so I had an intense memory relevant to the potential of this situation. I had to look at my leg, and I could sense that fear was not far away.

Thoughts happen very quickly, but it felt like my mind slowed down as a result of being fully aware. I heard a loud noise from inside the car and sensed there was something unusual about it. It was a scream, and was activating my alarm. As I shifted my attention to the noise I realized it was the scream of laughter. At least the car wasn't on fire. Did they know something I didn't? Unfortunately, my instinctive awareness immediately showed me they were not giving attention to me. I was back to square one. Back to the prospects of what the situation had in store for me.

My instinct, which includes curiosity, had taken over. I had to look at my leg. This time there was no fear. In this brief time my leg was feeling hot but had not yet begun to sting. I found myself looking down at my leg with a strangely calm resignation. This had the potential for disaster, but without fear it didn't seem so bad. I even felt a tingle of optimism that felt like an ability to cope with this event, whatever it turned out to be. Even when time seems to go slow, it's amazing how much goes through our minds.

My mind was completely open to possibilities, though leaning toward a repeat of my childhood experience. At this moment, my objective mind offered other information. Just before I felt these sensations on my leg, the person in the car in front of me had turned the motor on, and revved the engine. I had pulled up close behind this car, so it was only about 50 centimeters from the front of my car.

My instinct leapt at this realization. There was my explanation. My thoughts were trying to catch up, to make sense of it, to link the sequence of events. It was possible the car engine had ignited the petrol vapors, or maybe someone had lit a cigarette. I looked down at my leg to see the damage. This is when I saw the full consequences of the event. I got confirmation it was the car ignition that did it!

How did I know this? It was self-evident from my direct experience. My bare leg was completely exposed to the emissions from the muffler of the car in front of me. It was a modified exhaust for a hoon's car. The exhaust forced out a lot of air, carrying all the engine's emissions; enough wind to flatten my leg hairs and warm my skin as well. It's a wonder I didn't get black soot all over me! But strangely there was my leg, intact and not on fire. Yep, I got a laugh out of it, though no-one in the car had a clue what I was laughing about.

Under the circumstances, my instinct was in full flight and my fear could easily have been triggered. So why wasn't it? What was the mechanism for staying with the calm but alarmed instinct? I reviewed the experience, looking for an explanation. Funnily enough, it was my awareness of the laughter in the car which allowed me to remain frightened without triggering fear.

There are a couple of possible explanations for what happened. An observer could conclude I overrode my fear response because I didn't want to look silly in front of these people who were coming to my workshop. I can refute this one, because past experience tells me I still would have joined in the laughter had the fear emerged. All reactions are worth examining, and I don't suffer from false pride so much these days. Being precious about our scripts stops us from examining them. The belief associated with losing face certainly meets the criteria of a belief placed above goodwill. Besides, had I been concerned about losing face it would have been coming from fear.

The event had all the potential to go beyond alarm, and choosing to listen only to an instinct that felt okay to me, averted the experience of fear. It was a function of hearing the laughter from my passengers at just the right moment. This enabled me to see I had a choice in how I faced this unfolding event. I could meet the event with an unpleasant dread, or with a sharp but harmonious sense of alarm. Their laughter reminded me of my choice and on this occasion I chose wisely. When we resumed our travels, recounting my experience of "fright without fear" entertained us for the rest of the journey.

My instinct and thinking have led me to see fear as the primary construct by which we have gone wrong. Fear is a product of the objective mind of humans, and is not based on a natural sense of life afforded by the instinct. When we use fear, a distorted interpretation of events is guaranteed to follow. This means big trouble in paradise!

There is further evidence indicating fear is not an instinct. There are many pleasant expressions of instinct, including harmony, caring, nurturing, contentedness, happiness, hope, inspiration—too many to list. If fear is an expression of instinct, it would be the only one which is an unpleasant experience. This is a big call, so subject this idea to your own examination. In so doing, bear the following in mind; fear corrupts the interpretation of our experience. So when you examine your experience of anything, consider whether your fear has already tainted it. How can you tell when fear is active, in you or someone else? It does not feel comfortable or good to us.

I am convinced fear is at odds with our instinct. More specifically, giving attention to fear distracts us from the effect of instinct on the objective mind. It obscures the positive incentive of the instinct. For me, this observation was the most compelling piece of evidence that fear is not functional, and therefore not an expression of instinct. When we are gripped by fear, it causes us to become dysfunctional and reduces the likelihood of an appropriate response. The two most common expressions of fear are inaction and anxiety. Neither is functional, nor desirable, and they don't feel good.

A Culture of Fear

In terms of where we have gone wrong, everything hangs off this construct of fear. Our belief in fear is the seed of every experience that is unpleasant to us. All our woes are created by thinking based on and distorted by fear. Even the idea life is a problem or a bad experience, comes from fear. Perhaps worst of all, our loss of innocence comes from learning to conceive of fear; not from our first sexual experience. The enormity of it takes my breath away. Without trivializing the experience of fear, it is fair to say most people's basic perception of life is a "house of cards" built on a foundation of fear.

So let me talk more about fear and our misuse of it. Most people's perception of fear is that it controls them. Though self-control can be reasonably effective in managing fear, we seem to have no reliable way of living without fear. An experience of fear is always an unpleasant one. It consumes our thinking. Most of our beliefs are based on it. Fear is an epidemic in our world, and we believe we just have to live with it. It is likely, very few individuals live a day without some experience of fear. It has become a part of what life is about.

When I ask why we do unpleasant things to ourselves and others, the answer I get inspired by my instinct is "fear." We have learned to be fearful and from fear we have been taught to guard against our instinct. Why do we fear our instinct? It seems most people believe fear *is* our instinct. If this were so, instinct has made us do unpleasant things. Just look around you; across time and throughout the world, people have hated, raped and killed each other, and committed all manner of atrocities. It must be human nature; it must be instinctive.

But what if we have this wrong? Would you agree that if our cultural view of fear is wrong, this is a concern? Every one of us would want to be damn sure fear is an authentic instinct before we believed in it. What if fear is not an instinct and violence is not our nature? So there is your challenge. As for me, I am damn sure it is not. I'll begin by asking why fear is so prevalent in our experience of life.

Many ideas about fear seem rooted in the observation of a predatory universe; things feed on other things. Seeing animals feed on prey stirs the deepest of fears in us. Yet we humans are not regular prey for any predator in the world. To all intents and purposes we have no natural predators. There are a few animals which happily take a human that comes their way, but none systematically hunt us. Despite the fact humans are at the top of the food chain, we still tend to obsess about this aspect of nature.

Our fear leads us to conceive of unknown entities out to get us. This is the stuff of horror movies, in particular the predatory actions of humans toward other humans. Not satisfied with this, we apply this belief in predators to our own thinking process. The inhuman behavior of our own species is often taken to mean something feeds us unpleasant thoughts. This is superstition as it still exists today. The source of such thoughts is our belief in fear; what we call evil has another name!

Fear is justified everywhere in our culture. In particular, we turn our fearful thinking to things like death, regarding it as some sort of force constantly looking for an opportunity to take our life. We fear death is out there waiting to get us, in many different forms. At an early age we learn to fear, through what we are told and see demonstrated by our caregivers and culture. For instance, bad things come from pursuing too much fun up the hill with Jill, or from having a great fall which neither horses nor men could fix. It could be the cradle falling out of the tree when too much wind—trouble—blew, or something simple like the boogey man in the night. As a kid, I wasn't too sure about the intentions of Mr. Sandman or Jack Frost for that matter.

In the following discussion, keeping your sense of humor would be helpful, because this is where I take my biggest risk with you. Among the topics I have covered, this discussion about fear is most likely to challenge your beliefs. Differences of opinion are fine and even healthy, but where these differences are based on strongly held beliefs, there is a risk of rejecting other ideas about the subject. However, it is worth the risk because this topic is central to my explanation of where we have gone wrong. If you disagree strongly, laugh about it and move on to the next paragraph.

Why use Fear?

If fear is optional, why do we use it? What purpose does it serve? Why do we withhold attention, punish and do things which don't feel good to us? Doesn't this seem strange to you, particularly if each of these behaviors goes against our instinct?

Could it be that the construct of fear was designed for our own good? This sounds cynical, but I mean it sincerely. We have been taught fear is beneficial. In other words, since we experience fear we justify it as having value for our survival.

Why teach children to be fearful? Why do you think? My mind says "we think it will keep them safe." We are shown and encouraged to be fearful because we believe it is an instinct keeping us safe. Can you see the inconsistency in this? Feeling fearful is the opposite of feeling safe. How can fear give a sense of safety? You could rationalize it by saying the fear of something such as dark places, like an unlit street, keeps us safe by decreasing our chances of being attacked if we avoid it. However, this assumes more attacks take place in dark places, which apparently is not the case. Even if you avoided every place where you could be attacked, you are unlikely to feel safe because the fear of attack is dominating your thinking. Fear still rules.

If you think fear keeps us safe, try reframing the question. Ask yourself whether fear is the only way, or at least the best way, to keep oneself safe. If I do not fear danger, am I more at risk of harm than someone who does? It doesn't feel this way to me, so my response is "no". Respect for my health and well-being, not fear, leads me away from danger.

Fear is not even an accurate guide to what is dangerous. In fact there is a case to be made that fear actually puts people at greater risk of harm. For example, a proportion of people who are fearful deliberately put themselves in risky situations: to prove fear doesn't control them, to counteract the fear, to overcome the oppression fear causes, or for some other reason related to the fear.

However, the most significant point in this argument is, fear itself is a feeling of being unsafe. Has it occurred to you that when we are not experiencing fear, we feel safe and well? So which comes first, feeling unsafe or fear? If you sense fear before or at the same time as feeling unsafe, this is your evidence; fear is the cause of unpleasant experiences.

Rather than being an instinct to alert us to danger, fear itself is the danger in our experience. Fear tends to permeate our experience of life, causing us to feel unsafe quite often. Fear can be experienced hundreds of times a day, though sometimes it is barely noticeable; triggered by events such as crossing the street, someone approaching or talking to you uninvited, speaking your mind at work, hearing strange noises when trying to go to sleep, or even triggered by our own thoughts about horrible things, when nothing is actually happening. There are many who live with fear as their constant companion.

Fear is endorsed in our culture as a natural experience. On a cultural level, instilling fear is an accepted practice people use every day, at school, and in the workplace, though when it moves outside socially sanctioned norms it is called bullying. It is enshrined in law through punishment, such as being imprisoned as a means to modify our behavior. It is used in advertising to influence consumer behavior. If fear is behind our suffering, can you see how I have arrived at the view, fear is the true root of all evil?

The problem is that most of our beliefs are based on fear. Nonetheless, I have no doubt these are designed for our own good. A case in point is the parent who is fearful for their child's safety, and sees teaching fear to the child as the way to keep the child safe. For instance, children do impulsive things, like run onto the road without looking. At times such as this, it is important the child does what the parent says. After all, they are totally accountable for the child. If they yell "stop" with fear, the child needs to listen to their command; to do as they are told—or so they believe. However, when fear is conveyed to children, it distracts them from their instinct. If the child is on the road, the fear increases the likelihood the child will freeze and have less chance of dealing with the danger. Do you remember having any experiences like this?

What will be of greater benefit to the child, is clear access to their instinctive startle response; better referred to as alarm or being on high alert. The alternative is to yell out "stop" in a way which supports the child—without the fear. This would be more effective and favorable in touching the child's instinct of fright.

It is strange for us to willingly use the unpleasant experience called fear. Do you know of any scientific body of evidence indicating fearfulness works, or is better than fright? I don't. There is no evidence I know of, outside our beliefs. As mentioned above, transmission of fear is done with good intent. The parent wants the child to be safe, and our traditional, cultural beliefs say that exercising authority or control over the child, using punishment, and instilling fear, are the best ways to do this. Sometimes referred to as tough love, this way of caring for children was a solid belief structure of my parents' generation.

And why wouldn't we take on fear! We instinctively know our parents and caregivers love us. They would not be showing us this if it were wrong—would they? Although most children instinctively know something is wrong, what child has the capacity to mount a challenge to this lesson, and reject core cultural beliefs? Some children do go with their instinct and tell the parents they are wrong. Can you imagine, or do you remember as I do, the consequences? So at this point, we make a very, very important choice. Most of us chose to go against our true nature. We replaced our state of natural harmony and pleasure with dislike, fear, and often a deeply buried sense of begrudging the choice we made. As a consequence, we experienced an internal conflict of identity because we were not being true to ourselves.

When considered this way, the use of authority to over-ride our natural instinct and induce fear, however well intentioned, is a misuse of authority. For me, an illustrative definition of the misuse of authority is any word or action which implicitly or explicitly contains threat. To use fear to stand over a child is just that, a stand-over tactic to control. Bullying is a classic demonstration of this. Incidentally, I agree with the view that bullying in the workplace is an adult version of the schoolyard variety. Nonetheless, misuse of authority can only be addressed by rethinking the issue of fear. We seem unwilling to do so, and unaware of the consequences for our experience of life. This I will address in the solutions chapter.

The Extremities of Fear

Would it be an incentive for you to address the experience of fear, if I could show how abuse leads to abuse? We know people who were abused as children, are more likely to abuse others in adulthood, including children. Many don't, because as they grow up they challenge the beliefs associated with their experience. However, for those who do continue to verbally or physically abuse, the principles are the same as why we engage in any other unpleasant, fear-based behavior.

In brief, the child first experiences the abuse in their innocence. Their instinct shows them there is something wrong with what this person is doing; it is in contrast to their innocence. However, as part of the socialization process, most of us were taught not to listen to our instinctive sense of knowing—the part which feels good and right for us. From then on, all manner of misconceptions can occur. For instance, the person perpetrating the abuse may convey to the child that they are acting out of care for them. If this is accepted, the child has been given a corrupted view of how to express caring, which is often carried into adulthood. As an adult wanting to express caring, this corrupted belief or script is the one associated with how to express it—even though the instinct is still saying there is a better way to show caring.

Of course this is oversimplified, and many other factors can come into play. For instance, abuse is more likely to be passed on if the child lacks experiences of pleasant affection which would provide an alternative expression to the abuse. Also, when older some children abuse themselves rather than others, for example self-harming behavior. This is a complex topic which is beyond the scope of this book, but I want to make the point that the transmission of fear-based beliefs and behaviors affects many things in our lives. It also highlights the extent of the problem we have created for ourselves.

As a culture, we have assimilated a belief that inducing fear in children keeps them from harm. It is believed this will prevent them from falling prey to corruptions or perversions. In fact it does the opposite. The child's fear is coming from a learned belief representing a corruption of goodwill. The fear actually makes the child more susceptible to other corruptions: fear leads to fear, and corruption leads to corruption. Here, use of the term "corruption" means anything which does not instinctively feel good to us.

How is this so? Bear in mind, the perpetrator of harm is also acting out of fear. So if the child has learned not to listen to their genuine, instinctive dislike of fear, they are not consciously alarmed by another person's fear. The child's acceptance of fear is based on their experience of their caregivers' fear, which is often cited as being for their benefit, to keep them safe. With good intent and love for the parents, the child accepts the fear as valid. In so doing, the child has been taught a negative script about life; unpleasant emotion of fear is normal and keeps them safe.

But what is the implication? The child is likely to feel safe with the perpetrator. Their perception has been corrupted and they have become used to fear. If the child does not feel an abhorrence of fear, they are vulnerable; which I expect is the last thing the parents would want to achieve. Sometimes parents sense this vulnerability in their child and take extra steps to reinforce the fear, resulting in a child who is fearful of everything, including their own shadow. In the case of sexuality, of course, there is an added trap. If the instinctive alarm about the unpleasantness from the perpetrator is not acted on by the child, the onset of pleasure in the sexual experience makes it more difficult to change things. The pleasant experience temporarily counteracts the fear; the problem is, when the pleasant feeling is gone the fear intensifies.

This is what we grow up with. Fear will still be repulsive to us, but the familiarity with fear will lead us into the web of corruptions where fear is expressed as a normal part of life. Ironically, this is because we are trying to understand the fear and repulsion, based on our normal appetite to know. In adulthood, can you see where this could go in terms of testing ourselves with risk-taking behaviors, co-dependent relationships and extremes like sadism and masochism? What makes it more difficult to address the fear for example, is that we have multi-level corrupted scripts, for instance fear plus perseverance plus a belief we are undeserving. This is why it can seem hard to overcome our unhappiness.

So what is the alternative for our children? If the child retains a sense of natural pleasantness, shown by caregivers in their behavior and verbal expression, the child will recognize the fear in the perpetrator as an unpleasant experience, and make every effort to get away from it. They will act fearlessly. It is simple, but this is how instinct works. Unfortunately, this is not likely if the child comes to know fear well, and believes it is a part of caring; in this event the child will allow the fear to over-ride their goodwill and instinctive sense of knowing.

In summary, the simplest explanation of why we take on fear and abuse is because of our instinctive caring for the person showing the fear. It is our choice, misguided as it may be, to keep the fear we experience as a legitimate view of life. The fear based beliefs we have developed, have an unbalancing effect on us. This will remain the case until we are prepared to challenge this link; acknowledging our role in putting it there, and accepting there are better ways to express our caring. Then we are in a position to develop new beliefs and scripts which do not contain unpleasantness.

I think our belief in and use of fear, is the fundamental error of thinking that we have taken on board out of love and trust for our caregivers. If I am correct, this could help explain why our belief in fear flies beneath the radar, and for the most part goes unchallenged. So as my challenge, let me ask if you think the use of fear could be a good definition of abuse?

The Consequences of Controlling Fear

Let me wrap up the discussion of fear by coming back to our misuse of management strategies. We mostly use control strategies such as discipline, to keep a lid on fear. Wherever possible, we have replaced our instinct with scripts and beliefs about how to think, feel and act in the face of fear. It is essentially a misunderstanding, but the problem is deep-rooted and the consequences are very serious.

Controlling fear might seem like a good use of a mind that can conceive of anything. However, if fear is not all it is cracked up to be, then control is a basic misuse of beliefs to counter fear. Unfortunately, beliefs and counter-beliefs are insidious. Once the fear and control mechanisms have been instilled, a vicious cycle is in place. Any effort to move away from using control to counteract fear will expose us to the fear. This strengthens the belief in control as a coping mechanism.

What we have failed to see is that control mechanisms themselves are generally fear-based. It is an unpleasant experience for us to try and control ourselves. Also, it takes effort and is tiring. We justify it because it is the only tool we have to maintain peace and order in our mind. But there is an ironic twist. Most of the horrible things in life, for example bullying at school and in the workplace, are expressions of fear designed to combat fear. Bullying uses the principle "if you can't beat them, join them." In regard to fear, it means if I have no way of being fearless, I may as well use fear myself to get what I want from others.

In other words, we use fear to fight fear. Perhaps you are familiar with the saying "fight fire with fire?" Back-burning to control a fire can work very well. But the situation being discussed here is more like trying to dowse a fire with petrol rather than water. It cannot work. It can only spread the fire.

Fighting fear with fear continues to create a vicious cycle which keeps the horribleness in place. Another example most have experienced is the emotion of rage—heated anger. Rage seems to have a powerful effect of over-riding aspects of fear. Suddenly we don't feel the inhibiting effect of the fear. Used as a counter-script, some emotions can gives us a sense of control over the fear. This is because most people who know fear find rage intimidating—which it is.

So we use control to manage fear, but fear is also used to control one self and others. The cost; we live with fear. If you can verify this, you can safely say our strategy isn't working. I will go further and say it is fatally flawed. We cannot sustain a pleasant experience of life while we endorse unpleasantness. So is there a sensible alternative? I sure as hell hope so!

If we are to depose fear, we have to start by taking it away from center stage. This means replacing our use of the thinking mind as the primary faculty, in favor of the instinct and ultimately the will. I don't wish to scare you, but fear will never give you a solution, and neither will the thinking mind. We can still use the thinking mind to study, and come to understand how it all works, but this will not provide a solution to our dilemma with life.

I will end this discussion of fear by reframing one of the sayings about it. You have probably heard the philosophical saying "there is nothing to fear but fear itself." The real problem is our misunderstanding of fear itself. This saying can be interpreted in one of two ways. One interpretation is, there is nothing to fear, but we should fear the fear itself. The other is, there is nothing to fear, but there is fear. I am not sure which one the author intended, but I like the latter one because it acknowledges our capacity to experience fear without living by it.

Either way, if we use fear, then we suffer. Instead of focusing on the problem, let me rephrase this in the form of the solution; "there is nothing to know, but knowing itself." More importantly, in knowing there is no fear! As knowing is the primary expression of instinct, this is the theme for a later discussion of how to live a fearless life.

Summary

Fear has become a part of what we think life is about. However, our current use of fear is the source of our suffering.

It is useful to distinguish between two basic experiences, both of which are usually referred to as fear:

- I refer to one as fright; the other as fear
- One is functional; the other dysfunctional.
- One is instinctive; the other learned.
- One is not unpleasant; the other is always unpleasant.
- One is a function of the subjective mind; the other of the objective mind.
- When frightened the objective mind becomes clear; when fearful it becomes clouded.
- Fright is a proactive instinct, fear is a reactive response.
- Instinct is always switched on, causing us to be alert.

It is also useful to distinguish between two experiences which I refer to as feelings and emotions:

- Feelings are impressions in the subjective mind; emotions are expressions from the objective mind.
- Feelings are proactive and initiate action; emotions are a reactive response and follow thinking.
- Feeling is always pleasant; emotions can be unpleasant.
- Fright is a feeling; fear is an emotion.

We mistakenly believe fear is an instinct which helps keep us safe. In reality:

- Fear is fright corrupted by a belief.

- Fear is a product of the objective mind, not the subjective mind.
- If fear was an instinct it would be the only unpleasant one we experience. Fear in fact goes against our instinct.
- Fear leads people to put themselves more at risk.
- Fear is a dangerous experience, not an instinct to alert us to danger.
- Fear does not keep us safe, it is the source of feeling unsafe.
- When we are gripped by fear, it reduces the likelihood of an appropriate response.
- Fear does not feel good or right to us.
- Fear comes from a learned belief that is a corruption of goodwill.

Teaching children to fear is done with good, though misguided, intent. However, some of the implications of familiarizing children with fear are:

- If the child has learned fear from caregivers, they learn to ignore their instinctive abhorrence of fear.
- If a child does not listen to their instinctive dislike of fear, they will not run away from it.
- Fear makes a child susceptible to harm.
- Use of threat is a misuse of authority.

It may be that use of fear is the simplest definition of abuse.

SEVEN

BELIEF IN CONTROL

In previous chapters I described how beliefs contribute to our predicament. The main issue is not so much the beliefs themselves, but rather the extent to which our choices are based on them. Beliefs cause us problems when we place them above scrutiny in our daily experiences. An example discussed earlier was our cultural belief in manners. Such beliefs usually go unchallenged because they seem to be helpful. They don't necessarily stand out from other popular beliefs. In most instances we are not even aware they are elevated beliefs, so it is hard to imagine they could cause us harm.

There are many beliefs I could use to illustrate this, but I have chosen our belief in the benefit of "control" for closer examination. It *seems* innocent enough. Most people do it. So how could believing control is good, in fact be harmful? In our culture, self-control is widely advocated as the solution to many of our ills.

Far from being a solution, I see belief in control as central to the problem. The essence of the case against control is that the justification for using it is flawed. It is a belief based on the idea we are inclined to act badly; many say this is our natural inclination. If this were so, then self-control would be the answer. Seeing unpleasant things going on around us seems to justify the development of scripts and schemas to exercise control, so we too will not succumb to the inclination to do bad things.

Control has therefore become the means by which we manage unpleasant experiences. We develop it as a counter-script to cope with fear-based thoughts and behavior. Counter-scripts are strategies to address other core scripts or beliefs. Once a core belief in fear has been established, we need a means to deal with the situations activated by fear. Counter-scripts generally serve as a way to respond to fear, in a socially acceptable way. They allow us to feel competent in the face of unpleasant experiences. In other words, they help us cope with fear. The example I have already used to illustrate this, is our belief in self-control and control of others, particularly children's attention seeking behavior.

Unfortunately, counter-scripts such as control, also validate the fear-based belief they are counteracting. For instance, do you have a belief you are lazy because there are things you don't want to do, like go to work? This then requires a counter-script to make you do it. Once a control mechanism is in place, in this case making yourself do these things, we tend to lose sight of the core belief in laziness for two reasons. On one hand, when the counter-script is effective and our laziness is under control, things are going well and we have no motivation to change. In this situation, we have a vested interest in keeping the belief in controlling ourselves, because we think we have an effective way of dealing with life events like being lazy. It seems to make good sense not to change a system you find successful. If we changed our belief in control, we would have to start from scratch and learn to be successful all over again. That would put us out of our comfort zone. On the other hand, when things are not going well—we feel lazy and find it hard to make ourselves do anything—we tend to scrutinize the counter-script or coping strategy and see it lacking in some way. We conclude that more self-discipline or control is needed. If the fear-based thoughts are getting out of control, it seems the counter-script needs to be strengthened or another belief added. In so doing, we rarely challenge the root cause of the problem, namely the belief in being lazy, told to us in our upbringing due to a fear of being seen as "no-good". This is the situation with all of our beliefs which cause unpleasant experiences; all of which have a link to fear.

In general, control is a counter-script for fear. The justification for the belief in control is that fear has to be managed. Where there are beliefs based in fear, there you will find scripts based on control. The concept of control has gained popularity because it does quite a good job of keeping a lid on fear. However, consider this possibility; our belief in control makes the fear worse! This is because our counter-scripts like control are also developed from fear, in the above case from a fear of being seen as lazy or useless or no-good in some way.

The flaw is in thinking the emotion of fear is a valid one. As it is an unpleasant experience, we tend to fight against feeling this way. In response, we have used the objective mind to develop mental discipline and self-control. The end result is to believe only control can guide us away from unpleasantness. But this is not true. What *is* true is that without unpleasantness we don't need control!

I have chosen to focus on the example of belief in control for two reasons. First, this is one of the most damaging of all the beliefs we hold. Second, it is a concept linked to a lot of affiliated beliefs. Control, like fear, tends to be an enshrined belief, and as such is used to justify other beliefs about our unpleasant nature.

Dr. Warren Stanton

In Control versus In Charge

A belief in control is created by the intellect, to be used as an action plan, strategy or goal. This means it is thought-based and hence constitutes a belief structure, also known as a script or schema. This belief, once established, can be applied to any aspect of oneself or the environment.

Control tends to mean different things to different people. For this reason I will highlight the difference between two common meanings. There is a major difference between being in charge and being in control. Most people use these terms interchangeably, but I use "in charge" in the positive sense of being empowered, making constructive choices about what you want, and implementing them with confidence. I use "in control" in the negative sense, supported by common associations with the terms of blocking, restricting, and restraining. Being in control usually means having the power or authority to determine what will and will not happen. In this sense we talk about people being controlling.

I will highlight the difference in these terms by looking at the use of authority in a group situation. "In control" usually means one person has primary control of the group. If more than one person sees themselves as being in control, it can lead to conflict. This gives rise to the saying "too many leaders, not enough followers"; or the politically incorrect version used when I was a kid, "too many Chiefs and not enough Indians". The leader has the final say, exercising authoritarian control in the group.

In the case of being "in charge", each individual in the group is in charge of their own contribution—be it small or large. Each has responsibility for what they want to see happen, but having equality in the sense of every person being in charge—egalitarian. In this sense, everyone is both a leader and a follower. Many people believe a group of leaders cannot function effectively as a group. However, dysfunction arises when one or more do not accept each person as a leader; thinking they have priority over the others, and believing they are, or should be, in control.

Now consider the situation of people dealing only with themselves. Being in control means the objective mind is used to determine what will and will not happen. The body and mind, and often the environment as well, are expected to do only what the individual determines. Any variation from this is generally seen as a problem. On the other hand, being in charge means giving direction to the body and mind, but there is consultation about how things can best be done. In this way our wants are not forced upon our mind and body. We can note the limits of our minds and bodies and modify our behavior, for example when too much thinking causes stress, or how far you can turn your head before causing injury to you neck.

Now let's take a look at the use of control on the thought processes of our objective mind. To control one's thoughts means to block or avoid the occurrence of extraneous or undesirable thoughts. Generally, this is considered desirable. Single-minded focus on the task at hand is often credited with outcomes such as high performance in sport. In the case of mental health imbalance, managing unpleasant thoughts is considered a key strategy. Bear in mind, most people don't distinguish between being in control and being in charge, as I do. That distinction as already described, should be helpful to see where we have gone wrong.

Let me tell you a tale to illustrate the functional alternative to control. Consider the following account of Bell's invention of the telephone. Bell had encountered an obstacle to transmitting the voice down the line, which he could not resolve. At some time he met the inventor of the telegraph, Morse. During their discussion, Morse shared a piece of information unrelated to

Bell's problem, which later sparked Bell's insight into how he could fix the obstacle he faced. Like many before him, Bell solved his problem using his non-rational faculty or instinct which produces the "ah-hah" moment, when things fall into place as an insight or realization. Our ability to conceive of all possibilities unconstrained by thought is arguably the force behind every technological invention of our kind. Bell's story demonstrates that, while the objective mind is very good at recognizing and using information, it does not necessarily know what information will be useful.

A belief in control inhibits the creative "ah-hah" moment. Have you considered the consequences of trying to control your mind, when you want to resolve a simple problem, like how to motivate yourself to do work? The rationale for using control is based on the assumption you already know which bits of information are relevant. For example, you have to work to earn money so you can be part of society and not be a lazy, homeless bum—at least that is what I was told. I trust you can sense the fear in this belief. However, motivation comes from wanting to work, which is achieved by a realization you are not lazy. You feared you were, probably because someone told you this out of fear, when you didn't want to do what you were told. Using control to make yourself do work will increase your resentment of work, and reduce the likelihood of realizing you are not lazy.

So it is worthwhile asking yourself whether having your mind in control mode is necessarily a good thing. There are other consequences, for example you will have to live your life from beliefs. Your beliefs will have to guide your decision about the value of each idea you have. You can only accept information you believe in. This is what beliefs do for us. In this context, the purpose of control is to pre-screen ideas before they are taken into consideration. This way they don't take up as much time and effort. This is called a mind-set. The problem is that mind-sets harbor inflexibility and intolerance.

The flaw is in us assuming we already know what information is relevant or useful. If we reject information on the grounds we do not see its relevance, in many cases we can't move forward in our thinking. With this attitude we have little chance of finding satisfying answers to our questions. This is one way the use of control can do damage. If we stick to what we think we know, this limits our mind's potential. Put bluntly, we then have a closed mind. Can you see how this generalizes to all enshrined beliefs, social, political, religious or otherwise?

Having said control is a restriction, this does not mean restrictions can't ever be useful. There are instances when a restriction can have a positive function, such as being single-minded in a situation where there is *no* solution being sought to a problem. Think of a sports person who stays focused on the task at hand, thinking only about what they are going to achieve. This can enhance their performance.

Remember, the development of a belief in control has good intent behind it. Control is a mechanism made by humans, designed to protect us from fear. One way to avoid unpleasant experiences, and have a chance of succeeding in life, is to develop concepts and beliefs which seem to provide us with other options. This might even seem a sensible or a logical thing to do. Actually it *is* a logical thing to do, but should logic be in control?

The Harm Done by Choosing Control

The terms "focused," "concentration" and "discipline" are based on the concept of control, and we think we have to be focused and disciplined to succeed. For instance, it's currently popular to advocate for people to be in control, and there is good intent behind this catch-cry. It contains the idea of a person being empowered and having responsibility for their actions. I'm certainly not arguing against these desirable qualities; this is exactly what people have when they are in charge. My concern is whether control can achieve these qualities.

Although control has its place, for most applications in life it is very limiting. While it seems to do the job of keeping us on track, there is a cost. Control interferes with the spontaneous expression of both our subjective and objective minds, which interrupts the intelligent cooperation naturally occurring between them.

Operating under these limited conditions, how could you ever get satisfactory answers to questions about the meaning of life? Controlling your mind reduces its capacity to operate, and asking such questions is a major overload to the system. And don't say you don't want to know what meaning there is in life. If you think not, I will give any odds you like you are using a control mechanism called post-rationalization. Most counter-scripts are designed to stop the nagging question, legitimize the lack of an answer, or justify otherwise unacceptable answers.

So, the main problem arising from our belief in control is that it stops our minds from working freely together. You will have noted already the similarity between control and narrow-mindedness. We think having control makes us strong, rather than being susceptible to any ideas arising in our objective minds. With control we are able to pick and choose our beliefs. Nevertheless, we always have a choice whether to accept ideas or not, so why control them? If ideas are derived from our subjective life experience, then it makes sense to accept they have some validity. Controlling them will deprive us of useful information. Here is a question for you. We have set out to have control over our body, mind and instinct, but why would we want to control them? I ask this now so you might get an answer, not so I can respond to it just yet.

I discovered another flaw to do with control which I had better mention. Put simply, control is not possible! We have an incredible influence on most things but no real control. Controlling the movement of the body or the direction of a river is exerting influence, not exercising control. We use natural laws to change the course of events. This is not control. The joke is that everyone instinctively knows control can't be achieved, and this is a primary cause of our insecurity in life. Though I have to admit, in my teenage years I was very dedicated toward trying to achieve control—frustrated too.

True control of an event would mean being the sole determinant of it. Moving of our limbs might seem to be something over which we have complete control, yet this is clearly not the case given the structure and formation of the body. The body has design limitations, as a matter of necessity. We can influence the body within its design parameters, for example, increasing flexibility to perform amazing feats of acrobatics, but we can never train our heads to turn 180 degrees! You can restrict your mind, limit its functioning, make it seem orderly or disorderly, but you cannot actually control it. You can use it, harness it, influence it, you can point it in a particular direction, but you cannot control it.

For us to have control essentially means the body and mind do only what we say. This we cannot achieve, no matter how strongly we believe otherwise, and all the effort we put into trying to do so is futile. Frustration and despair are direct results of persistently trying to control the events of life. If we block information or thoughts we restrict our ability to have influence. So control, far from being a functional, desirable thing to do in everyday life, is an overtly dysfunctional thing to do. We need to extend the wise saying "time and tide wait for no-one" to recognize the many other things over which we have no control, including the functioning of our mind. In fact, "life waits for no-one."

Would it surprise you to hear that trying to control your mind by blocking thoughts can cause imbalance? Let me give you a personal example to highlight this. Throughout most of my youth I was plagued by heavy, unpleasant, negative thoughts. The effect they had on me was obvious, leading my mother to suggest I seek help. The thoughts were very intrusive and try as I might, I could not stop them. This was ruining my life, and a lot of my time, energy, and self-concept was wrapped up with my inability to deal with these thoughts. I was very fearful of what was going on in my mind, desperate to find a solution or a way out, and quite unsettled by my emotional responses. I tried just about everything and nothing seemed to work; drugs made it worse. My inability to resolve these thoughts and feelings continued to escalate in my early 20's while at university, until I reached a point where I accepted I couldn't fix it and I just had to give in. Now, in this situation my objective mind presented all sorts of fearful ideas to me, like having a breakdown, going mad or ending my life. However, because there was nothing else I was willing to try I resigned myself to failure, and accepted whatever was to be my fate. It was all over. The negative thoughts had won.

What followed was one of the most incredible experiences in my life up to that point. I encountered a strong positive thought, enough to alter my negative mood. This was new to me. I tried to duplicate it. I waited for the negative thoughts and feelings to re-occur and once more gave in to them—in thought, not action. Once again I had a positive thought. Then an astounding insight hit me. So much so, I subsided into a fit of laughter. I rolled around on the ground for what felt like a half an hour, laughing hysterically and trying to stop my stomach bursting from the laughter.

What was my insight? I had spent the past 20 years of my life, or as many of them as I had been aware of my thoughts, fearing these negative ideas and trying to control them. I had been told in all areas of my upbringing, it was wrong to have negative thoughts and I was bad to have them. To be a good person I was told I had to be a good boy. If I failed, it was obvious this would bring shame on my parents; to be accepted I had to do everything I could to stop such thoughts. This I diligently set about doing. This example, by the way, also illustrates how as young children we take on such beliefs. This one, which I'd picked up at a very young age, was still ruling me at age 20, whether I was conscious of it or not. Also, at the same time I was trying to be acceptable to my peers—who strangely seemed to be less concerned about having bad thoughts. I was known to be very strong willed, and thought I had done a pretty good job of blocking the source of these negative thoughts.

Thinking without Control

In that moment of insight I saw something very important about the functioning of my mind. Every negative thought was followed by a positive thought, and every positive thought was followed by a negative one. As I began to examine this insight, it proved true from my observation of the thinking process. Now I could see, using control to stop the negative thought from happening meant I was then stuck with this negative thought.

Whenever I had a really negative thought, I would try to stop my thoughts right there, not allowing any more thoughts to form. Of course this was not sensible or balanced, and my efforts to control my mind were sending me spinning in a downward spiral of unpleasant thoughts.

The mind-blowing part of the insight was, by getting stuck on controlling the negativity I had been blocking the next positive thought. Much the same as putting all the weight on one side of a see-saw will not allow it to balance. Without input from the positive side of my thoughts, my interpretation of what my mind was saying had been weighted heavily on one side and totally negative. My life changed irreversibly from that day on. My fears came true; it **was** all over, but not quite in the way I had been thinking! The information I had been getting from my mind was correct—it was going to be all over—but it was the struggle which was over, not my life. I no longer needed to hang on to the belief I had to control my thoughts or my mind. What a relief.

Now let's examine "positive" and "negative" thoughts in more detail. Our mind, as discussed previously, can be understood as operating on complementary poles of thinking—like magnetic polarity. In this description of the thought process, as an alternating series of positive and negative thoughts, I am using the term "positive" to mean a positive pole, experienced as **constructive** thoughts, and the term "negative" to mean a negative pole, experienced as **deconstructive** thoughts.

However, our belief is that negative polarity thoughts are destructive, rather than deconstructive. We even call it "negative thinking", meaning it gets in the way of us doing things. There is a fundamental misunderstanding here about the effect of fear on our thinking. It is our fearful attitudes and beliefs about the negative pole of our mind which turn the deconstructive, negative thoughts into unpleasant, destructive ones. Let me highlight this with a bold statement; a belief in the destructive nature of the objective mind is the foundation of our views about mental health disorder.

We have created a misunderstanding about its bi-polar nature. This is another contentious statement because we have labeled a serious mental health disorder as bi-polar—it used to be called manic-depressive disorder. However, I am using the term to suggest our objective mind does have two poles, which are positive and negative in polarity or charge; borrowing from the terminology of electromagnetics. In terms of the functioning of the objective mind it acts like a pendulum, swinging from one pole to the other. Each pole provides a contrast, acting as a springboard for the next thought of opposite polarity. That is what dual polarity is all about. With the introduction of fear, the pendulum can swing more intensely; meaning our thoughts have too much effect on our mental and emotional state.

You can verify the bi-polar nature of your objective mind by listening to your thoughts. Each positive thought is followed by a negative one, followed by a positive one, and so on, as long as we don't try to interfere. As I will illustrate, without fear, neither positive nor negative thoughts are unpleasant. With these poles of the thinking process, we progress toward a solution.

The objective mind, with its thoughts of positive and negative polarity, is there to serve us. In the following example, when thinking about getting ready for a meeting, my self-talk or thinking process went something like this: It is too hot to bother (–ve), I could have a swim (+ve), I haven't got time (–ve), I need to cool off (+ve), I'll be late for the meeting (–ve), I will have a quick swim (+ve), I have too much to do (–ve), I can have a swim for 20 minutes (+ve), I only have an hour left (–ve), the rest of my preparation will only take 30 minutes (+ve), I have to allow more time for reading it (–ve), okay I will swim for 10 minutes. This goes on, back and forth until enough information has been processed to make a choice. I concluded there was sufficient time for a quick swim. Had fear been introduced, the negative thoughts would appear destructive; I would have doubted my choice.

Without a negative fear-based attitude, the negative polarity thoughts help us in our endeavor to find a solution. Yet common beliefs wrongly equate negative polarity thoughts with bad thoughts. Thus we see the negative polarity of our thought process as undesirable. We have come to view negative polarity thoughts as trying to destroy or undermine our positive thinking. In some quarters these thoughts are considered to come from some bad part of us. This belief is responsible for a major misunderstanding, which has affected most people's ideas about how our mind should work, and left them thinking their mind is not working properly. The magnitude of the error in this belief never fails to take my breath away. It is my hope I can give you a glimpse of this, so you may see the extent to which it has undermined our naturally joyful experience of life.

Thinking becomes one-sided or obsessive if both sides of the self-talk are not treated equally. Just as in group dynamics, if one person believes they need to be in control, the group's balance and harmony is under threat. If we believe our mind's negative polarity is more accurate, or the positive polarity is fooling us, it inhibits decision making and harmonious action. In more extreme forms this represents repression of our thoughts, which can depress us in affect and emotion. We tend to describe persistent negative polarity thoughts as obsessive. However, if we favor the positive polarity while ignoring the negative polarity, this also makes it more difficult to settle on a balanced course of action. Too much priority on positive polarity thoughts can lead to "chasing rainbows," and in a more extreme form this is manic thinking.

In the process of making a choice using the two polarities of our mind, we may have no idea which side will prevail. The answer could come from either side. The point being that either way, the thought processes are helping us reach a satisfactory conclusion. Consider another example, this time thinking about buying a car. The self-talk might go like this: I would like to buy a BMW (+ve), I don't have enough money (–ve), I can sell the second car as well (+ve), I will have to share a car (–ve), at which point the positive polarity concedes it wouldn't work, so the choice was based on the negative polarity giving the more salient information. Alternatively, at the point of thinking about sharing the car, the thought may occur to replace the second car with a cheaper used car. Then the negative polarity may concede to the purchase. Another likely outcome is for the qualities of the car to be broken down, to understand what it is about the BMW that really attracts me. For example, if the shape of the car is the primary attraction, a cheaper car with a similar look could be purchased. At the time a Mitsubishi Lancer somehow reminded me of a BMW!

Negative thoughts are deconstructive, not destructive. They function to examine the creative output of the positive polarity and separate the "seed from the chaff." In addition, the deconstructive thought provides the opportunity for our positive polarity to agree or disagree with what has been discarded. By doing this, the positive polarity provides further constructive direction for achieving what we want. This continues until we can see what it is we want, and the means by which we can pursue it. The same principle applies in all areas of our thinking. If you think your mind does not produce solutions or satisfying answers, look for controlling beliefs inhibiting the process. As a simple example, if you have expectations about the car you want to buy, you won't be open to other possibilities, and you risk disappointment if your expectations are not met.

So what is going on when the outcome is an unpleasant experience? In summary, my argument is that unpleasantness is a function of our beliefs. Fear-based beliefs, including a need to be in control of our mind, have a destabilizing effect on us. In the above example from my own life, instilled beliefs were making my objective mind appear dysfunctional. It is like an unbalanced set of scales, weighed down on the negative side by the attitude it is wrong to have negative thoughts. Fortunately, the thought processes are not actually unbalanced by our efforts to control them. They go on doing what they do, swinging from positive to negative. However, this adds to our frustration if we believe the mind shouldn't be producing what we mistakenly see as destructive ideas. In the face of our inability to achieve control, we can end up experiencing emotions such as hopelessness, fuelling our belief that life is an unbearably unpleasant experience. This is only one scenario for how our lives could play out.

Alternatively, we can think realistically, treating both sides of the thinking process in our objective mind as equals. Both poles of the thought processes are designed to assist us. Both are respected for the roles they play. Both are listened to and responded to by the other polarity. This does not require us to believe they are equals. If the thought processes are allowed to do their job, they function in this way naturally. One is constructive, the other deconstructive. Neither is destructive.

Luckily for us we cannot control our thoughts. Consider the implications for a moment, if we could eliminate the negative polarity thoughts. This really would make us a dysfunctional species, because it would eliminate the very function by which we interact with the physical world. By analogy, controlling our mind is like believing nature got it wrong by not allowing us to see through the back of our heads. In response, we try to create a device which could turn our heads 180 degrees. With the body, we seem to be more willing to listen to the signal when it is reaching its design limitations; for example pain warns us the body's limit is breached. However, in the case of our minds we don't seem willing to listen to the signs or heed the warnings—this signal being the suffering. We seem to think it is normal to have mental pain.

There is irony in this situation—some say justice. The frustration and futility caused by efforts to control ourselves is correct and accurate feedback. It is the signal that what we are doing, in this case trying to control our mind, is futile and a gross misuse of our mental capacity. It is amazing how we will go through hell before challenging the belief causing the unpleasant experience. The belief we must challenge here is that our deconstructive, negative polarity thoughts are bad or destructive. Could it be, negative polarity thoughts actually help us see what is good for us; or in terms of the above discussion, what is in accord with our will? I know a heap of objections might come from people's beliefs about how our mind works, and I am happy at some later time to respond to every one of them. In the meantime let me make an overarching comment. If our will is *not* goodwill we are a lost cause and fighting a losing battle, however you think of it. If our nature *is* goodwill, then we have no need to control it, or our minds.

Summary

Our predicament arises from placing beliefs above the scrutiny of our daily experiences. Fear and control are two of the most common beliefs to be elevated in this manner.

A belief in control seems innocent, but the justification for using it is flawed:

- Seeing bad things going on is used to justify control.
- Control is a counter-script to block, restrict or suppress fear.

- Counter-scripts validate the core belief they are counter-acting.
- We end up believing that control can keep us away from the unpleasantness of fear.
- Control mechanisms including "focusing," "concentration" and "discipline", reduce the information or choices to be made, but foster a closed mind.
- Control is useful in some circumstances, such as high performance in sport.

It is useful to differentiate between being in control and being in charge:

- Being in charge is empowering; trying to be in control is futile.
- In a group setting, dysfunction happens when one or more persons believe they have control.
- When all participants are in charge, everyone takes on the roles of both leader and follower.
- What we do have is incredible influence over ourselves and the world.

In the thinking process, a key flaw of control is to believe we always know what information is relevant and what is not. This suppresses our natural creativity:

- We use beliefs to undermine our natural thought process.
- Our thoughts alternate between positive polarity and negative polarity.
- One side is constructive, the other is deconstructive – neither is destructive.
- Thinking becomes obsessive or manic when the two sides of our self-talk are not treated as equals.

- The flaw in efforts to "control" is that it is not possible.

For most applications in life, control is debilitating:

- Belief in control interferes with the balanced operation of our mind.
- We have incredible influence over everything, but no control.
- Frustration and despair are direct results of persistently trying to control life events.
- Our fear-based beliefs used to control our mind are the cause of unpleasantness.
- Ironically, the unpleasantness is a signal that we are misusing our mind.

If our nature is goodwill, then we have no need to control ourselves.

EIGHT

CHOICE OF BELIEF OR INSTINCT

Science provides us with a lot of information about the processes of the human brain, but little understanding of the human experience, including beliefs. When we do not understand something, we defer to beliefs. Unfortunately these beliefs are often poor interpretations, particularly if based on fear. It is important to challenge our beliefs if we want answers to meaningful questions about life.

One challenging question to ask is; "why do we have unpleasant experiences?" In every moment we have a choice, to react from a place of morbid fear or resonate with our instinct. This is the deciding factor between having unpleasant experiences or pleasant ones. There may be other factors involved, but our beliefs and attitudes are at the heart of the matter. When we overlay our natural experience of life events with beliefs, they have the potential to corrupt the experience. When these beliefs are not in accord with our goodwill, we will have an unpleasant experience. Therefore, the beliefs we choose to live by determine whether we predominantly experience mental health or mental discord.

It is in our hands, so let's talk about choosing to have pleasant experiences in life. I want to present some examples of how instinct provides a better alternative to beliefs. The examples relate to our overuse of control and how we would benefit from reframing our perceptions on the basis of goodwill. An approach based on instinctive goodwill could lead to a whole new foundation for positive psychology and living without fear.

Challenging our Belief in Discipline

One of our most significant control mechanisms is belief in the necessity for discipline. Everywhere we look we find human endeavor based on disciplines. We have disciplines in thinking, as in philosophy and positive thinking, in moral codes of conduct, in physical disciplines including sport, in education, and in professions such as science, and on it goes. The concept of discipline pervades most areas of our life. We hold in great esteem the idea of being disciplined in thought and action.

We have made discipline a remedy for our ills. Wherever there is a problem, discipline will fix it. This form of control is intended to keep us on the "straight and narrow," both in the positive form of "keeping ourselves on track" by being single-minded, and in the negative form of "punishment for transgressions" when we stray. It is one of the basic concepts most people advocate and live by. But have you ever wondered where we got the idea discipline is good? Could it be flawed? Let's have a look.

Most people would probably agree, discipline is not our natural state, and is learned. All disciplines, schools of thought, techniques, in fact any thought structures we use, are developed in the objective mind. Hence, they are all the product of the human mind. This point alone should have your alarm bells ringing, though it doesn't mean all thought structures are wrong or bad for us.

Disciplines like science are based on objective thinking and evidence, and refute the notion of beliefs. Science urges us to stick to objective explanations of events, to avoid the trap of subjective interpretations based on beliefs. However, this scientific view is itself a belief.

The misunderstanding here is thinking beliefs are linked to subjectivity. A purely subjective impression is based in instinct, and does not involve beliefs or interpretations of events. Interpretation is a function of the objective mind. So, it is our objective explanation of events which is open to personal interpretation. Opinions are explanations in the form of simple beliefs, developed by the same mind which does the objective reasoning. Invoking the principles of quantum physics once more, I can happily say objective observation is in fact part of the natural subjective sense of life! It is an arbitrary belief to regard objectivity as independent of subjectivity.

The question for me is whether being disciplined is better than living by my instinct. Do I have a natural inclination toward discipline? I can't find any, so the response I get is a big fat "no!" Many people choose discipline because it seems to give order to their lives. It helps them achieve things, plan things, or dare I say, control their lives. In most cases this application of discipline is designed to counteract a view of their world as unruly, lazy or fearful. Note, in saying this I do not mean everyone who uses structure in their life is a control freak. People who train for sport, do repetitive tasks or use other developed structures can do it for the love of it. This gives the appearance of discipline, but is not the same as discipline, at least in the sense I am using the term.

Discipline is a control mechanism which provides rules for us to function in thought and action. It is based on an idea there is no natural order in life, and we have no natural interest in life. Therefore, without discipline our world would fall apart. Now, the scary thing about this is, if you have a view of life as being unruly, then abandoning discipline will provide evidence of your life falling apart. Discipline is used to counteract the belief in a chaotic world, and sure enough, without it the unruly world of your fears will re-surface. Thus, people who embrace a belief in discipline think they have proof life is unruly. This is enough to cause most people to revert back to discipline to regain their ordered reality.

The error in thinking occurs if we do not challenge the underlying belief that life is unruly. Other common beliefs in need of challenge are, we are lazy and our resentment of work is natural. I personally regard such beliefs as being so far from the truth as to be laughable. Could experiences of unruliness and laziness be concepts made by humans, and not represent our actual subjective sense of life?

The goal of self-exploration is to challenge such beliefs, by testing whether the subjective sense of life has a harmony to it and is stimulating. If we find it translates into a pleasant experience, we have started the process of proving our lives are not naturally unruly or unmotivated. In so doing, we are moving beyond belief! If we then begin to abandon use of these unpleasant beliefs—the unruly view of life as well as the need for discipline—and our life doesn't fall apart, discipline would be seen as unnecessary. What you have instead is an experience of freedom.

Here is a question for you to consider. Throughout history, have we benefited more from disciplined thought or free thought? What does your instinct say? What do your beliefs say? What do your fears tell you? Free thought has enhanced our lifestyle. It allows us to use our creative capacity to explore "where no-one has gone before." I am confident it has been sufficiently documented;

free thought results in more rapid advancement of technology and civilization than disciplined thought.

If you follow my reasoning about discipline being a control mechanism, can you see we also use it to manage or counteract fear? The previous discussion of how we relate to fear also indicates this relationship can be changed; without fear, there is no need for discipline and control. Without either of these, the prospect of a solution to our suffering is at hand. For the sake of further discussion of a solution, I ask you to challenge the belief that discipline or control is the solution.

Want versus Need

Two related concepts corrupted in the name of control are "want" and "need." In Western culture it is acceptable to have needs. When we define something as a need, we think it is necessary for us to fill the need and this gives us more motivation. As a simple example, I am making a cup of tea and run out of milk; if it seems I need milk, I will immediately head for the shop. Wants, on the other hand, are treated with suspicion. Those which are functional such as "I want a drink" or "I want to get the job finished" are generally seen as okay because they express a goal we wish to achieve. However, most wants such as "I want a new car" or "I want attention" are seen as arising from the ego, and considered suspect. In general, wanting is believed to come from a person's dissatisfaction. Consequently, wants are seen as optional extras which aren't necessary to fulfill, unlike needs. Yet the idea of having needs is one of those enshrined beliefs I would like to challenge.

First, let me break down the concept of wanting. There is little debate about us wanting things, and some of these are not good for us. The relevant question is whether it is bad or undesirable to want. I think most people would believe wanting something is a product of the objective mind, but I see it as more complex than that. If we divide "want" into its two components, namely the wanting and the thing we want, we have a better chance of seeing there is more to it. We certainly decide on the things we want, the object of wanting, but do we decide on the wanting itself?

When we are hungry we want food. We choose to look for food, and we choose what food we'll eat. From want we choose what we think will satisfy our appetite. Our appetite comes from instinct, and so does the prompt to search for food. However, how we go about the search and select the food we want to eat is conceived in the objective mind. This is where things can get skewed; when a belief comes into play, what we want may no longer be based on our instinct to thrive. For example, if I believe I am lazy, my search for food will be restricted to the easiest and closest things I can find to eat, even if it is not what I feel like. If I direct my want to things not in accord with my instinct, the object of want will be ill-conceived, but the wanting itself is fine. On the other hand, if my instinctive appetite guides my choice, I am prompted to get what I really feel like eating; which is more likely to be influenced by what will nourish my body. That is, I am motivated by want rather than need.

Instinct expressed as want feels genuinely good. If we want things that enrich our lives, bring us enjoyment or provide some functional gain to life, such as food or money to live on, then "want" is a totally pleasant experience. Any change in this experience is a product of the objective mind. For example, what happens if we think happiness is based on having an expensive house or car, particularly one beyond our means? Believing our happiness depends on something worldly or physical, turns the want into a "must have," otherwise known as a "need." Such expectations usually result in unhappiness, or a sense of feeling deprived.

The wanting, before we attach it to something, comes naturally to us. Want is sensed physically and experienced in the objective mind, but it is not a bad thing. It is the source of motivation from which we develop a goal and strategy to achieve something, using our thought processes. In sum, want is our natural sense of motivation based on our instinctive appetite. When we want to do something, it comes easily to us. If we listen to this appetite, the motivation is part of the want. We don't have to make ourselves pursue things we want. Hence, no need for control.

In particular, my experience of wanting is that it is there all the time. It is there even when there isn't anything I want. The wanting itself is not based on a belief. For me, it is an instinctive inclination to create, a directive of the will to thrive. It is my source of motivation, my reason for living. Nothing in our minds happens without want! It is a pleasant experience, and a major piece of the solution for our suffering.

Want is perceived as bad when it is corrupted by a belief which is not in accord with our will. It is not the wanting itself which is bad, or the object of wanting. It is not even the belief about the thing we want. It is bad when the belief causes the experience to be unpleasant. For instance, have you felt the disappointment of not getting something you wanted? Disappointment happens when you have some expectation or belief about the thing you want, for example you deserve it. A variation on this is to believe you don't deserve it, which would mean the disappointment was there before you even decided what you want. In response, we use counter beliefs to protect ourselves. Our negative view of want is a control mechanism which we use to try to counter the unpleasant effect of being disappointed. By blaming our instinctive wanting, we fool ourselves into not challenging the belief causing the disappointment. Now, most people no longer allow themselves to want.

When we override want with a disharmonious belief, fortunately the want itself is not tainted by the belief. The sense of want remains a simple appetite. It is the **perception** of want that is tainted. When we get to the chapter on solutions, the importance of this will become apparent. Our unpleasant fear-based beliefs corrupt our perception of wanting. In effect, the want now appears to be something it isn't. If I want a new car, but fear I must have an expensive car to appear successful, I have overridden a pleasant experience of want with an unpleasant perception—a created psychological need.

Now let's break down the concept of need. Most people believe we have needs. There is even a famous theory suggesting we have a hierarchy of needs. So what are needs? Perhaps a clean definition is that needs are the requirements for survival. The things we need are things we cannot do without.

There are two types of needs I would like to discuss. One is psychological needs the other is physical or biological needs. Other types of needs, such as social needs, and emotional needs, can be reframed according to the discussion of these two types.

Psychological needs: I will start with the easier of the two to analyze. In the above discussion of want, those adept at reading between the lines, will have seen I am of the view we have no inherent psychological needs. What we have are wants, the natural appetite from the instinct. We are social beings and instinctively do want social contact, but do we need it? Would we cease to exist without social contact? Well, no, it is apparent people do live without social contact, some preferring it. We want to do well, to be happy, to do what is asked of us, to have or not have children, to feel good about ourselves and to prosper. But we do not need to. We can live without these things. Most people do. You want proof? Happiness and joy are not dependent on having material things, and evidence of this can be found in your moments of happiness. So let's ask some hard questions about the necessities of life; can you live in joy without a roof over your head? Yes, I have seen photos of kids living in a dump with rags on their backs, laughing their heads off. Now the tough one; can you live in joy without food and water? Yes—until the apparent need of the physical body catches up with you.

Psychological needs are a product of the objective mind. They are created by humans. Want starts out as a pleasant appetite; all appetites are harmonious, discussed again in relation to physical needs. A belief in "need" corrupts the wanting by putting a twist in the expression of it. What started out as a nice sense of wanting is burdened by a disharmonious belief, introducing emotions like dissatisfaction, frustration, and lacking. In more extreme forms, psychological needs are expressed as neediness, dependence, and depression, just to stay a little contentious. Then we develop other beliefs to provide a consistent view of the world. Next thing you know, love is a need!

Physical needs: I could live with the view we do have physical needs. Physical needs include those based in the biological and physiological system. I am not sure whether to include the emotional system, but I am referring to any system related to our physical body so am inclined to include it. There are different ways to look at physical needs. The obvious and sensible way is to accept there are physical needs, such as hunger and other appetites prompting us to eat, breathe, think, and procreate, to name a few. The concept of need is based on the observation we cannot survive without them. The end result of this line of reasoning is we keep the term "need" to refer to the physical.

What seems interesting is, needs are the things we seek to control. Why is that? Is it because our needs are out of control? I suggest we have turned our wants into needs, and by doing so have created a monster which then needs to be controlled. With the aid of fear, we have made our instinctive appetites like hunger and the sexual appetite, seem like things which control us. This in turn justifies the use of control to keep them in abeyance. Here is the twist. If needs are distorted wants, then perhaps we can do something other than control them.

Nonetheless, I still have a concern about physical appetites being called needs. I wish to reframe where the need lies, in a similar sense to reframing the meaning of a "problem." My concern with calling them needs is that it opens the door to believing our instinct controls us. This type of reasoning is used to support the argument we are not free agents, and therefore do not have free choice. In this case, the psychological concept of need would still be dictating how we live our lives.

Instead, I want to challenge the perspective that physical needs leave us no choice, by asking who has the need. When we are hungry we often say "I need to eat." It is okay for the word "need" to convey the essential nature of the appetite, but once it becomes "my" need, it also conveys a psychological dependence. If I ask who has the need I can separate the sense of "me" from the sense of need. Using a reductionist approach to what is "me," most people agree they have a body but they are not the body. If this is an acceptable conclusion, then it is the body which has the need not me. My body needs food, water, and air to stay alive. Given I want to continue living I will care for my body, by choosing to provide it with the essentials of life. Clearly I choose to do this. So far so good—needs do not take away our choice.

The more difficult aspect of this issue is in challenging whether the body has needs. Does the body breathe because it feels the need to, or does it breathe because it has an instinct to sustain life? Look closely at the sense of hunger. It is not experienced as need. Only I can perceive it as a need, so without "me" there is still no need. I think a better term for this is "appetite." The body has an appetite for life. This term can include physical appetites, mental, emotional, and social appetites, even an appetite to live. This links our experiences with our instinct in a healthy way, without creating a perception of neediness.

I acknowledge there are many more questions to ask in relation to this philosophical debate; more than I wish to take up at present. However, in all instances I find it difficult to establish the basis of need. There is a question which puts "need" in its place; do we need to live? I have no sense of needing to live, I want to live. A person who feels they need to live believes they need to achieve something while alive, and hence have to stay alive. This is a created psychological condition of need based on the belief. Even if I accept my want to live is based on an instinct, the instinct does not "make" me stay alive. Instinct does not control us. I can starve myself to death if I choose. Rather, the relationship between myself, my body, and my instinct is one of intelligent co-operation.

The Prisoner's Dilemma

The choice between belief and instinct is evident in the following story, a variation on a logic game referred to as the "prisoner's dilemma," which shows the vicious cycle we can get into with exclusive use of the thinking mind. Study this story closely; it describes how to live a fearless life.

My version of the hypothetical story is as follows. Two prisoners arrested and charged with a particular murder are in prison, facing execution for the crime. From examining the evidence, the warden knows only one of the prisoners committed the murder. Being a fair-minded man, he approaches the prisoners and makes an offer. He says if one of them owns up to the murder, the other one can go free. The imprisoned men are known to each other. The one who is innocent knows the one who undoubtedly committed the murder, is a pathological liar. He certainly won't confess to the murder. This creates a dilemma for the innocent man as there seems no way out of the situation.

Consider the innocent prisoner's situation in deciding what to say to the warden. If he tells the truth, both will deny committing the murder and both will die. If he says he did commit the murder, he will die anyway. So there is no apparent solution to save his life. It seems to be a hopeless situation, and all that seems left to do is accept he is going to die. No matter which answer he gives, the innocent prisoner faces death. Since either option leads to the same result, the innocent prisoner may as well not even give the warden an answer.

But all is not lost. There is a way to resolve the dilemma about which answer to give. What is more, the principle behind this is the solution to all vicious cycles. The solution is to go to a different level of thinking about the problem, in other words to reframe it. The prisoner can find an answer by changing the framework on which the problem is based.

The most important thing to understand about this situation is what makes it a dilemma. It is the assumption that the only acceptable outcome for the prisoner is to avoid his death. I can think of two ways the prisoner can reframe the situation to give the warden an answer—one of them even has a chance of saving his life!

How can the prisoner reframe the situation to enable him to choose an answer? The first option would be to choose an outcome which lets him make the most of his life, irrespective of how long that will be. From this point of view, his two choices are to tell the truth and die knowing he is an honest person, or to say he did it and give the liar another chance to make something of his life. This form of reframing involves going to a higher-order principle about life and using it to make your choice. It works by placing the point of view outside or above the perception causing the dilemma and sense of hopelessness. In this scenario, the choice the innocent man makes is not about trying to avert his death, but about putting meaning into his life, including the possibility of achieving something with his death. In regard to our dilemmas, of course the outcome may not be so severe. In any case, re-framing does allow a choice to be made, breaking the vicious cycle.

However, there can be a hiccup in this approach to breaking deadlocks. The approach works by using a belief as the justification for making a choice. By adopting a belief about "making the most of his life," the prisoner internalizes the reason for his choice. This way out of a dilemma only works if he sticks to the created belief and thinks no more about it, irrespective of the outcome. He runs a great risk if he starts to think further about what will happen, such as whether admitting to the murder will work in changing the other prisoner's life. If he looks for a guarantee about the outcomes of his action, it will undermine his reframing of the situation and he will experience doubt.

There is a risk with this approach because it is based on a control mechanism. For the effect to persist, we have to lock into the reason or belief and never question it. This is done by using the belief to control the thought processes. Any thought to the contrary will need to be over-ridden in favor of the belief. However, it is natural to want to know our sacrifice was going to be of benefit, so these thoughts will occur. When they do, we are faced with the possibility our sacrifice may come to no avail. Confessing to the murder may work if the pathological liar is influenced by knowing the innocent person gave up his life for him. On the other hand, psychological principles suggest this is an unlikely outcome. The one who is lying is doing so to achieve what he wants, which was presumably reinforced with some success through his life. If he gets off the murder charge by lying, he will have further reinforcement it works, and will be even more likely to lie in future!

So is there another way to reframe this dilemma which could lead to a better outcome? Yes, for me the answer to the dilemma is emphatically that he tells the truth. But the reason is not because he would prefer to die an honest person. Nor is the reason based on any adopted moral values, such as "honesty is the best policy." The reason why the innocent person should tell the truth in this situation is; it maximizes the likelihood he will **not** be executed. Pause for a moment and ask yourself—your instinctive sense of knowing—why this would be the case?

The hidden part of this scenario making it a dilemma is the prisoner's efforts to control the outcome. The dilemma is created by the belief that avoiding death is the only desired outcome. As neither action seems to achieve this outcome, he appears to be in a logical bind, literally at a dead end. Breaking the dilemma by changing his expectations about the outcome, so there is meaning in his choice, allows the prisoner to regain a sense of control. However, this is still a control mechanism. As such, there is still the prospect of a dilemma if he thinks about the outcome.

Is there a way to reframe the dilemma which is not a control mechanism? Yes, by not having an expected outcome. This is a better way to get out of the mental trap because it is not subject to interference from thoughts presenting other outcomes. How would this fix the dilemma for the prisoner? How might it save his life? I will explain the mechanism from two different perspectives. While I hope I can present these perspectives with logic, I have to warn you neither is based in logic!

The way to reframe the dilemma free of control, relies on the assertion our true nature is goodwill. If you look at the experience of your own life, I hope you agree we seem to favor or have more of an appetite for what is enjoyable. I know many people do not think of this as their true nature. However, if you can identify this disposition as an instinct, you have proof of where the solutions come from. If you can further identify that being horrible or unsavory does not come so easily, and requires a trigger or belief for it to happen, then you have proof this is not our true nature.

In the context of the prisoner's dilemma or any vicious cycle of thinking, a sense of goodwill will allow you to proceed. To follow our instinct is to have no expectations about the outcome, and is therefore not a control mechanism. Without the control mechanism, there is no need to think about whether the outcome will be achieved. There will be no doubting thoughts about what is going to happen. Therefore, there is no dilemma about what to say to the warden. "I didn't do it, sir," is the answer.

So how does this increase his chances of not being executed? Assume the sense of goodwill is our true nature. The warden has already demonstrated his goodwill in offering to let one person live. If the warden knows goodwill, he is more likely to recognize it in another person. Therefore, it may be possible for him to sense which prisoner is being honest and which one is telling a lie. This could result in the warden letting the innocent prisoner go free. Though less likely, the other prisoner may even take this opportunity to respond from goodwill. So if the innocent prisoner tells the truth there is a chance he will be spared.

There are at least five explanations of how this can work, any or all of which could work together. First, our behavior has some level of correlation with our mind. If the warden is an astute observer of human behavior, and knows how he behaves when telling the truth, he has a good chance of sensing who appears innocent based on non-verbal cues such as the prisoner's tone of voice. Second, it is generally accepted that humans have empathy. Using this, the warden knows how he feels when telling the truth. Therefore, he may be able to perceive a difference between someone telling the truth and someone telling a lie from how he feels about the person. Do you ever get impressions of people when they are talking to you?

The other possible pathways get increasingly more contentious. A third possibility is based on this idea; what we conceive in our mind is energetic in nature and has an effect on other people. In this scenario, our affect is not just our appearance, but a vibratory signal we give off which affects others. Does our empathy include feeling the energetic effect of others on us? A lot of people say it does. A common example cited is being able to feel the atmosphere in a room when you walk in, particularly if it is unpleasant. As the saying goes, "you could cut the air with a knife." I don't want to get too caught up in the mechanism of this, but it is likely non-verbal communication means more than action and tone of voice. The point of contention is less about whether humans produce an electromagnetic field, and more about how much other people are affected by it. It seems likely we use all three of these perceptual systems in support of each other, to assist in making choices. If we are affected by others in this way, then by telling the truth the innocence of this prisoner may be felt by the warden. This could lead him to decide in favor of the innocent man and set him free.

The fourth possible mechanism is even more contentious, though acceptable to many people. It is an extension of the third one, which says we do have a faculty allowing us to perceive unspoken information. This is referred to as intuition, a specific type of instinct with which we sense things like danger or fear. If we accept animals have radar systems, it is at least conceivable we have a similar system, even if we don't put much trust in it. It is at least common folklore we have a sixth sense.

The remaining pathway is probably the most contentious, but I will mention it for the sake of completeness. The fifth possible pathway is via the Jungian concept of a collective intelligence. The concept behind this is, we are all connected by a species-specific common mind, deep in our mind's subconscious. This concept of a species-specific collective mind is similar to discussion of morphic resonance or fields.[3] The rapid transmission of information among animal species can be used to describe this mechanism. Essentially, when a new behavior occurs, say in how a particular bird cracks open a nut or opens a milk bottle, the behavior is taken up by other members of the flock until some sort of critical mass occurs in the number of birds behaving in this way. At this point the behavior does a quantum leap and begins to spread rapidly, showing up in the behavior of other flocks of the same species which haven't had contact with the initiating flock. This has been attributed to the existence of a shared mind, which in the case of the prisoner, makes it imperative he tell the truth. Let me leave this one as speculative, but the concept of us all being linked through a collective subconscious or deep subjective sense has a tantalizing ring to it!

By any one of these mechanisms, goodwill maximizes our chance of survival. A cynic might say this explanation is over-simplified. However, it works. Further, one of my discoveries in life is that simple is better. The law of parsimony says "if you have two options which seem comparable, always choose the simpler." The cynic, in maintaining this is over simplified, is suffering from their own cynicism. People sometimes argue against a simple solution being right, on the grounds it would have been thought of before now if it were really that simple. Yet the reply is; it has been working all the time. The area in which we think it is not working is the part of our lives we have complicated with beliefs. Many people have worked it out or just do it instinctively. It's not

---

[3] see R Sheldrake, *Psychological Perspectives*, 1987, vol. 18, pages 9–25

like no-one has thought of, it just doesn't get talked about because it doesn't require intellect to work it out!

Is it wiser to frame our experience in terms of our goodwill and instinct to thrive, or from our beliefs in fear and control? In terms of the following discussion, it is a choice between living primarily from the subjective mind or objective mind. Framing our experience from subjective awareness of our will, seems to have certain benefits beyond what our beliefs have to offer.

Positive Thinking

Often, I hear criticism of the idea of reframing everything as a positive. The common expression "life isn't a bed of roses" is meant to convey the idea life is not all sweet-smelling. However, in my view it would probably be better used to convey how life seems to most people—some sweet smells yet full of thorns. Another popular saying which reflects this is "life wasn't meant to be easy." These sayings pretty much reflect the prevailing view for most people, at least in Western culture. I will respond to both of these beliefs, but first I want to give a general comment about the version of positive psychology I am presenting.

The old positive thinking form of positive psychology is based on counteraction of beliefs which generate unpleasant thoughts. It goes something like this; if I feel bad about myself, but say "I feel good", I will accept this suggestion and actually start to feel good about myself. It can work, but only by counteracting the belief making you feel bad about yourself. The belief causing you to feel bad is not resolved, and will raise its ugly head again. So you need to make a commitment to always counter its effect. If you don't, you are no better off than before.

A lot of positive psychology practice is based on strategies to counteract using control. This is a management approach that does not seek resolution of the original belief. I can understand the viewpoint from which this comes. Resolution of issues is usually achieved only after years of treatment, requiring extensive finances and human resources. A management approach achieves effective outcomes in a much shorter time-frame. People get on with their lives. This viewpoint assumes all resolutions are time consuming and may not be achievable, which I wish to challenge later. The question I am asking is; can a simple sense of goodwill empower people to challenge their fear-based beliefs, and enable them do it in their own time?

Most people view positive psychology as the use of positive thinking and values—beliefs by another name. If we can see life as either a glass half empty or half full, it is preferable to take the positive view. It seems a straightforward choice. Another old saying which reflects this kind of thinking is "every cloud has a silver lining" meaning it will all turn out for the best.

Affirmations are a more active version of these sayings, by which we generate a belief in present time. An example is to stand in front of the mirror and repeatedly say to yourself, "I feel good today", or a statement of intent such as "I am a winner." Some people get good results with this method, at least for a while. It works if we accept the suggestion we repeat to ourselves, and believe it will happen—we have created the reality. This in turn spreads to our emotions and we start to feel good.

This approach to positive psychology is still based on using beliefs. There is nothing wrong with using beliefs, but as we've already discussed, to have your view of life based on them is of major concern. If positive psychology really had this mechanism as its centerpiece, I would join the ranks of those complaining about always having to turn their thoughts into positive ones.

People tend to get tired of counteracting their fear-based beliefs with manufactured positive comments, as this is not really what they believe. It can seem arbitrary to keep saying positive affirmations, and sooner or later we revert to the old belief. A pessimist would say you are just fooling yourself; better to "call a spade a spade," than to forever call it something it is not, in order to make yourself feel better. A cynical view of positive thinking sees it as "burying your head in the sand" or sometimes "self-medicating." Life is full of unpleasantness and to think otherwise is to be unrealistic or naïve or "off the planet" isn't it?

Let me briefly jump to the defense of this form of positive thinking. I admit if you do not change the old belief causing the unpleasantness, it will come to seem like an uphill battle. However, if repeated rehearsal of a strategy allows you to develop a new belief, this can become a new habitual pattern of thinking. This is an underlying principle of cognitive psychology. To respond to the pessimist, if this results in us feeling better or enjoying life more, that can't be a bad thing. People take drugs for this effect. So if you have an ability to change your experience of life for the better, go for it!

However, this is not the version of positive psychology I am advocating. It can be an add-on component, but my concerns rest with the main focus on thoughts or beliefs. In a lot of cases, the new beliefs are used as counter-scripts, to balance out the effect of the original beliefs based in fear. This is a reasonable management strategy and does provide benefits. In addition, it sometimes results in resolution of a script containing the unpleasant affect. However, this approach does not use the full capacity of our mind, only the thoughts and faculties of the objective mind. If we are not using the capacity of our instinctive mind, the effect is limited.

The limitation to this old positive thinking approach to positive psychology is this; it has no independent point of reference. If the thoughts do not have a direct life experience to call upon, the resulting counter-scripts are arbitrary beliefs. As such, they are unstable and require high maintenance, so the positive effect is highly likely to break down with time. With this approach, there are no grounds to decide what type of script will give us a pleasant experience. So what else is there to base our thinking on? If you have identified an inclination toward being pleasant, have you tried using this as your base?

There are many detractors from the positive thinking approach, but I am not in agreement with them either. On occasion, I get short of patience with people who blindly follow a view of life handed down to them by someone else. I couldn't count how many times people have responded to a positive statement of mine, with statements like; "life isn't a bed of roses you know." My answer is, "NO, I don't know life stinks, and how the &%$# did you arrive at this view? If life seems difficult, it is because you believe life is difficult, and think like that as well. Me, I experience life as amazing and think accordingly."

However, my experience of life is not based on a belief. I do not **believe** life is amazing. I sense it this way innately—through instinct. I am saying you do as well. Even those who believe life is an unpleasant experience, innately sense it as pleasant. When it seems difficult or unpleasant, we are falling into the trap of following beliefs which are not based on a direct impression of our nature. Unfortunately for the believer, once the belief has corrupted the perception of a life event, there appears to be plenty of evidence to support the belief. This is commonly referred to as a self-fulfilling prophesy. Once we have accepted an interpretation of particular life events as unpleasant, we find support and justification for our view in the expression of others who also believe life is unpleasant.

Life Wasn't Meant to be Easy

Living by beliefs makes our life experiences difficult to understand. To illustrate this, let me take up my concerns about the saying "life wasn't meant to be easy." The recent resurrection of this truism is attributed to a politician, but it goes back a lot further than that. It is the type of comment and belief I grew up with. Yet I knew from the first time I heard it, there was something not right about it. This statement is flawed though explaining why is a bit tricky, because at the same time it is true; life was not meant to be easy. Describing a saying as both true and flawed sounds like an oxymoron, so let me set this up carefully. Understanding the flaw in this statement goes a long way to explaining the pickle we are in with our belief structures.

I pointed to the answer earlier when discussing morality and sexuality. In summary, I was told there was no morality in a stiff dick. This statement implies the sexual instinct overrides morality, and thus an aroused male will not act morally. Somehow, this did not seem right to me and yet the statement seemed obviously true; a stiff dick does not have any morality. It took me several years to solve the dilemma because I would not accept the statement could be true. In doing this, I was blocking further inspiration from my instinctive sense of knowing, which was telling me there was something wrong with the statement. Finally, I decided I must be wrong and I accepted the obvious truth in the statement. Only then did I get my solution. If I make the statement in the form of its implication, the error may be more obvious. The implication of "there is no morality in a stiff dick" is "there is no morality in a sexually aroused person." But this interpretation is wrong; there is no morality in a stiff dick, but there is morality in the person wearing it. What was wrong was the implication attributed to the statement.

How then, can the statement "life wasn't meant to be easy," be both true and flawed? Is anyone getting an answer from their instinct? Once again, the explanation has to do with how you interpret the meaning of the statement. Most people understand this statement to mean life is meant to be difficult. The meaning is implicit rather than explicit, because the statement is put in negative form. In this form it is easy to agree with. However, if it is made explicit as "life was meant to be hard," would you still agree with it?

While it seems a truism that life was not meant to be easy, do you think life was meant to be difficult? I find myself suddenly disagreeing with the explicit version of the statement; though I am not speaking for you. You may agree with the view life was meant to be difficult. However, I am suddenly in conflict; agreeing with one version, disagreeing with the other. How can this be? What am I seeing wrong with the second version which doesn't show in the first version? Put yourself in my position and go over these statements again. How could I agree with the first statement—life was not meant to be easy—and disagree with the second statement —life was meant to be difficult? This holds the key to understanding how we are misled by our beliefs, so give it some thought.

If this doesn't help you solve my dilemma, try using the opposing view. What happens if you consider the idea "life wasn't meant to be difficult"? Do you agree with this? I did. Now make it explicit. Do you agree "life was meant to be easy?" I do not. Many people agree with both versions, but I am implying you too should be in conflict with your responses to these statements. If you agree with both, I am saying you have been misled by your beliefs.

Let me try to untangle the dilemma for you. If I disagree with the statement "life was meant to be difficult," you would normally think I would agree with the opposing view "life was meant to be easy." This is logical. If you look at these two statements objectively, they are the opposite of each other and by logic only one can be true. But, I disagree with both statements. If I disagree with both, am I being illogical?

Yet there is a perfectly good solution to the dilemma. Both these statements are flawed because both start with a hidden belief—an assumption—life is "meant to be" a particular way, either easy or difficult. So the error causing my dilemma is the concept life is "meant" to be. I disagree with both statements on this ground.

The solution is simple, and summed up in a saying already commonly used; "life is what you make it." Life can be easy if you make it this way, or it can be difficult if you make it that way. From your choice of beliefs, you have made it how it is for you. Yes, you weren't alone in making it easy or difficult—or a bit of both. We were shown in our upbringing how life was for our parents, caregivers, relatives, and friends. Our experiences were readily interpreted for us with the "wisdom" of other people's interpretations, usually through traditional sayings such as the ones I have just analyzed. People use such beliefs in social conversation, pretty much on a daily basis.

Listening to the Objective or Subjective Mind

As this next topic is an important part of the solution, I want to link it back to earlier comments. What have we used as a reference for making these common sayings? Basically, these beliefs are interpretations of life events. Interpretations are made using the thought processes; in particular our imagination, the wonderful capacity to image things in the objective mind.

Most of us believe our objective thoughts provide the best point of view. I think this is folly. Our culture urges us to base our interpretations and self-identity on evidence provided by objective reasoning, images and beliefs. However, as our interpretations become more abstract, they become further removed from personal experiences of life. Although disciplined thinking can reduce errors of interpretation in abstract beliefs, it introduces another error; it treats our subjective impressions and innate sense of self as invalid. Consequently, the majority of our beliefs have no link to the impressions of our nature found in the subjective mind.

This can be highlighted further with the sayings we commonly use. Think for a moment about the origin of the common sayings we were discussing above. Where do beliefs come from; for example life isn't a bed of roses, or life isn't meant to be easy? Didn't somebody make them up? This might seem a dismissive comment, but I don't mean it that way; we make most things up. That is what we are good at. We use the objective mind to conceive how life is, so we can better interact with it and understand it. Someone or other used the creative capacity of their mind to conceive each of these ideas. So I mean this in a constructive way. We do make things up. The question is, are they true?

When you look at different beliefs, often they are not congruous or consistent with each other. For example, it is obvious these two sayings are in conflict; life is "meant to be" a certain way and at the same time "what you make it." The difference in these sayings is a source of confusion. They represent two different philosophies about life and ultimately cannot be integrated. We can try to make them relevant to different situations, but who has ever said when one or the other applies, or for which events neither applies. If we keep both these sayings among our beliefs, life will seem inconsistent to us.

The more our beliefs are made up out of thin air, without being derived from a direct, personal experience, the greater the likelihood they will be based on another belief. Without a reference which is separate to the thought processes of our objective mind, we are at the mercy of our thoughts. Without such a reference, the belief is arbitrary and may mislead us. The inherent danger is that we then make our experiences fit our beliefs. Can you see where this gets us into trouble, if the core belief does not actually reflect our natural sense of life?

So beliefs and sayings should have reference to a personal sense of life, by which they can be verified. The appropriate reference point is our subjective impressions, where there is no trouble or unpleasantness. This event is occurring in our awareness and does not involve thinking. In other words, the subjective mind provides access to our instinct without use of beliefs or fear. It is easy to verify; are you aware of existing without thinking? Try it now. You can listen to a noise without thinking. If your head is full of thoughts, look behind them or between them. It is obvious there is more than thinking making up your experience.

The natural order is to have an instinctive impression of an event, then think about it, thus creating our experience. We have an instinctive want to understand these events, before we think. Even thinking itself is an instinctive act. Then, we engage the objective faculty of reasoning to interpret the events and develop beliefs. We only interpret a relatively small proportion of them, mostly those which affect the practicalities of our daily living.

The subjective impressions happening in our awareness have more to offer than the beliefs created in our objective mind. Consider this question; what is an experience without a subjective sense of self? For example, if a child observes a person turn a tap to get water, they can believe water is obtained by someone turning a tap. However, a subjective self is necessary for growth and learning. The subjective component allows the child to transfer the information to see they can get water this way. With no subjective self, the child thinks water comes out only when another person turns the tap. Luckily, children are not based in their objective mind or else they wouldn't learn much of value! Without use of subjectivity, our explanations of life experiences are shallow.

Therefore, while using the objective mind to understand our personal life experience, the best reference point is our subjective self. Our beliefs work for us when they have a subjective impression as their foundation. So what do I make of objective explanations about why we have unpleasant experiences in life? Explanations based on beliefs which do not contain a sense of self, are invalid. In fact our subjective impressions are critical, because they confirm our sense of self is based in goodwill, not fear. Expressed by the objective mind, this becomes our direct, personal experience of life.

Let me refer back to our personal experience when it comes to the saying "life wasn't meant to be easy." No-one ever experiences what is "meant to be" independent of thought; it is always a created image. We infer "meant to be" from retrospective interpretation of life events. An interpretation of life as "meant to be" a certain way is based on a belief there is an intention for life, external to humanity. Statements like "life was meant to be" can only be based on beliefs otherwise we would not have free choice. Let me highlight this by saying it again. No-one directly experiences the meaning behind the word "meant". It seems people don't accept responsibility for the amazing ways they use their minds. Alternatively, many people may want **not** to have this responsibility! This is a free choice though. There is no escaping our amazing capacity to do just that!

The difficulty in explaining this solution is that it does not come from logic, reasoning or use of any objective faculty of our mind. I say difficult, because it is not obvious enough for those who run their lives from objectivity, or from beliefs. In order to see the solution to the contradictions and confusion in my life, I had to go beyond logic and beyond belief to bring another perspective to bear. This perspective is based on the will, the instinct to thrive. As it is not based in positive thinking, in my mind this requires a new form of positive psychology.

Summary

We have lots of information about our mind, but little understanding of the human experience:

- Our understanding is clouded by our abstract beliefs.
- It is important to challenge beliefs because they often misguide the course of our lives.
- When we choose beliefs over natural impressions they change how we interpret the event.
- When a belief is not in accord with our goodwill, we have an unpleasant experience.

Differences in meaning between the terms "want" and "need" show where things have gone wrong:

- Wanting is a direction from the will to thrive, and is a pleasant experience.
- Wanting comes naturally to us and is there all the time, even when there is no particular thing wanted.
- Nothing happens in our minds without want.
- Wanting is an appetite, and our source of motivation to use the thought processes.
- We do not have to discipline ourselves to do what we want.

- Want is corrupted when our attitude is not based on our goodwill.
- Needs are seen as things we cannot live without.
- If I have a body but am not this body, it is the body which has the need and not me.
- As I want to be alive, I care for my body; no-one maintains we need to be alive.
- Psychological needs are a corruption of want, caused by using the objective mind to overlay wants with fear-based beliefs.
- If we have needs, this suggests we aren't free agents and don't have free choice.
- Turning wants into needs creates a monster in need of control.

Is it wiser to follow our instinct or our beliefs?

- Thoughts and beliefs are not inherently wrong, but if not consistent with our instinct they cause us grief.
- The current approach to positive thinking is based on beliefs. Its limitation is not having a reference point that is beyond belief.
- Living your life based on beliefs is alarming, and carries an inherent danger we will make our experiences fit our beliefs, rather than developing our beliefs from our experiences.
- One of our significant control mechanisms is our belief in discipline.
- Discipline is not a natural state, it is learned.
- All disciplines, schools of thought and techniques, are developed with the thinking mind.
- Objective observation requires a subjective sense of self to be valid.

- In the context of a vicious cycle, an instinctive sense of goodwill allows you to proceed.

The difficulty in explaining this solution is that it doesn't come from logic, or from reasoning or use of any objective faculty of our mind. This requires a new form of positive psychology.

NINE

Living the Natural Solution

Let's get to the details of a solution to the great dilemma of life. There are two actions enabling us to live a life of joy, rather than unpleasantness. The first is to unseat fear from its throne in our thinking mind. Second, and of greater importance, is to frame our experience with our instinctive sense of goodwill. This means installing the products of instinct in our thinking mind, the main features of which are a sense of knowing and a pleasant feeling. This is the solution in operation. The question is; how do we do this?

Creating Ill-health

An understanding of the problem is a start down the road to recovery. So, let's briefly go back to the idea that unpleasant experiences indicate simple misuse of our objective, conscious mind. We have an objective mind which can conceive of anything, but we believe we have immunity when it comes to what we do with it. The truth is, when we conceive in fear it creates an unpleasant experience. This is a straightforward consequence of misusing our minds. Believing in fear locks us into our mind with this unpleasantness. Ironically, we are misinterpreting the indicator which shows we are misusing our mind—the fear.

Mental ill-health comes from constructed beliefs which are not grounded in the pleasant experience of our will. When we experience common mental health disorders, like stress, anxiety and depression, it doesn't automatically mean there is something wrong with our mind. In most cases our minds are working perfectly. Rather, it is how it is being utilized which results in suffering. The "problem" is caused by what we feed our mind; much the same as the health of the physical body depends on what we feed it. It's a software problem with the capacity to distort the hardware. Notably, this does not discount the organic source of some disorders, such as hereditary, dietary, physical trauma, or substance abuse.

We believe the experience of fear is legitimate. As a result, we believe the unpleasant things we experience are there against our choice. This belief allows us to dissociate from the effects of the fear. We complete the vicious cycle by attributing unpleasantness to some other cause; our "nature" being the most commonly used scapegoat. We generally regard this undesirable aspect of our thinking, as coming from something which leads us to do bad things. From there on, it is inconceivable we could be in charge of our minds. To cap it off, we cement the problem in place, when assuming unpleasant experiences are mostly biologically based. When we suffer, our minds are just not working as they should!

Even though our instinct and goodwill prompt us to correct the unpleasantness, we choose our fear-based beliefs instead, believing fear is our true instinct. We hold on to the very beliefs causing the suffering, and devise counter-scripts to try and control the effects these fear-based beliefs are having on us. We certainly have done a good job of burying the source of the suffering, rather than acknowledging it. It seems we cannot come to terms with the reason this approach fails us; namely because it is against our true nature.

In sum, we create beliefs not in accord with our will. Some might say this is ill-will, but it is simply a choice to listen to fear instead of our instinct. ***We have chosen fear as our guide to life, and our belief in fear and efforts to control it is the source of our suffering.*** Unfortunately, to the extent we succeed in managing fear, we have a vested interest in not rocking the boat. This often prevents us from challenging our belief structures, particularly those related to control.

This is what we are up against when seeking a solution. We prefer thought based solutions because it seems easier to control our thoughts rather than our instinct. How wrong we are. Neither is subject to control. The solution involves being free of our effort to control. I will outline a process for doing so now and in the following chapter. How to deal with fear when we let go of control is of major concern for many people. Consequently, I want to start with this part of the solution and examine how we can put fear in its rightful place.

Deposing Fear from the Throne

The Nature of the Beast

Fear is a lie. When we are fearful we cannot see the truth because the fear makes everything seem something it is not. If fear and the dysfunction it causes is not an instinct, we are living our lives as a lie. When we follow fear, we believe in a lie.

More specifically, fear turns things into a lie. Fear reverses the positive-negative poles of our thinking. Seen through the lens of our fear, everything appears the opposite to what is genuinely good for us. Hope becomes doubt and love becomes hate. If fear is endorsed as valid, everything is turned on its head; "ass about face" as the saying goes. For instance, many people who live with fear like to portray themselves as "bad," and portray "good" to be "too good to be true." When fear has its dysfunctional grip on us, everything seems counter-intuitive. That is why it seems hard to get away from fear. Fear interferes with us instinctively seeing a way out. When present, fear governs our experience of life, and the boat is belly up!

How do you turn the boat the right way up? Sorting out the fear and control would help. However, merely to stop "wronging" ourselves is not going to set it right. Such an approach would be reactive, whereas a proactive approach is called for. The good news is that our instinct is continually prompting the system to right itself. If we listen to our instinct, the fear can be put where it belongs—to sleep. The truth is to be found in the effect of the will on the instinct. It is the sense of thriving, experienced as everything feeling genuinely good to us. This is the only way to undo the lie representing fear; and it is the only way to get answers that satisfy.

The discussion and examples related thus far have given away any element of surprise about what I see as the solution. So let me paraphrase a simple statement putting this in perspective. **Fear goes against my will.** Recognizing this was a profound experience for me. It meant I could have a pleasant experience of life, even if others choose to follow fear. But I still remember the story of the prisoner's dilemma. Living by the truth of my will is essential to my continued healthy existence. Also, I understand my continued physical existence is not guaranteed. Life does not come with a warranty! Wanting a guarantee is just another control mechanism. The best I can do is to enjoy the life I have, while

I have it. This gives me a sense of innocence and freedom. The solution then, rests with following our instinct, fed of course by our true natural self; the will.

In a nutshell

Let me succinctly describe the mess we have created, and the solution. We have a will, which by nature is expressed as goodwill. We have a subjective mind housing the instinct, one aspect of which is awareness. Awareness knows a sense of harmony, indicating life is not a problem. Our objective mind can conceive of anything. We use the objective mind to conceive from fear—the dysfunctional variety—because we can. Yet we believe fear is a natural part of life. From fear we distrust what comes naturally. This leads us to discard input from the subjective mind, instinct, and will. By doing this we imprison ourselves in fear. To try and solve the dilemma, we use the objective mind to construct solutions in the form of beliefs. These beliefs are mostly fear based control mechanisms or scripts. These solutions do not work. In fact, they cause more unpleasant experiences of life. This is because fear is the source of our unpleasant experiences. However, by becoming subjective and listening to and wanting the instinctive goodwill, the fear is put in its place. Then we have a pleasant experience of life. There you have it, in a nutshell.

Freeing Our Mind of Fear

We need to reframe the function of fear, and get away from using fear the way we do. We seem to have a fatal attraction to this experience, though it is more a case of not knowing what we can do about it. Let's start with an acknowledgement; fear has a practical function. Well, that is not quite true. It is not the fear which is practical, but our ability to conceive and experience it. How is this possible?

Our objective mind is there to be of service, but it can conceive of fear. The voice of instinct is not fear, but thoughts of staying away from fear are its words. Have you considered how this could serve us?

Surely there is a functional role for the fear? Why else would we be able to experience it? The best we have done so far is to bear it, or lump it in with our idea of a survival instinct. It must be there to keep us alive. Yet when the fear gets into the thinking mind it produces mayhem. From this point of view it seems the objective, conscious mind is working against us.

Let's look at an alternative function for our ability to conceive fear; one more down to earth. I'll use physical pain as a model. Pain is a response from an intelligent system seeking to sustain life. Generally, pain is not regarded as instinct, but as a signal. If we are in pain from a cut, this is a signal our physical system is compromised. The healing action which follows on from pain is very much pro-life, remembering there is no guarantee the system can always correct it. Pain is a noxious stimulus, uniquely different to a pleasurable one. After all, if it were a pleasant or neutral experience we wouldn't mind bleeding to death.

What if fear serves our mental system in the same way as pain serves the physical system? I am going to be bold and suggest fear is a signal from the objective mind, indicating we are at that very moment doing something which is compromising our continued existence. When we think in a way which produces an unpleasant experience, this hurt registers as fear. In other words, when we think without goodwill, there is an imminent and immediate danger to our mental health and our continued existence. Our mind, like our body, is an intelligent system, giving feedback when we are compromising its nature and hence its health.

This is such a simple idea, yet it fits perfectly. Fear is not some kind of punishment; that's a fear-based interpretation. Our ability to experience fear is a mechanism to give us feedback when we are not listening to our will-based instinct. In my life I have heard many suggestions of how to deal with fear, but none quite like this. In other words there is a practical purpose to having a mind which can conceive of anything.

It is an extremely radical idea, highlighting the basis of our misunderstanding about how our minds work. If it is true, then we should change the whole foundation of what we are doing with our minds. Why? Because it means whether or not we suffer unpleasant experiences, is entirely in our hands. It is a most radical thought, because if we respected this function of our mind to conceive fear, like physical pain, we would seek to avoid it. We wouldn't touch fear with a ten-foot barge pole.

When our mind registers fear we should be taking note and heading in the other direction. Fear is **not** in our best interest. Our ability to conceive of fear isn't there to control us though. It is a backup system to let us know when we are not listening to our will. We should appreciate this function. If your mind is used in this fashion, it will change the course of your life. That *is* a guarantee!

The Solution to Release Fear and Control

At this point, I want to present some diverse examples of how things would be different without fear and control. This means reframing some of our cherished ideas, such as our attitude toward our thoughts, our belief about the survival instinct, and how we treat children. Let's start with our fear about thoughts.

Our belief that fear comes from instinct, gets us into all sorts of trouble. It means when fear speaks, we think we ought to listen. So when we have thoughts that trigger fear, we embark on a rollercoaster ride. To illustrate this, imagine standing on the edge of a sheer cliff. A seemingly creative, positive thought enters your objective mind; you could easily jump off here. This can feel like an idea to try it. I would venture to say most people have, at some time, had a similar thought when facing a potentially dangerous situation. Next you recognize that jumping of the cliff could kill you. This triggers a fear reaction, and you are now shocked and dismayed you would think of such a thing. You quickly step back and control your mind by reminding yourself there is a lot to live for. You leave the cliff-top believing you cannot trust your own mind, if it would have you thinking of doing such a thing.

Can you see how the point of departure from "normal" thinking occurred? When the fear was invited in to corrupt the natural process of constructive and deconstructive poles of thinking, the thoughts were seen as bad. What would have happened if the fear did not activate? Our mind's job is to show us the truth in any situation. So from curiosity, the positive polarity will ask every question there is to ask and the negative polarity will respond. The outcome in this situation could go something like this: I could easily jump off this cliff (+ve). It's a long way down (-ve). Is there anything stopping me (+ve)? Not really—and that is true (-ve). Now in the absence of the fear, the thoughts carry on with the negative polarity having a deconstructive role. While looking down to the bottom of the cliff, the thought occurs; what would happen if I did jump (+ve). You will die—again true (-ve). What if I die (+ve)? You will be missed (-ve)—and miss out on life! Notably, the negative polarity gives good direction if the creative thought has undesirable consequences.

So where does the process of thinking lead to in the absence of fear? In all cases the objective mind points to the truth in accord with our goodwill. The two poles of thinking help us find answers. The positive, creative side of our thoughts comes up with all sorts of ideas, without considering the consequences. That is the role of the negative polarity. In this scenario, the deconstructive polarity responded to the creative idea to jump off the cliff, by helping see life is worth living. The net result is, we get reinforcement life is good, a far cry from listening to fear.

However, fear changes the course of these events. In the example above, a creative thought appears to put our life at risk. With the introduction of fear, it would go something like this. See if you can spot where the fear comes in. I could easily jump off this cliff. Yes, there is nothing stopping you. What would happen if I did? You would die. Do I want to do it? No. Am I afraid of dying? No. Prove it. How? Make the jump. That's crazy. No. How could I do that? If I jump out far enough I will miss the rocks and land in the water. From fear the action is now being contemplated, though hopefully common sense from the instinct and goodwill still prevail.

In the absence of fear, objective reasoning works because the negative polarity thoughts are deconstructive, not destructive. The positive polarity thoughts present the unrestricted, creative side, such as an idea to do something. The negative polarity thoughts deconstruct it by presenting an alternative idea, for instance why you wouldn't do it. In this way we get to choose our course of action. Rather than controlling our thoughts, the process of choosing would benefit from us letting the information come into our mind so we can think about it, and conceive its relationship to our situation. Then we may see the relevance to our situation more clearly. That is of course, provided we don't believe in fear. Fear lies to us, and listening to it unbalances our thought processes.

This last proviso is very important. If you choose to entertain unpleasant notions in your mind, it makes it harder to deal with the fear, anxiety, stress, depression, or whatever else the unpleasantness has in store for you. So when I say let the thoughts into your mind, I mean the ones spurred by the instinct and goodwill, not the ones in memory corrupted by fear. Also, do not go chasing after unpleasant scripts in memory, unless you are confident of these two things: you are presently in touch with the instinctive sense of a good feeling, and you can and will stay in touch with it, if and when you encounter an unpleasant script. If you are not sure or it does not feel safe, this is best done with the guidance of a trained counsellor.

Instilling the Input from Instinct

Free Choice to Express the Solution with Beliefs

Does this mean we should abandon beliefs? No, that would be going to the other extreme. Beliefs themselves are not the problem. It is our misuse of them which causes our predicament. The fundamental mistake is to elevate beliefs above the natural instinct of our will and our sense of knowing.

Use of the objective mind, including the development of scripts and belief structures, is how we interface with the world. The thinking mind enables interpretation of life events. This is how we comprehend how the world works, and how we come to know ourselves. Interpretation of events is important for us, because it allows us to express our will. Nevertheless, in going beyond this point with abstract thought, we should be very, very careful it meets our instinct.

Using the objective conscious mind properly means using it as your will intends. This means bringing the objective and subjective minds into alignment to enable your will to be expressed. I suggest this happens through expression of our true instinct. However, the objective mind is the one interfacing with the environment, and we are not controlled by instinct, so choice is involved.

The marriage of the minds happens by being willing with the subjective mind, wanting with the objective mind, and making a conscious choice of what you want. Your choice of what you give attention is of paramount importance. The will and instinct are already doing what they do best. Our awareness gives off the signature call of our will—a sense of harmony, or any other pleasant feeling. For that part we do not have to do anything. However, in order for us to experience this harmony in our objective mind and daily living, it is essential to do three things: first, want the objective mind to bring attention to our subjective impressions, second, freely give attention to our awareness of the harmony there—rather than to our capacity to conceive fear—and third, choose to express the harmony or pleasant sense in thought and behavior. Making this choice simply means you listen to what feels pleasant. You note what becomes unpleasant in everyday living and you do not entertain it. This is really the only choice we ever have to make, though it is played out in every life experience, through the positive and negative poles of the thinking process.

A distinction between the terms "will" and "volition" may help at this point. Volition, related to the word voluntary, is associated with our choice; the ability to create options in the objective mind and freely select among them. On the other hand, our will can be regarded as the source of instinct in the subjective mind. We could debate whether or not will is itself an instinct, but it doesn't show itself that way to me. In fact it feels like the will *is* me. Subjectively, I sense the core me as a source of power. When I listen to my will with the objective mind I feel empowered.

In this sense, volition means free choice. One of the more difficult ideas to get a handle on is the prospect of our objective mind not being controlled by anything, not even our will. In other words, as strange as it may seem, we have an instinct to think but we are not required to think; otherwise meditation would not be possible. Thinking is an activity we engage in to develop plans and goals, construct action plans, store and access them in memory. We choose to use our thought processes. In this sense all thoughts are volitional. They are the product of receiving stimulus through the physical senses and constructing—creating—ideas to interpret them.

An argument used to refute free choice is that some of our thinking seems automatic. It seems like this because many thoughts come from memory. Once we have stored an action plan or response strategy in memory, it doesn't take much effort to bring thought and memories into the conscious space of the objective mind. If we have developed a strong habitual pattern, this seems to happen before we get time to think about it. So most people who use their thinking mind in isolation of their awareness, miss the critical moment when they choose to allow a belief into their objective mind. I will give more detail about this in the next chapter.

There is an extension of this argument. I am aware some people believe they have no choice over thought. However, this isn't supported from personal experience. What most people mean by this is that they cannot control their thoughts. Yet the compulsive thinking most people experience is the result of an instruction to their intellect to control everything: including perceptions, ideas, responses, and choices. It really is like banging your head against a brick wall. It is an exercise in futility resulting in extreme frustration. Direct, personal experience indicates we can choose to be aware without thought. Again, ask people who meditate.

Some people argue we are not free to choose. However, even to arrive at the idea you are being controlled is a choice. We can appear to have no choice because we have chosen to look at life this way; to create the reality of others controlling us. Examples abound of people's retorts to this, but the arguments behind most of them are similar. A common example is, if I am arrested and thrown in jail, I no longer have a choice. Such an argument confuses whether my choice is related to physical liberty or freedom. If my liberty is taken away I still have the freedom to choose whether to give my attention to the output of my goodwill; remembering the story of the prisoner's dilemma. If the choice is between what feels okay and what feels unpleasant, I always have this choice to feel okay under all circumstances. In this sense, the infamous saying is true—they can take my liberty, but they cannot take my freedom.

Realizing we have free choice enables us to properly use the objective mind. Just about everyone accepts we can freely choose what we do, be it to comply with social norms, engage in unhealthy behaviors or break the law of the land. Having free choice means nothing controls our mind. Not even our own will forces our choice; or else it wouldn't be goodwill. This means we are free to conceive and believe whatever we like.

Choosing to use your mind to act in accord with your will is a primary part of the solution. However, it is not a case of simply deciding you will do this and all is well. In order to re-instate choice to its rightful place above the intellect, it has to be wanted and exercised continuously. It is easier than it may sound. In other words, by choice you tune in to your awareness of the subjective impressions. By doing this, awareness detects a sense of harmony, which can then be expressed by wanting to show it. Who isn't attracted to pleasantness in life? Some people describe harmony as a neutral experience, which is still not an unpleasant one.

In terms of the experience you want to create, your will manifested through instinct is the only input you have which is not based on a belief. Therefore, it is a fitting reference point for how to think, and how to live your life. This enables you to choose to construct scripts and beliefs consistent with your true nature.

A potential obstacle with belief structures is they are stored in memory. I'm not making a demon of the memory. The memory function has a role to play, which is to present back to us the ways we have previously dealt with life events; taking account of our successes and failures. Memory also allows us to recognize what we are doing, so we don't have to start from scratch each time a situation arises. The problem is that memory is equally effective at retrieving unpleasant experiences as pleasant ones. So, when we experience unpleasantness, these are the times to go back to the drawing board and choose a pleasant one. If we continue to use belief structures not based on goodwill, we have no means to get away from the unpleasantness.

Goodwill versus Control

Let me show you what life could be like without fear, using an aspect of child-rearing as an example. The topic of boundaries is currently a hot one. My views on this topic may ruffle a few feathers, but we should be prepared to challenge any of our cherished beliefs. If there is any chance it is doing children harm, we should be more than willing to examine it at any time and any place. The case I wish to make is that placing boundaries on children and insisting they adhere to them, does harm.

A common application for boundaries is in managing children's behavior. A highly recommended principle by experts in the field is to establish a clear boundary of what is acceptable and what is not. This seems reasonable as a basis for communication and guidance for the child. As an added bonus, it seems to work. In fact it seems to work quite well, so why would I be concerned about it? How could this be doing harm? I'll pause while you see what answer comes from your subjective mind. The answer mine gives is, because establishing boundaries usually involves fear. How does setting boundaries involve fear? Let me count the ways!

Essentially, the concept of boundaries is a control mechanism. It is a means of showing the child what is expected of them, usually defined as what is acceptable to the adult. This is accompanied by consequences, usually in the form of rewards for compliance and punishments for non-compliance. If managed well, this can be as simple as giving or with-holding parental approval. Our belief in boundaries is based on the idea that children need structure, and discipline is required to control unruly behavior. I have said plenty about this topic, so here I will focus on other aspects of it.

The component of boundary-setting doing the most harm is this; boundaries are imposed on the child. Discipline is good for us, isn't it? This belief is supported by what others believe and what is conveyed in our culture. Children do not have an effective say in the matter, even when asked if they agree. Where is the harm in setting a boundary? It is in the threat, whether implied, or explicit.

By definition, imposing a boundary means if it is over-stepped, there will be consequences. Can you see the fear yet? The control mechanism is designed to over-ride the child's choice. Any person, child or adult, would find this intimidating. You might argue, the child has a choice to do or not do what the parent wants, but really the child is being instructed to defer to the parent's choice or suffer the consequences. They have not been consulted or involved in setting the boundary, and their choice doesn't matter. The child has in effect been deprived, and will feel that way, whether they do what the parent wants or not.

Think about what the child is being taught. Putting a boundary in place sets the wrong example for the child. Instead of teaching the child to accept the consequences of their choices, it does the exact opposite. It is teaching them to do the right thing according to what others think. It is teaching them, what they want doesn't matter; it is teaching them to fear. Boundaries are set in place because the parent fears for the child. A boundary imposed by one person on another is, and always will be, unpleasant to the person on whom it is imposed. No person genuinely likes this, no matter how much it is dressed up as caring. Most often the fear is hidden by the parent's good intention. Does it matter if the child doesn't like it? Absolutely! This is the signal their goodwill has been compromised. In my view, the use of threat or fear is abusive. When we attempt to deprive others of choice we are psychologically assaulting them.

Now I want to speak of what the alternative would be like. It would certainly revolve around the child's choice and their will, with no discipline, no fear, and no control. If this seems scary, hang in there, it is not as you might think.

Without boundaries, interaction with a child, as with any other person, would be based on the two principles of effective communication. These are, to ask questions and form agreements. Both are expressions of our instinctive goodwill. Rather than assault the child with your view, consult the child so they feel involved. In every situation ask what they want to do and say what you want to do. Even tricky things like what time they could go to bed. If it is agreeable to you, form an agreement with the child. If it feels unpleasant, continue to negotiate until you find a mutual agreement which is pleasant. Make sure an agreement is formed as quickly as possible to establish this as the basis of communication. Remember, it is not about controlling the child to get your way.

Agreements are the basis of further communication between the adult and child. If the agreement is followed, a positive relationship and way to get what you want is reinforced. If it is not followed, then negotiation begins by asking questions. Why wasn't it followed? Will it be followed if I agree next time? Can you see I am giving you what you want? Will you give me what I want? If not, you could attempt a bit of reverse psychology by attempting to form an agreement in which you don't give them what they want. For example, let's agree you don't get a story at bedtime and I don't get a hug goodnight. The child soon sees the benefits of giving other people what they want. It is in their best interests to do so, and it is not based on manipulation.

The key to the success of agreements is they are based on a two-party consensus. With any proposed event, if one of the parties doesn't agree, it doesn't happen. A controlling person will see this as them not getting what they want, but what they miss seeing is the power of consensus. You do not have to give the child what is wanted if the child is not following what was agreed on. In this way the child learns to stick to agreements, and you both get what you want. It is based on self- direction, not the adult setting boundaries.

If this is done with goodwill, the right message is conveyed to the child. If the child is exposed to goodwill, rest assured they will respond in kind, because it is in accord with their nature. This caring interaction can easily be seen between mothers and babies. Naturally, before the child can make complex choices like what they want to wear, it is okay to speak on the child's behalf.

It goes wrong once the child has been taught to believe in fear. If fear has been instilled, it can take time to reestablish a pleasant basis to the interaction.

Agreements have all the positive attributes of boundaries, but they differ because the child or other party is involved in the decision. It is a mutual choice not containing fear or any level of intimidation. The child is respected and will feel this way. This also maximizes the likelihood of the child extending respect to you. Both parties will feel good about the interaction, and the child will feel in charge of their destiny. In this way the child learns self-regulation. This gives the child a good example of how to be happy and get what they want. It teaches them to ask of others and form agreements with them. In particular, it teaches children to give of their goodwill to other people.

Their will is the solution! Of course, it is the same will as yours. In the big picture, listening to and acting upon this will gives us confirmation life is good. Showing this to children teaches them about their instinct, and reinforces they know what is good for them. They learn to listen to themselves and others. This is known as intelligent cooperation; the creative potential of your will acting in accord with the will of the child. This is a will not corrupted by fear in its expression. The upshot of this is, when the child listens to their sense of knowing, they will get answers that satisfy them.

Let me put you to the test by asking a trick question. Do you think children should be allowed to do whatever they want? Now, before you trundle out the old belief structure and say "of course not," review some of the earlier discussion. Remember in particular, the error in the statement "life was not meant to be easy." We get misled by statements like this, when we fail to question the hidden assumptions on which they are based. So, where is the trick in this question?

I am saying children should do exactly what they want. Actually, I am saying they do follow what they want and this is how it should be. Our job is simply to guide them to do what they want based on their goodwill. Without fear, appropriate choices are made, such as telling the truth or at least being true to themselves. So the trick or error in the question, "do you think children should be allowed to do what they want" is in the words "allow" and "should." It is our place to advise the child, not to decide and enforce what the child should do. That is a control mechanism. Yes, it is designed to stop unpleasantness, but it actually reinforces the view fear is legitimate. It does nothing to undermine the unpleasantness and fear. From unpleasantness, children are more likely to make bad choices and act accordingly. This is the damage we are doing to children.

So how should we interact with children, and anyone else for that matter? My answer to this question has got me into hot water with a number of well-meaning health professionals. Some people find this idea offensive, many others are dismissive of it. Nevertheless, I will stand by it because my quality of life depends on it. Teach kids to listen to their knowing. Treat them as equals. Treat them as you do a friend.

Summary

The nature of fear:

- It is our choice to listen to fear rather than our instinct.
- Fear makes everything seem what it is not.
- When we follow fear we believe in a lie.
- We believe we have impunity from the effects of misusing our mind.

Reframing fear:

- Fear has a practical function of feedback, like physical pain.
- Pain is feedback to an intelligent system seeking to sustain life.
- Fear is an indicator that the objective mind is being misused.
- It is a backup system to let us know when we are not listening to our will.

Knowing your will is the solution:

- In terms of the experience you are having, your will manifested through instinct is the primary source of input.
- In expression it is goodwill, and way beyond belief.
- Alignment of the objective and subjective minds enables expression of goodwill.
- In communication, goodwill has two principles – to ask questions and to form agreements.
- Listening to and acting on your goodwill gives children the message that life is good.
- Show children they know what is good, so they can listen and respond in kind.
- Treat every child as an equal and as a friend.

TEN

KNOWING YOUR WILL

We can now discuss the primary part of the solution in more detail. I have more to say about the roles of the will, awareness, and instinct of the subjective mind, as well as the wanting, thinking, attention, and memory faculties of the objective mind. If we did not use fear in our thinking, how would these minds relate? In particular, how do we come to have pleasant experiences of life?

No matter what is said, for each of us the evidence comes from our own self-exploration. Exploration of your instinct is arguably the best way to know your will, and find out you can live without fear. See if you can relate the following discussion to your impressions of life. In particular, you require confirmation of the following experience; in the absence of fear there is an innate pleasant experience of life to be had. You could do this by taking a walk in the forest and communing with nature, or possibly by not watching the news on television, so your mind is not fed with fear. More easily, you could just become subjective and see if the event going on there feels harmonious. The question I want you to ask is, "how would our sense of knowing deliver this pleasant experience?"

Instinct without Fear

First, we need a better definition of instinct. Do you wonder what our instinct would feel like if fear was not part of it? Survival instinct is the term used to describe our primary urge. In my mind, it is problematic if we regard instinct as being only for survival, rather than something broader like "for existence." They seem very similar, in the sense survival means continued existence. Except, pro-existence has a broader, more life enhancing meaning than survival, one that can take us out of the clutches of fear and control.

The concept of survival has been developed to explain, among other things, how fear controls us for our benefit. If fear is considered a natural sense for humans, then the concept of survival is a very attractive explanation of why we experience fear. It steps in when needed and makes us do things instinctively to survive. Seen in this way, fear seems to be part of our instinctive responses. Without a definition of fear as being instinct, we would be hard pressed to explain why we have unpleasant experiences in life.

But reference to our instinct as the survival instinct sells it short in a very big way. The term "survival" implies we are fighting for our lives. Out there in the world, or in there in the human being, is an adversary with forces that would lead to our demise at the drop of a hat! Is this what your instinct tells you? I don't think so. This is a fear-based belief. It is not our instinct to fear for our life. It is our instinct to sustain and support our life. Our instinct caters for continued existence. It is our beliefs about life and death for example, which contain the ideas associated with fear.

Calling it a survival instinct is based on our fear of death. This is not said to trivialize fear. It is an incredibly potent experience.

However, I do want to suggest it is a misunderstanding of life events. The experience of fear is a created one, and like all created realities should be challenged. Changing it is another matter! It is important to try though, as the consequences are immense. What would it mean to you, to have an instinct without fear?

It seems to me our system instinctively wants to ***thrive***, not just survive. This is an important distinction, because "just surviving" implies it is against the odds. Do you think we are lucky to be alive? In fact, the odds are hugely in our favor, suggesting instinct does a good job. A better description of instinct would be an inclination to grow and flourish. Our instinct, including fright, is pro-existence and not based in fear. Here is the link to our will being goodwill. The will is creative, and the source of harmonious impressions of life. If it were not, it wouldn't be favoring our existence. ***In particular, acting from goodwill dissolves disharmony, thus supporting our existence.***

Our instinct is pro-life. Think of some of our instinctive appetites like sleeping and thinking. None contain a sense of anything being set against you. If you want to speak, laugh or just scratch your head, does it feel like this is surviving or thriving? When you are hungry and want food, does it feel pleasant or unpleasant?

So if fear is a capacity of the objective mind and not our instinct, how would things work then? Consider the idea that our instinct does not control us, and is rooted in goodwill. The concept of pro-existence encompasses all of this. What is more, our goodwill is the indicator of how things work to favor and enhance life. This is experienced as an incentive to do what is naturally good and affirming for our continued existence. In the hierarchy of life processes, will manifesting as goodwill is behind the instinct to do what is to our betterment. This is our true intent—not intention. This intent informs our instinctive want, and want informs our thinking. In the natural order of things everything works fine. That is, until we use our thinking to create something not in accord with our will. At the risk of repeating myself, then there are problems in paradise! So the concept of pro-existence is a more appropriate term for this broader view of life, encompassing the idea all is well, including our ability to conceive fear.

The Direction of Instinct

There are some implications worth noting here. We talk about instinct alerting us to danger. We also talk about fear doing the same. A challenging question to guide your self-exploration is whether in fact fear does alert us to danger? A way to examine this is to look closely at how instinct operates. Could it be that our instinct always points toward a pro-action not a re-action? In this case, instinct does not directly tell us what is wrong. The instinctive appetites, for example hunger and fright, do not tell us what is against our continued existence. They show us what is consistent with our continued existence. Then we see clearly if what we have in mind is life sustaining or not. This is vastly different to our usual ideas about instinct; an example of this is, fear alerts us to danger, so we should listen to it.

If our instinct is to thrive, when we are fearful, the fear itself is the danger. This distinction should, at the very least, lead us to use different terms for an instinctive fright versus dysfunctional fear, because "never the twain shall meet." Instinct prompts us forward, toward growth, and hence away from anything which does not meet the creative drive of the will. This includes fear. Our instinct leads us onward, whereas fear retards us. Have you ever noticed if you are frightened of fear? This may seem like a minor point, but this distinction is right at the heart of the solution. If you can confirm you are frightened of fear, you have your proof; fear is not part of our instinct.

Our instinct is not telling us our life is under threat; fear does this. The instinct is a blueprint of our will, showing us which way will continue our growth and harmonious existence. This includes feeling happy, being friendly and wanting sex. These impulses do not make us look over our shoulder. It does not cause us anything unpleasant in our experience of life. Only the conception of fear does this!

Instinct operates continuously. It is an initiative we each meet the world with, rather than a response to the world. Instinct is our guiding force, experienced as **want**. It gives us the impetus to do what we do, including the means to thrive in the world and the curiosity and interest to explore it. The phrase "to do what we do" is not to be confused with "how" we do it. How we do what we do is a function of the scripts and belief structures we have built up over time, particularly our early childhood years.

So with my instinct in place I am always able. This pro-life sense both motivates me to engage in the act of living, and gives me the means to do so. This includes my appetites, my inclinations, my sense of well-being, and the natural use of whatever faculties are at my disposal. Dare I say this includes the impulse to engage in thinking? We do not learn to think; we learn what to think. It may be that instinct has nothing to do with learning, other than prompting us to do it. Isn't it curiosity which interests us to learn?

My instinct monitors the world through the physical senses, and in a manner of speaking, my instinct knows what is good for me. Simplified, this means my instinct is being served if I am experiencing harmony. If a sudden and unexpected loud noise happens, my instinct instigates a startle action, causing a release of adrenalin to help me deal with an extreme event. This is not fear or disharmony as we usually define it.

The instinct gives us a reference for how to live. Instinct keeps us in touch with our sense of goodwill, which is the solution for all situations. For example, if we come across someone who is sad, we are inclined to be kind. It also sets in motion a healing action to overcome unpleasant experiences. If we permit the will to "do what it does best," we are inclined to laugh about our misfortunes. During this experience, control is exposed as a fear-based strategy. Without fear and control, the alternative experience is increased creativity, a feeling of well-being, and a sense of strength and power.

What do we do now? How can we sustain a pleasant experience of life? Basically, we have to reinstate the natural collaboration between our objective and subjective minds. This is done by consulting our true nature, the instinctive experience of harmony and knowing, which shows us the way. Rather than relying on the objective mind, we remain connected to our instinct and will. Since our true nature is goodwill, we do not need to control ourselves: no discipline, no control, no fear.

The good news is that everyone follows the solution to some degree. Most people are happy to eat and procreate for example. Our will seeds our instinct to thrive. Our instinct in turn seeds our want; expressed in thoughts and deeds. Where it is not working, is in the part of our lives where we consider beliefs to be more significant than instinct. This idea may raise a lot of objections about matters such as undisciplined behavior, which I will shortly address. But let me say, the solution does not involve fear or unruly behavior.

An End to Suffering

With fear in its rightful place as a backup system, we are free to explore how to undo the corrupting effect it has had on us.

This is not as easy as it sounds because we are so used to listening to fear, as if it had something meaningful to say. Fear has turned the world of our objective mind upside down. Experiences are distorted, causing everything to seem as it is not. In this way, fear appears to block our way out.

Keep in mind, the solution is already in place. It is our will: represented as a sense of knowing, felt as subjective harmony or goodwill, and experienced as a want to create and thrive. The solution is activated by the choice to listen to our instinct—rather than fear—and the want for instinct to be in charge.

This is done by becoming subjective. Whenever we are doing this, the objective mind is not running the show. When this happens, the function of fear stays in the background where it belongs. The subjective mind is revealed anew and the solution can be felt once again. In sum, by letting go of control and giving no attention to fear, what we are left with is the will-based instinct of the subjective mind.

When you are being subjective, have you noticed the impression you get about life is not unpleasant? This is the core piece of information you should confirm in your experience. It means unpleasant experiences occur in our objective mind. Once armed with this, the solution is put in place by using our subjective impressions as the reference point for what we want. This enables us to use beliefs to construct a reality based on a sense of harmony. There you have it—no rocket science involved, and 25 years of formal education for me to arrive at a view a child already knows!

So how do we resolve or at least minimize our suffering? We do it by wanting to base our thinking on the impressions in our subjective mind, in particular our goodwill. Yes, this means giving more emphasis to our nature than our thoughts. Living from our subjective mind is the key to living a fearless life, and one which gives satisfying answers to questions. The subjective mind always gives a viewpoint based on a sense of harmony independent of fear. What is more, our instinct guides us to listen to the will. While listening to the will expressed in the subjective mind, we experience freedom from fear. This you can verify in your own experience. Have you ever examined what you are doing when you don't feel fearful?

An example given by a lady who has attended some of my workshops was about an emergency situation in her medical based workplace, when an unintentional injury resulted in a client bleeding uncontrollably. Someone's life was in her hands and she knew the situation called for fast immediate action. With literally only moments to spare, an instinctive urge enabled her to stay calm and be in charge of the situation. This allowed her to draw on her experience, resulting in a positive outcome for the person affected. Most others on the scene became fearful, and were unable to function optimally until given direction. In her account of the event, she said it was obvious that instinctive intelligence in action, free from fear, meant she could think clearly. This laid the foundation for saving a life, which was an empowering experience for her.

Our will, expressed as intelligence through our instinctive sense of knowing, then operates the thinking mind. This instinct always shows us what is true, in what we have conceived in our mind and developed in our beliefs. You always get an answer. Whether you choose to listen to it is another matter! If you do choose to listen, being able to sense the instinct before any belief takes over, requires use of a faculty other than thought. This is the role of awareness.

An in-depth examination of how my minds work, led me to differentiate between awareness and consciousness. Awareness is a more subjective sense than consciousness, indicating it is a faculty of the subjective or instinctive mind. When we use it, we are in the subjective mind. The main difference is that pleasant and unpleasant experiences come and go in the objective mind, but awareness itself doesn't change. In particular, awareness has a harmony linked to it, a natural core sense of feeling good, which is always going on behind the scenes of the thinking mind. So, greater use of our awareness is an important ingredient in the recipe for creating a pleasant experience of life. This is discussed more in the next chapter. But there are no surprises, just a specific application for what is already being done naturally.

Our natural impression of life, untouched by fear, is a pleasant one. This is not a belief; it is an easily demonstrated, reliable and repeatable experience everyone is capable of. It is one I willingly show whoever is willing to look. On the basis of these innate pleasant impressions, if I use my mind to express this in a pleasant script, I have created a pleasant reality for myself. If I choose to create a script containing unhappiness or discontent, or any other unpleasant conception, I have introduced an unpleasantness into my life.

It seems obvious, doesn't it? When I create something unpleasant, I am the first to suffer from this misuse of my mind. This is my system showing me I have constructed something not in accord with my will. Of course it is aided and assisted by the unpleasant treatment from others, who look at the world through expressions of their own fear-based beliefs. In combination, this makes us both victims and perpetrators of all things horrible, which we carry forward in our scripts stored in memory.

Take the time to become aware of the effect your thinking mind has on you. If we choose to think unpleasant thoughts by fully engaging the imagination, that wonderfully creative part of our mind, it does affect us negatively. If you think this way, you will create an unpleasant emotional state and unbalance your bio-chemistry. This emotion in turn will seed other unpleasant thoughts. Note, if an unpleasant thought does not change your emotional state, it probably means you were already experiencing an unpleasant emotional state. Sometimes you may not be conscious of this, because you can get accustomed to feeling unpleasant.

As obvious as it sounds, the next comment was a bombshell for me. When I use my thinking mind to conceive, think and act in accord with my will, I do not suffer! I am well aware this is a big call. However, it is completely verifiable in your own experience; how you can do this is taken up in the next chapter.

The end-of-suffering is a moment-to-moment experience. When I listen to, and express my instinctive goodwill, I do not suffer an unpleasant experience. This happens for as many moments as I choose to do this. However, my mind will always be able to conceive of fear, and I wouldn't want it any other way. If I am living a fearless life, do I experience fear in my life? Yes, on rare occasions I am still silly enough to choose fear. There are two reasons why this is possible.

First, I am still free to conceive of fear. The will does not control me or make me listen. This is good if I know the unpleasantness means I am no longer doing my will. I'll risk laboring this point to clarify a common misconception about fear. The fact we can conceive of fear does not mean fear is good for us. We have a tendency to falsely attribute fear with intelligence. Do not think fear is teaching you to listen to the will; that idea is based in fear. ***Fear is a signpost, not a teacher.*** And it is not the primary guidance system for a pleasant life. It is a backup system activated when the primary one has not been exercised. The primary system is your free choice to give attention to the will-based instinct.

The second reason I sometimes experience unpleasantness is due to my memory. The beliefs and scripts, representing my past unpleasant ways of dealing with life events, are stored in memory. When triggered by a stimulus, fear and suffering is less than half a second away. This is the time it takes for a habitual response pattern to be retrieved from memory into the working space of the objective mind. These are critical moments; when I do not choose the instinctive goodwill, I still suffer. If I choose my goodwill, I do not suffer when these beliefs are exposed. It is in my hands to choose not to suffer, and it is my choice for how long this will happen. And so it is for you.

So there are two parts to the solution. One is to "flick the switch" and listen to the will-based instinct as an ongoing meaningful way of life. The other is to clean out the memory store of fear-based scripts. This is a work in progress that can take many years; which is okay considering how many years it took to create them in the first place. The point is, right now you can live without fear and suffering, while challenging belief structures you have developed through fear. The key is to not have the backup system of fear come into play, even when challenging the fear based scripts. This is discussed more in the following section on attaining and maintaining good mental health.

Listening to Instinct

Answers that truly satisfy are formed in the objective mind, based on input from your will and instinctive sense of knowing, appearing in the awareness of the subjective mind. This being the case, how do you know whether or not an idea was inspired from your instinct?

Perhaps the answer to the question you asked was not motivated by your instinct. You could have read on this topic or watched a documentary about it. That is, your response may have come from an opinion or belief rather than input from your instinct. If your mind acknowledged the answer as a matter of fact, then it probably came from your beliefs. Bear in mind it is also possible for both instinct and belief to be involved. You can get an indication from your instinct and back it up with a belief.

But how do you know if your instinct was involved? Well, the simple answer is your instinct is always involved if you are listening to it. It is continuously in action sampling the environment through the senses and giving us direction. Instinct is proactive, not reactive. Apart from our choice not to listen to our instinct, there isn't anything we do which doesn't involve instinct!

Is there a way to tell when you listen to your instinct? I'll give you some hints shortly. If you knew which bit was the impulse of instinct, at least you might know if you were listening to it. In all likelihood you do listen to it, at least some of the time. I doubt there is anyone who chooses to listen exclusively to the objective mind. In fact, I think such a feat is not possible. Could you ignore instinct and yet continue to live? We clearly use both the subjective and objective minds, but we have instructed the objective mind to dominate.

How can we tell the difference between instinct and belief? Here are some quick and easy hints. Examples you could try fitting with these differences are; hunger and your choice of food, relationships and your choice of partners, wisdom and how you speak to a stranger.

1. Listening to instinct has a sense of spontaneity and ease to it. Holding beliefs requires effort in thinking, and often makes matters difficult.
2. Instinctive urges feel genuinely good, so we like them. Beliefs are an "acquired taste", sometimes distasteful to others.

3. With instinct, you don't have to rationalize your choice. On the other hand you do with beliefs, as they are based on ideas.
4. What is in accord with instinct is what we actually want. Beliefs require interpretation to provide a course of action, often against our better judgment.
5. Your sense of knowing gives confirmation of your instinctive impulses, but not your beliefs; choices based in instinct are satisfying when acted upon.
6. The will-based instinct contains a genuine sense of you, not found in beliefs or images. With the above examples still in mind, this sense of you is felt as an affinity to the food or person. If you don't know what this feels like, you are in worse shape than I thought! That is a tongue-in-cheek comment of course; instinctively we know our unique sense of self.

It would be helpful to be able to separate out the instinctive component. This would enable you to give it precedence, assuming you choose to do so. There is a cue to tell you which is instinct. Everyone knows it, but most people only occasionally use it because they do not value it for everyday living. Having taken belief structures onboard and elevated them to the status of control mechanisms, we have learned to place more value on these created realities. For the most part our instinct is relegated to our physical system, for example the physiological appetites of hunger and sexuality. It is little recognized that we have similar appetites of the mind, including our natural appetite to want to understand the world we live in, to experience pleasantness rather than unpleasantness, and my favorite, to explore our own existence and come to know ourselves!

What is the instinctive sense like? ***It is a sense of attraction.*** Do you recognize your appetite for pleasantness as a sense of attraction? Instinct doesn't cause an attraction to things—the appetites it causes ***are*** the attraction. And not a fear-based distortion of what is attractive, but a genuine sense of attraction giving us a good feeling about whatever it points us to. Can you feel your lack of attraction to unpleasant things? No-one in their right mind wants to experience unpleasantness.

Let me clarify this further. The following point about attraction seems subtle, but the implications are huge. Instinct puts out a signal, and the things meeting it appear attractive to us. This includes actions, thoughts, and feelings. For example, certain thoughts are attractive to us, such as the idea of success. Our will causes an instinctive attraction to whatever is in our best interests. When we are thirsty the taste of water is more appealing, even though it doesn't have a taste. When we are hungry, food looks attractive to us. As the sight and smell of food makes us salivate, we tend to think the attraction was a response to the sight of the food. This interpretation is not quite accurate

Instinct is an ongoing sense of attraction. Would you like some proof? Look into the subjective impression you are having right now, and ask if you have an attraction to life. Think of it like a magnet attracting metal. This attraction is happening before it is mirrored back to us in food, our success, or in the qualities of another person. It is continuously active and sensing the world. It is attracting us to act, in other words prompting action. It is even attracting us to think. The ideas we conceive in our mind hit on the attraction, causing the attraction to be intensified. In the case of food, at a certain level of intensity we salivate.

The difference between "initiating" an action and "responding" with an action is important, when we get down to developing a coherent story of our life. This difference is captured by the terms proactive and reactive. The idea of the instinct being proactive and thoughts being reactive is not just a matter of terminology; there is a meaningful difference. It means instinct leads the way, and moves us away from fear. Instinct does not react to the environment. It is an innate intelligence, pointing out the path of attraction to our continued, enhanced existence. Hence this is another way to tell if you are listening to instinct rather than fear. **Instinct is not reactive, fear is. Instinct does not feel unpleasant, fear does.**

Earlier I posed the question, "which is of more benefit to us, disciplined or free thought?" When you read the question, which choice attracted you? Of course, free thought is more attractive. But this is not by chance. It is not attractive just because it is the easier option. It is attractive because it is in accord with our instinct—innate intelligence. This is how we get answers that satisfy. However, the source and nature of this attraction is one of our misunderstandings.

A person with a strong commitment to discipline may answer in favor of discipline. But I can say without fear of contradiction, if you had in fact listened to your instinct you would have favored the option of free thought. A pragmatic person might argue an attraction to free thought happens because we learned to like it, not because it is our instinct. An argument could be developed around this point of view, but it is a hard case to make. You could equally say we learned to be good, and to do and say things to be liked by others. But why does being liked, appeal to us? Did we learn this too? I don't think so. Being liked is pro-life and a clear indication of attraction—there is not much chance of having an intimate relationship with someone who doesn't like you.

Here is another question for you. This is a tricky one to answer. Is it in our nature to dislike? Or, did we learn to dislike? Most of us felt disliked early in life, so it seems like innate knowledge; but yes, we did learn to dislike. Where is my proof? I know I have experienced dislike, but when I ask my instinct if it is my nature to dislike, it shows me no sign of it. To me, this means dislike is learned. So let me add a word of caution as you seek an answer that rings true for you. The following point is critical. It holds a lot of things together, and answers how we know if we are listening to the instinct. Actually, it is what makes it safe to listen to our instinct.

Instinct does not say "no", in the sense of being opposed. This might trigger your disbelief at first. Keep in mind it is okay to say no, if for instance someone offered you something you didn't want. So, how can instinct work if it doesn't say "no?" This is the most significant thing about the instinct; it always points you in the best direction to thrive, and it feels good to us. Instinct does not initiate unpleasantness. Unlike fear, instinct will not cause us to feel abhorrence, malice or contempt, or anything which doesn't show us where our continued existence is favored. In the case of fear, we have no attraction to it. Fear is psychologically painful to us, and it is appropriate for us to be frightened of it.

If instinct doesn't say "no", how does it work to provide an answer to every single genuine question we ask? If the question is not in accord with your will, we do not get an answer from instinct. This is how we know the question is not recognized. For example, if I pose the question "is it my instinct to be unpleasant" I do not get an attraction to the question, hence it is left unanswered. If I pose the question "is it my instinct to be pleasant?" I get an affirmative urge—attraction—accompanied by a pleasant feeling—instinct met. In this case the instinct prompts my thinking mind to form the answer "yes". The answer comes naturally, so it feels different to pre-conceived ideas in memory. When the question is not in accord with my instinct, it does not relate to the question. I do not get an unpleasant feeling; I get no feeling. I can interpret this as "no" if I want.

A blank response does not mean you don't know, it means the question is not understood. By analogy, it is like someone asking you a question in a foreign language you don't understand. In this scenario, have you noticed what happens in your mind? My mind goes blank; I don't know what to say to the person. Similarly, the language of fear is foreign to the language of instinct. Thinking we have to understand fear, we have become bi-lingual. Now when fear talks, we answer in the language of fear. My advice to you is this; if you wish to live a fearless life, use the universal language of instinctive goodwill.

There you have it. One of the most startling insights I had while studying my mind was this; my sense of pleasantness indicated when I was listening to instinct. Think about the implications for you. A pleasant experience is your affirmation. If you do not get it, you know what instinct is saying by its absence. Somehow the idea in your mind is not formulated correctly. If you hear a direct "no" in your mind accompanied by a slightly unpleasant feeling, you are using the language of fear. All you have to do is keep asking questions until you get a pleasant subjective feeling. On the other hand, if you believe pleasant feelings are not genuine or not to be trusted, then you have set yourself up for a lot of misery. Rather than that, see if you can find a pleasant feeling from asking questions, even difficult ones such as "does fear lead me to distrust pleasant feelings". This is difficult because you have to be careful not to listen to the fear when you use its name. With regard to another difficult question, "where do the unpleasant feelings come from", I am pleased with the answer "fear." How do I know when fear is speaking? For me, a pleasant feeling comes from the following answers. I have no attraction to fear. I do not comprehend fear. I am frightened of fear, and want to turn away from it.

The Source of Instinct

Many people say they do not know their will. But instinctively they do; they just don't recognize it consciously. Your will is there "doing its thing" to keep the minds alive. It tirelessly urges us through instinct to think, to investigate, to understand, to care, to act—in sum to do our will. Try reviewing what you have done today, and look for choices that came easily to you or felt pleasing. It manifests as a deep, good feeling. However, the source of instinct is more direct than a deep, good feeling within you or about you; it is a deep, good sense of you. Actually, it is even more direct than this; it is a good, deep feeling that *is* you.

So the key to the solution is; ***the will is you***. It is our core sense of self. In this way it deposes the need for fear of our-selves and our minds. It also means we don't need to control ourselves, nor explain life as controlled by something else.

How do you know it is you? It fills you with a strong sense of your own empowered existence. It is the means by which you feel confirmed, recognized and acknowledged. By this I mean feeling right and authentic. You know this is you, because your instinctive sense of knowing feels recognized. Your will is the essence of you, and this core creates a good feeling, 24 hours a day 7 days a week. Your will is the source of all the natural experiences you have in life. You have access to feeling good no matter what is going on around you or within you. If you still wonder how you will know it when you feel it, come to one of my workshops and I will show you what it is like when fully engaged. In this event, when you experience it you will know; it is unmistakable, and unmistakably good!

This is why the solution is so simple. If our will-based instinct seeds our expression, the events of life are pleasant for us. For the most part we do not experience fear, nor do we suffer. It probably doesn't matter too much if will is viewed as our core instinct, as long as we don't see it as something separate from or outside of us. I favor thinking of it as a third mind because this sense of me seems to be there all the time, to be behind or beyond even my instinct. For me, this is what philosophical thinkers refer to as the unmoved mover.

How do you find your will? You know how some silly jokes stick with you? One from my childhood came in a booklet on "waiter" jokes, consisting mostly of one-liners between a waiter and a patron. The one which stuck with me is a good analogy for how you find your will; and how to find yourself. The joke goes as follows: Waiter: "How did you find your steak sir?" Patron: "Well, I just lifted up a chip and there it was!" The obvious meaning is that the patron is complaining about the small size of the portion. Even with the small portions one sometimes receives at a restaurant, the idea of the steak getting lost under a chip is ludicrous. Now for me this joke has another meaning, irrespective of what the author intended, in which the chip also symbolizes resentment. When we are resentful of something, it is said we have a "chip on our shoulder." The steak is symbolic of enjoyment in life. The response of the patron to the waiter also said to me—"well I just lifted up my chip (resentment) and there it (enjoyment) was." I guess I also found this funny because it captured my experience of life at the time.

It is hard for some people to grasp the idea there is a part of them feeling good all the time. Instinctively, people can relate to this, but when things are going badly it can seem there is no part of us feeling good. That part is buried under a whole load of chips. But it only seems this way because we are giving our attention to what doesn't feel good, namely the expression of fear. When we do this, the unpleasantness sensed in the objective mind invades our thinking and emotional state, increasing our suffering.

What is more, expressed beliefs affect and infect others. Most of us may know this, but I don't think we see just how serious the consequences are for us. When these beliefs are not based on a sense of goodwill, they have a corrupting influence. Can you relate to a situation of feeling good, then someone vents anger at you, and you find you are suddenly angry? Although we don't like it, we allow it to happen, based on other equally misguided beliefs. For instance, do you believe it is too hard to change the unpleasant experiences in your life? Since we are talking about simple choice, it isn't hard; as the starting point, we just have to be genuinely willing!

Have you ever wondered about the source of our sense of humor? Isn't it there all the time? Even in the most unpleasant situations, we often seem able to laugh. While working as a researcher in my late 30's, I remember doing a presentation to a community services club, introducing a skin cancer prevention program. As I was feeling bold about giving the talk, I planned to start with a joke. It was relevant to changing people's behavior, but it came with a risk because it was another of my childhood jokes, which I was about to deliver to a large group of educated, older males. One minute into the presentation, which was about getting people to check their skin for early signs of skin cancer, I delivered the following joke: How many psychologists does it take to change a light bulb? Answer: Just one, but the light bulb has really got to want to change. Now to my surprise, it went over reasonably well, but as an anecdote about humor, the best was still to come. At the same meeting, a representative of a well-known Australian folk festival, was making a presentation about relocating the site of the festival; a very serious matter for the community. During his talk, on the spur of the moment and to everyone's delight, he delivered the following joke: How many folk musicians does it take to change a light bulb? Answer: Two, one to change the bulb and one to sing about how good the old one was! This totally set the scene for the most enjoyable formal evening I have ever attended.

If we look on the funny side of life, we can have a good feeling all or most of the time. It would be handy if this could be done deliberately, rather than happening by accident. Let's try it? If you become subjective and think of the range of expressions of goodwill being like radio frequencies, can you tune in to your instinctive sense of fun? In general, this means using awareness to sustain any pleasant impression found in the subjective moment. This is aided by choosing to willingly give attention to our fun loving nature. It is an invitation for instinct to show us the way. This can also correct our unpleasant expressions, including the ones in memory. Further practical details about this will be discussed shortly in the context of mindfulness meditation.

In the meantime, here is a challenge for you. Watch your reactions really closely whenever something horrible is expressed by you or another. See if you notice in that first brief instant, you get an urge to correct it. It lasts for less than a second—until a belief or script cuts in. In this brief moment, if you can detect there is no unpleasantness in what you are sensing, you are on your way to living a fearless life. This is the answer; using your awareness to sustain that moment.

From there it is a matter of meeting everyday life with this moment. Continue to observe closely, and you can feel the effect of the script cut in. Inspect even more closely, and you can see the unpleasant experience happening when the script is not consistent with the urge you got in the first brief moment. If the thought or script is consistent with a caring instinct, then you go on having a pleasant experience. If the script is not based in goodwill, then in about another half a second, an unpleasant experience begins to manifest.

In sum, we create a pleasant life experience by engaging the objective mind to serve the harmonious impressions in the subjective mind. This happens by being subjective, and choosing to give attention to our awareness. An important part of the solution is realizing we do not have to find the harmony. Our awareness itself *is* the embodiment and sense of harmony. When we sense the harmony in awareness we are in a position to think in accord with it. If the harmony seeds our thinking, the fear is not activated. In this way we respect the ability to conceive fear, as an indicator of when we are not giving our attention to harmony. What is more, being instinctively frightened of fear makes it easy to not go there.

Use of awareness is an important ingredient, but perhaps not like most people would think. The discussion to follow suggests our current use of awareness to approach good mental health would benefit from further development. A new form of positive psychology is there for the making.

Summary

The nature of instinct:

- Instinct is pro-existence.
- We are not fighting for our lives against the odds.
- Instinct prompts us forward to growth, and leads us away from fear.
- The action of goodwill also dissolves disharmony; this is how it supports our existence.
- Instinct is always in operation as a driving force, giving us the impetus to do what we do.
- If I am experiencing harmony, my instinct is being served.

The solution is delivered by our instinct:

- The solution is to listen to our will rather than the voice of fear.
- If we listen to instinct the fear can be put in its place.
- When there is no fear we start to get answers that satisfy.
- The intelligence of our will operates through our instinctive sense of knowing.
- The sense of knowing highlights whether our will is met by what we have in mind.
- Pleasant and unpleasant experiences come and go in the objective mind; whereas awareness has a continual sense of harmony.
- You are free to conceive of fear at any moment—instinct prompts you not to.
- The end of suffering is a moment to moment chosen experience, not a guaranteed condition.

Your goodwill is the essence of you, sensed as power:

- Acting in accord with your will prompts you to change some of your beliefs.
- Beliefs and scripts based on fear are stored in memory and are easily brought to mind.
- Cleaning out unpleasant scripts from the memory store is a work in progress.

The instinct to listen to ourselves is how we get answers that satisfy. How do we know the voice of instinct?

- Instinct is a sense of attraction, prompting us to act and to think.

- Appropriate ideas in our mind hit on the attraction and intensify it.
- A sense of liking is an indicator of when we are listening to instinct.
- We have no natural attraction to fear.

Expressing your will as goodwill puts the solution in place:

- When we listen to our will, it deposes fear of ourselves and our minds.
- The solution is created in daily living by sustaining the initial instinctive moment of awareness, and meeting life with this.
- If you can sense the harmony in awareness, you're in a position to think in accord with it.
- If harmony seeds our thinking, fear is not activated.

In moments when I use my mind to think and act in accord with my will, I do not suffer.

ELEVEN

WELL-BEING BEYOND BELIEF

In earlier discussion about the role of fear, I said we have a choice about how to view fear. If we choose not to believe in fear, we are free to use our objective mind to make our personal reality a pleasant one. At the same time, unpleasantness coming from others who are using fear, still goes on around us. In this situation it is easy to slip into choosing a similar fear-based mindset. However, we have free choice. Exercising choice to think in accord with our will instead of with fear is the key to a pleasant experience of life. This is the required primary action for living without fear and knowing the meaning of life. Secondary, is the management of our belief structures, schemas, or scripts, particularly the fear-based ones. I think there are different meanings for these three terms, which represent a hierarchy of relatively more complex concepts, but here I will refer to them as scripts.

Before discussing this in detail, let me add a caveat about script-based, created realities. It is hotly debated how far scripts go in explaining the unpleasant part of the human condition. In the sum total of all unpleasant things we experience, I see the vast majority of them being based in learned scripts. Irrespective of how much suffering is due to scripts, it is these I discuss below because they involve choice.

Choosing Wisely

Accessing either well-being in the subjective mind, or fear in the objective mind, is a matter of choice. It is important to understand, choice enables a pleasant experience of life.

We choose what we entertain in our objective mind. Our choice is exercised by giving attention. This is irrefutable because it is verifiable in our own experience. Everything we do involves a choice. Acting on a thought involves choice, as does not acting on instinct. Even believing we have no choice involves choice. In other words, there isn't anything which has absolute control over what we choose.

The majority of the time, we use the objective, conscious mind to choose. Choice can be defined as the conscious act of giving attention. In practice, this means giving attention to one event in preference to another. Whatever we give our attention becomes the event we then entertain in the objective mind. Everything else follows on from there in terms of our thinking, imagining, and conceiving. All these activities, including choice, are the capabilities of the objective mind energized by our instinct. We have an instinct to choose, to think, and to want, but the instinct does not control us, so we are free to choose what we want. Nothing happens in our personal reality without voluntary attention—choice—which is why the choices we make are so important.

The most significant choice we make is to what we give our attention. Giving attention to the content of our awareness is absolutely the best thing we can do with it. Awareness, a quality of the subjective mind, is the link between our will and the objective mind. Awareness is tuned into our will, so it carries an immediate sense of harmony, representing the effect of the will on our subjective mind. This harmony, found in all facets of goodwill, can then be directed to the objective, thinking mind for creative expression. In a nutshell, this is how we have pleasant experiences.

What is in awareness is our direct impression of life, without filters or corruption. The harmony produced by the will is ever-present there, even when we conceive of fear in the objective mind. When it seems as though harmony is missing, we are giving attention to the fear or other functions of the objective mind, instead of to the subjective sense of harmony.

Part of the proof for me is that subjective senses or feelings are never unpleasant. When you become subjective, you tune in to a place or state which has no unpleasantness associated with it. Have you ever experienced this? If not, try it! Granted, if you have been using your thinking mind to attain control, the thoughts will interfere with this experience. In this case it can take courage to let go of control.

Technically, this sense of subjectivity is not a created state of mind, but a naturally occurring sense. It is awareness itself. In subjectivity we also sense our core self or actual self, which I maintain is the will. Being aware of our own existence, feels genuinely good. This enables us to have an innate sense of harmony, strength, belonging, and caring; before we create them as our objective reality.

Previously I mentioned the objective and subjective minds normally act cooperatively. Giving attention to awareness is how we enable the cooperative connection between them. These two minds complement each other. When we objectively conceive of the subjective sense of goodwill, it is like delicious nectar enlivening our taste buds—perhaps more like chocolate for some.

Our harmonious awareness does not interfere with our thinking. In fact, it facilitates it. If I give my attention to the awareness of the subjective mind, I experience a freedom to think what I like—literally to think whatever is to my liking. What is more, when I am based in my awareness, I am not obliged to use my thinking processes. I can simply enjoy listening to a bird singing. My choice to give attention to ideas about the bird, or other matters which interest me, is an added event. Awareness also shows me I am having a pleasant experience, in this case enjoyment of the bird's song. Best of all, awareness of any pleasant experience indicates my will is being served.

The way these minds cooperate is the key to maintaining pleasant life experiences. Awareness is a creative seed or life force, while attention is nurturing, providing the oxygen or fuel for growth. Thus, when given to awareness, attention fuels the natural subjective sense of harmony. Then I can easily use my conscious mind to conceive in thoughts and deeds, based on this pleasant sense of life. Awareness brings life to events, producing precepts—basic thinking—and attention brings them to form as concepts—advanced thinking with images.

See if you can prove that attention brings subjective impressions to life. Try this "quick quiz", without giving yourself or me a hard time if it doesn't work immediately. Look for a sense of harmony or any pleasant feeling in you—it is there. When you find this subtle sense, freely give it your undivided attention for 10 seconds without concentrating on it—just be open and aware of it. Then describe what happens during this time. Does the pleasant sense change, increase in intensity, expand or seem to be more obvious?

Before describing this direct path to well-being, I will relate two other experiences found from exploring my subjective mind.

These are the most helpful pieces of information I can tell you about how to have a pleasant experience of life. If you are not yet conscious of these events, think of them as a theory to explain why it is at least possible to have pleasant experiences.

First, the subjective mind operates as a range of frequencies. We can use our awareness to tune into any of these frequencies and sense the impressions of our will. Until we do this, these impressions are undetected. When we become subjective—tune in—we sense a type of neutral harmony or calmness, around the mid-point of this range of frequencies. Using our awareness, we can move up and down this range and induce or tune into different types of pleasant impressions. If we go up into the higher frequencies, we can sense an innate kindness, higher again a sense of happiness, and still higher a sense of joy or delight; bearing in mind this has nothing to do with thinking or images in the objective mind. Similarly, we can go down this frequency range to be aware of a sense of contentment, lower down a sense of assuredness, still lower a sense of nurtured and authenticity, and at a very low frequency a sense of power and core self. This discovery astounded me. It means we can access any pleasant sense we want. We are then free to express it with our objective mind, resulting in an objectively pleasant experience. In doing so, we create a pleasant reality for ourselves. In some circles, accessing these impressions is done with visualization. However, when people are taught to visualize, this often involves images, which can conceal the innate impressions.

The second experience was equally astounding to me. If you scan the range of subjective impressions looking for fear, you cannot find it. When you try this, be sure not to use images or memories. If you remain subjective, there is no unpleasantness. This means we cannot induce fear; it is not to be found in the subjective mind. In fact, the more you attempt to find fear while remaining subjective, the more remote fear will feel to you. This confirms fear is related to the objective mind, and therefore is not part of our instinct. As previously mentioned, the language of fear is foreign to our instinct. You have to think or use images to experience fear. The clear implication is that it's not compulsory to live with fear. With these two ideas in mind, let me talk about the direct path to well-being.

Mindfulness-based Positive Psychology

The topics I've discussed so far support a positive psychology approach to life. However, I am going to take them further, to develop a different direction for positive psychology. On the way, I'll show the implications for creating "mental health order," since dealing with mental health disorder is a field I have been involved in as a health professional. In this section I will summarize the features of my approach, link it to a branch of current psychological practice, and provide a brief framework for self-help practitioners and health professionals. If you find some of this to be complex, just take it slowly. It is an important part of the story, demonstrating how you can tap into your source of fearless living, and then show others how to do the same.

Mindfulness is the act of bringing attention to an event in the present moment. It is being used increasingly in psychological practice. Better use of attention allows us to become more conscious of our personal experiences, including information about life events, our reactions to them in the form of scripts and beliefs, and their effect on us, particularly how they change. Understanding that events run their course, gives us the option of waiting until they pass. In essence, mindfulness is the use of attention to deal with life and its unpleasant events. Recent research shows the benefits of using mindfulness for a range of mental health conditions. There are now a number of psychological treatments which use this approach; you can find these by searching the internet and journal literature using the term "mindfulness."

A mindfulness approach to life events probably should be called neo-positive psychology, because it substantially revamps the basic idea of positive psychology. Until fairly recently positive psychology was based in the thought processes, using techniques such as holding healthy values and beliefs, and consciously thinking positive thoughts to feel better about oneself. Affirmations, for example, are a way of giving suggestions to our mind, which can change how we feel. Nonetheless, this form of positive thinking is a control mechanism.

A mindfulness approach accesses the natural abilities of attention and awareness, which are not part of our thought processes. Attention is our ability to attend to selected events, enabling use of the thinking mind to produce and retrieve relevant ideas and beliefs about these events. Awareness is an unbiased, non-judgmental, pre-thought capability, allowing us to perceive the effect of what we are thinking, and sense our instinctive impressions of how to thrive. This gives us an alternative to having the thinking mind running the show. Mindfulness bridges the gap we have made between the objective and subjective minds.

However, knowing mindfulness works is not enough. I want to be more specific about why and how it works. Gaining a clear understanding of the mechanism of effect could let us use it more effectively. The central distinction, which most people overlook, is the difference between "attention" and "awareness." Most people use these terms interchangeably, saying that giving attention results in increased awareness of an event. This statement needs to be reframed, as confusion in the use of these terms disguises the function of mindfulness.

Mindfulness Viewed as Giving Attention

First, let's examine how mindfulness works in addressing life events. There would be little debate over a definition of mindfulness as the use of attention. Attention is the most significant capability of our objective mind. It is the only faculty which is 100 per cent at our disposal. Early writings about mindfulness referred to it as "paying attention." But this keeps attention in the realm of a control mechanism. ***Attention can only be given.*** It does not cost anything; if given freely the positive effect on us is enormous.

Attention is enabling, because it is the doorway to the faculties of the objective mind. Giving attention is actively choosing the event we deem relevant to us. Whatever we choose to give our attention, can be processed. Processing a sensory perception means developing an image, enabling thought, and activating the memory processes, resulting in formation of a script or selection of an existing one. So attention allows us to be conscious of our perceptions and responses, including the fear-based ones which constitute our unpleasant experiences.

Mindfulness of an unpleasant event means giving attention to the effect of a script, without engaging thoughts about it. Just as we can listen to a bird singing, we can observe tightness in the stomach or an unpleasant emotional state, resulting from getting stressed or frustrated at work that day. This is done at the physical sensory level, so as not to further affect our thinking. Mindfulness observes the passage of the unpleasant script before it has fully infected the thinking mind. By being mindful we can be conscious of the effects of a script, and see it change. Observing the effect come and go, confirms it is temporary and therefore manageable.

Here is where the distinction between attention and awareness comes into play. I have questions about every aspect of this description of mindfulness. Can we give attention without thought, does attention observe, keeping us apart from the script? For me these functions are the role of awareness, not attention. Awareness is the connection to harmony, while attention opens the event to the thinking mind.

All our experiences are fuelled by attention. Whatever event you give attention to becomes your personal reality. If you consciously listen—give attention—to a passing bus or phone ringing, this event is on your mind and then in your thoughts. On the other hand, whatever event you do not give attention dies. Even within the objective mind at the level of our thinking, if you do not give a thought any attention it does not leave a trace in memory; the thought effectively dies. So mindfulness is really about *not* giving attention.

If awareness of our subjective impressions allows fear to stay asleep, there is a further implication. Consider how mindfulness manages unpleasant thoughts. A script or thought allowed "to pass through to the keeper" withers. If you keep sensations like anger or frustration at a sensory level you are less affected by the input. This provides an opportunity to cope with the script producing the frustration. The question I have about this is whether keeping experiences at a sensory level, also enables us to have a direct impact on the script? If awareness provides a pleasant impression, and giving this attention opens it up to expression with our imagination, thoughts and behavior, isn't this our solution?

I am interested in how to use mindfulness to change scripts; also called schemas and beliefs. I think most people would acknowledge, scripts are products of our thinking mind and therefore of our creation. Consequently they can be changed, the same as any other habitual, seemingly automatic, response pattern. Most current applications of mindfulness in psychology are directed at managing unpleasant conditions. The hidden assumption behind a management approach is that unpleasant experiences are not likely to be resolved by being mindful of them; and the hidden assumption behind this is, the unpleasant experiences are not of our creation.

Attention to the conscious event is not enough to induce a pleasant experience. Therefore, the initial use of mindfulness in psychology is not directed toward finding or creating pleasant experiences. It is more about seeing off the unpleasant ones. In this sense mindfulness-based positive psychology is not proactively looking for something better. Recent applications of mindfulness are looking to address this by adding positive scripts, such as acceptance.

The question I have in mind, is how best to deal directly with a script causing an unpleasant experience like frustration, without using a counter-script? Your choice determines which scripts are activated in the conscious mind. Working with this idea, if the script were in accord with your goodwill, you would choose to let it in. If it were not in accord, you would look for something else. In this case, choice is an expression of power; using it can put you out of the reach of fear. More importantly, any pleasant expression of your will does the job, not just the ones selected from our cultural values and beliefs. For example, when someone makes a mistake at work, you can choose to stay with your subjective impression of understanding, in preference to annoyance about the time being wasted.

In sum, the path to well-being is paved with choice, attention, subjectivity, and awareness. I am pretty sure not a single event in the objective mind becomes conscious without attention. Yet in the subjective mind, things are going on without it, specifically our frequency range of pleasant impressions governed by awareness. Separately, these minds are useful but uninspiring. Actively bring them together, and like poles of a battery, sparks fly. Hence, choosing to give attention to awareness, and expressing the impressions you find there, is the most effective means to accomplish a pleasant experience of life. Use of mindfulness to achieve this more efficiently, is based on a distinction between attention and awareness. Understanding them as entirely different abilities enables us to use subjective awareness and objective attention, to proactively change our experience. This is being in charge of your mind, an important ability if you want to live a fearless life.

A New Direction for Mindfulness

This enhanced mindfulness approach to mental health specifies the difference and relationship between awareness and conscious attention. Currently, advocates of mindfulness tend not to distinguish between attention, consciousness, and awareness, often referring to attention as conscious awareness. In my terminology, the appropriate description for current applications of mindfulness is the use of conscious attention. Consciousness and attention are strongly related. However, as already mentioned, I regard awareness as separate from these other faculties. The case for this distinction is as follows:

1. Conscious attention and awareness are housed in different minds; the former are faculties of the objective mind, whereas awareness is an instinctive sense in the subjective mind.
2. Attention can be focused, or concentrated, onto a chosen piece of information or event such as eating a raisin—as done in mindfulness exercises. Increased attention to an event seems to make us more conscious of it. In contrast, I am unable to focus my awareness. I can only give attention to it.

3. Attention is at our disposal to give. Being subject to voluntary use is a good criterion for defining qualities of the objective mind. This includes attention, perception with the physical senses, memory, learning, imagination, and the thought processes.
4. The faculties of the objective mind involve choice, which is not the case with awareness. We can choose not to use the faculties of the objective mind but the subjective mind is always engaged, even if we direct our attention elsewhere.
5. Qualities of the objective mind are responsive to faculties of the subjective mind, especially the instinctive appetites, including the desire to sleep.
6. Faculties which disappear during sleep belong to the objective mind. Consciousness and attention may seem constant, but only when we are awake! So consciousness is not continuous.
7. Attributes of the objective mind, such as attention, are subject to change (e.g. the effect of sleep), whereas awareness does not change. It is an ongoing harmonious sense.
8. Awareness exists prior to giving attention. Awareness prompts our attention as in waking us from sleep to respond to a noise. Consequently, if awareness contains a sense of harmony, it enables attention to be given to changing the unfolding event.
9. Awareness is more closely associated with the core sense of self than attention. If we give attention to the subjective impressions in awareness, this is what keeps our subjective sense of self separate from the reaction of the thinking mind. This enables us to choose to not get caught up reacting to scripts and belief structures. In this sense,

harmonious awareness is our natural coping ability; our resilience.

Clarifying the difference between awareness and attention opens up the possibility of a process with more applications than the current practice of mindfulness. The practical difference is to move our attention from observing conscious objective experiences—life events—to our subjective impressions in awareness, including our will, instinct, and innate sense of well-being. Awareness of these qualities, in particular the range of innate pleasant impressions available to us including nurturing, love, contentedness and delight, provides the basis of a new direction for mindfulness. The potential benefits include breaking the vicious cycle of scripts rather than being repeatedly subjected to them. The story of the prisoner's dilemma, presented in an earlier chapter, is an example of this.

Awareness is a quality of the subjective mind, having nothing to do with consciousness. I am reluctant to call awareness a state as this suggests it is induced. I prefer the term condition—the human condition if you like. It allows our intelligence to assimilate what is happening to us. Awareness is the means by which we experience life events as meaningful. It provides access to the faculties of our thinking mind, including the memory storehouse. It enables us to create realities, and therefore to influence by choice the content of our experience.

It can be argued that awareness is the "agent of change" and consciousness in the process. Passively, whatever we are conscious of makes up the content of our experience. Actively, as quantum physics would have it, observation changes the event. So when we are aware of something, we can observe it. In doing so, we are changing it. As a concrete example, when you become aware of being stressed or resentful you can give it attention, bringing it into consciousness. This allows the content of the script to be retrieved from memory, and when revealed in the objective mind, it loses its power as an incentive for reaction. This is the same process used to change any habitual behavior or routine, for example the sequence of physical actions you employ when cleaning your teeth. When brought into the realm of conscious choice, the script can be resolved or changed. Do you remember how you broke bad habits when you were a child? It is fundamentally a matter of wanting to change the behavior, then bringing all your attention to a new behavior when the old one presents itself.

In discussing how to make changes, there is another important feature of awareness. The faculty of awareness doesn't change as our physical sensory perceptions change. I wish I could say it is the "thing" which doesn't change in our experience. But it is not a tangible thing, in the same sense as instinct also isn't something tangible. Awareness is not subject to the actions of the thinking mind, or affected by giving attention to a stimulus in the environment. The hardest part is verifying it is there when we are asleep, because we have varying degrees of consciousness during sleep. This is probably why we think they are the same thing.

We think we can't be aware if we are not conscious, but this is not true. It can be a bit tricky to verify you are aware of things you are not conscious of, so I'm relying on you to explore this at length for yourself. For me, it makes sense there is something going on beneath the conscious frequency band, or else we could not wake up in the morning! A common, similar example is being selectively tuned into the noises of a sleeping child and stirring from sleep only when you hear these sounds. Another supporting piece of evidence is vivid dreaming; being aware you are dreaming and also aware your objective mind is still asleep. However, you can verify whether or not your awareness changes when physical perceptions change. All events change the content of the experience you are having. While this is happening, check if your sense of awareness stays the same. Does it? Furthermore, if you can confirm awareness is there when you are asleep, then it is safe to say it is continuous—at least while we are alive.

The following statement is contentious, but I think it warrants your consideration. It is contentious because it is difficult to verify. I propose, awareness is continuous but it might not be a constant. The constant I can't get beyond in my exploration of subjective awareness is the will. As I said earlier, the will could be considered a third mind; described in philosophical terms as the "unmoved mover." Whether or not it is the will or a mind or something else we can debate. What is apparent to me, although the will is not a tangible something, it causes or motivates occurrences in my subjective mind, such as the instinctive appetites. Consequently, our will enables us to change the products of the objective mind. Awareness provides the means.

Awareness also allows us to see which scripts are not in accord with the will. As the impressions of the will are pleasant ones, those not in accord are detected as unpleasantness or fear. As the instinct does the bidding of the will, we are then prompted to make a change: to do something different. For instance, if someone speaks about someone else in an unpleasant way, we are prompted by instinct to say something which provides a pleasant alternative. At that point we then choose, either to listen to the instinct and say something pleasant, or stick to a script and perhaps believe it's none of our business. Basically we can choose to use the faculties of the objective mind to change whatever is changeable, namely the belief structures of the thinking mind. This is "full living."

Mindfulness Existence (ME)

Bringing mindfulness to our sense of existence puts a whole new spin on that old negative expression "it's all about me, Me, ME!" The approach of being mindful of our natural subjective impressions has certain advantages over the approach of being mindful of our interactions with the environment. The main advantages are to enjoy:

1. A direct and immediate subjective sense of a good feeling, like friendliness or kindness.
2. A choice of what to entertain in the thinking mind, such as happy thoughts.
3. An independent position from which to challenge old scripts, for example resentment.
4. A reference point on which to base new scripts, such as goodwill.
5. A means to change the environment, in particular the unpleasant scripts used by others.
6. And mindfulness of our pleasant interactions with the environment, such as the sound of birds chirping. Notably, there is no cost.

These advantages come from proactive mindfulness rather than reactive or passive mindfulness. A passive approach means waiting until the unpleasant sensation passes; an active approach means doing something to reinstall a sense of pleasantness. The active approach enables choice. The net effect of using the awareness of the subjective mind is to put the thinking mind back in its rightful place, which is serving the awareness. By doing this we reinstate free choice in the objective mind, which in turn increases our sense of being in charge—able to influence. Living this way, we have all the influence in the world, but no control.

Awareness is not only proactive but also impartial. Because it is in the subjective mind it is not subject to bias from scripts and belief structures. Awareness of an unpleasant sensation allows the natural harmony of our subjective mind to meet the unpleasant experience without it infecting our thinking mind. Programs based on a mindfulness approach bridge the gap between the natural coping ability of our mind and the traditional approaches usually referred to as treatment or therapy. Mindfulness also enables intelligent co-operation of the objective mind with the subjective mind.

The enhanced approach I am describing here applies mindfulness to a very specific part of us, namely our true nature of goodwill. As previously discussed, our will is expressed through instinct, in particular our sense of knowing. This unique part of our life event is the very essence of our existence.

The philosophy of our existence has been reflected in psychology as the theory of existentialism. It sounds complex, but fundamentally this refers to your sense of existence, be it as an individual speck of dust or as the center of the universe. The main criticism of this theory is that no-one has been able to turn the theory into psychological practice. It has therefore stayed in the realm of theory. I think the advent of mindfulness is the means by which existentialism can be brought into practice. I call this practical way to access the impressions of our sense of existence a Mindful Existence (ME) approach.

There are two parts to ME. The first is to use mindfulness to be aware of the core sense of self. I am referring to this as the will, an un-manifested potential which gives rise to a range of instinctive pleasant impressions, collectively referred to as goodwill. The second part is to challenge belief structures by discussion of their nature and their effect on us, and how to create alternatives which do not cause us disharmony.

Let me insert a caveat. The following discussion is not intended as a complete statement about this approach. These are my thoughts about what is possible; a start for those who see value in them and wish to explore ME further. In Appendix A, health practitioners who wish to apply ME will find similar content to the remainder of this chapter, expressed as instructions for working with another person.

Let me make the following distinction about the two parts of ME. The first is the use of the faculty of awareness to sense the "part of us feeling good all the time"; the effect of our will on the subjective mind. It is suitable for anyone to examine and explore this sense of well-being. The second part is the use of cognitive challenge to address existing belief structures, in particular the beliefs causing disharmony and unpleasantness in our experience of life. Those with a good level of awareness may be able to do this part for themselves, but they have to be sure to keep their eye on the source of well-being. This is not so easy when a script or belief structure has been triggered. For this part, some people may wish to consult a suitable health practitioner with appropriate training in motivational interviewing, in applying cognitive challenge to beliefs, and dealing with difficult or adverse situations.

There are three main outcomes from employing ME. First, connecting with our instinct and will, which results in a pleasant impression of life; second, having a base from which to examine our expressions and stored scripts, especially those not serving us well; and third, resolving unpleasant experiences, rather than just countering them. These are added benefits from the proposed new direction for mindfulness, beyond current practice, so I will expand on them.

First and foremost is to establish a connection with our instinct and will. This provides a reference point to our direct sense of life, which can immediately be used to promote good mental health and a sense of well-being. It happens instantaneously because our true nature—instinctive sense of harmony—is there all the time. However, when our scripts or belief structures are activated, we generally tend to give them our attention, thereby obscuring our innate sense of well-being. For example, when experiencing dislike for a blunt comment made by a friend, most people are busy getting into the dislike rather than their caring for the friend. Giving attention back to the core sense of self enables the pleasant effect of our will to be impressed upon us, and in turn expressed. We can then act from kindness rather than hurt. Some people say it is a neutral experience, but at least it does not have unpleasantness or fear in it. Although this pleasant experience is continuous, not everyone notices it straight away. This is because we have been taught to control ourselves; mainly in an attempt to combat fear. How quickly people notice the effect of their instinct, is a function of how willing they are to let go of control. When you "let yourself be" and refrain from calling up disharmonious beliefs, the effect your pleasant subjective impressions are having on you, is more noticeable. In this sense it is our default condition, our birthright. Listening to your primary instinct by giving it your attention allows you to feel the effect of the will. "You know it by its fruit." In other words you have to allow your will to "have its way with you" before you sense the pleasant effect. Some people find this a scary idea, because it means letting go of control.

The second outcome of giving our attention to goodwill is that it provides a reference point, from which we can be much more effective in changing unpleasant scripts and belief structures. In the example of disliking a comment made by a friend, we can challenge our belief in having to get even, and ask if they could speak to you as a friend. Of course this means inherently trusting your intelligent system knows exactly what it is doing. If you feel good in yourself, then you are less likely to believe the unpleasant thoughts and scripts. In particular, the sense of goodwill provides a means for you to write new scripts, establishing new responses in accord with your will.

The most striking effect of giving attention to the instinctive impressions of the will is a strong sense of empowerment. It might seem strange, but as I mentioned earlier, being out of control is to feel in charge. The meaning people usually place on being out of control stems again from beliefs, suggesting some scary, unpleasant and chaotic state. However, when we are not exercising control, our will comes to the fore and we are prompted to do harmonious things. Chaos does not rule, and anarchy is just another script!

Our will gives us a sense we have great influence on whatever we let it flow toward, namely the events of everyday life. As the will feels good to us, it generates a sense we can enjoy life and cope with others unpleasant scripts. It also promotes a healthy sense of worth and self-esteem, which is independent of events triggering our own fear-based scripts.

Finally, with this approach we can talk about resolving unpleasant experiences, not just managing them with counter beliefs. The most significant part of letting the will face off against scripts is this; you get confirmation of the will having the power to overcome any script developed with the thinking mind. If a person is listening to their will, they can acknowledge awareness of the unpleasantness, and change the way they interpret it, in *exactly* the same way they created the unpleasant version. It seems the explanation for this is based on the will generating at a different frequency to the thought structures. When the two come together, the frequency of the will has the capacity to encompass the thought structure of the belief, and undo it if it is not an expression of the will.

The benefit of ME is that the person has a pleasant impression to attend to while the unpleasant script comes into the objective mind. This generates confidence about taking on the unpleasant scripts and the experiences they produce. It can give people a new perspective about their mind and their sense of self, which leads them away from fearing it. Imagine the possibilities of a constant involved in the core self, which happens to give us a natural sense of well-being not based in thinking, but which our thinking mind can manifest. Happy days are here again!

Some of the ideas presented here may have been mentioned by others, but ME differs in the way these ideas are put together. As such, some features call for different terminology. The first is to think of ME as an approach rather than therapy. This is an important distinction, because the terms "therapy" and "treatment" reflect a view of the presenting issue as a problem, with an implication something is wrong with our mind. This viewpoint is something I want to distance myself from as far as possible. A lifestyle approach to good mental health is consistent with the view that most perceived problems are caused by us doing something harmful with our mind. Remember, biological and physiological causes of disorder are not under consideration here.

There is a current move to take the stigma out of mental health problems. I cannot conceive how this can be done effectively while thinking of them as problems. Over the years I have heard many people say something along the following lines; "I don't know what the matter is with me. I seem to be unhappy all the time. I never used to be like this." Usually, the unhappiness has been there for some time. When we are young we simply learn to keep the unhappiness at bay by "sitting on it" and getting on with our lives. As we get older we get tired of putting so much energy into pushing our unhappiness away. We start to let it into our objective mind to examine it with our awareness, but it makes us unhappy.

Unfortunately, most people misinterpret this situation as there being something wrong with them. The truth is this it is part of the healing process. The increasing unhappiness is showing the extent of the problem; a similar mechanism to the inflammation surrounding a skin infection. When an unpleasant event arises, it is an opportunity to change the belief supporting it.

Instead, we can begin with a different view. The unpleasantness we feel comes from using our mind in a way that is causing us harm. From a positive psychology approach, you can choose to use your mind in a different way—a way which reduces harm. What is even more important, you already have the solution. With this in mind, the view there is something wrong with you is disempowering. Thinking of a positive psychology process as an approach, or even a way of life, gets us away from both the stigma and the problem view of life. We are all exploring our nature, and we do so as equals.

Furthermore, our instinct is pro-life, prompting us to make changes for our benefit. Mindfulness of our will prompts us to develop new scripts, in accord with the sense of goodwill, which is impressed upon us all the time as instinct. We clearly have the capacity to change our scripts, whether we produce new ones, edit or rewrite the old ones, or simply abandon those which no longer serve us. Ironically, scripts get in the way of us doing this. Take, for example, the prospect of abandoning a belief. Most of us have experienced feeling abandoned. The most common response to this hurt is to develop a counter-script; a belief we would not abandon anyone or anything in the world. However, a consequence of this script is that we can find it hard to abandon the things in our mind, as well as in our life, because it hurts us! On the other hand, if we listen to our goodwill, we can feel okay about abandoning such beliefs.

ME in Practice

The following self-help guidelines will help you start to engage in your own self-exploration using ME. They are useful to read and re-read, until you are totally familiar with the content. Health practitioners will also find the content of Appendix A, useful to explain the process to a client.

These guidelines are an introduction to the mindfulness component of ME. This approach differs from a clinical approach in which your unpleasant experiences or presenting issue is the focus of discussion. ME is a well-being approach which has a focus on your strengths, and showing a positive way to deal with any experience you face in life. The idea is to know more about how your mind works and increase your skills and confidence to address unpleasant experiences. This is achieved using a self-exploration process, centered on your faculty of awareness.

Awareness allows us to monitor what we are sensing in the present moment—to be mindful of events. There are a number of programs available which use a mindfulness approach. The difference with ME is that mindfulness is used to be aware of our core self and instinctive pleasant impressions of life.

The idea behind this approach is that there is a core part of you feeling good all the time, which is a sense of what feels genuinely good and right for us. We commonly refer to this as our natural sense of well-being or goodwill. This is what we are born with. I think of this as our birthright. Arguably, it is the source of what we genuinely want in our lives; a sense of calm, peace of mind, contentedness, simple joy of living; a sense of completeness, belonging, and caring; and most importantly, a deep, authentic sense of you.

You should regard these comments as my opinion. I don't want you to believe me. These things will not be true for you, until you are experiencing them. What I would like you to do is confirm you have the ability to tune in to a sense of harmony and well-being. If you can verify it, this natural event provides a pleasant condition to literally keep in mind when addressing unpleasant experiences. In this way you will be able to address the issues you wish to change, while remaining grounded in your sense of well-being.

If we are born with this sense of well-being, what goes wrong? As we grow older we have many and varied experiences of the world, and we interpret some of them in ways which are not in accord with our goodwill. Misinterpretations are also reinforced by how we see others respond to us, and in the responses we are taught. These interpretations become our belief structures, or scripts, stored in memory. We learn to see the world in different ways, and some of these ways do not feel good to us. This means a lot of our unpleasant experiences are learned. They are corruptions of our natural sense that life is good. You only have to look at an infant to be reminded of our wonderful nature. So a part of what we can do is to challenge the scripts we find unpleasant, because they do us harm. In their place, we can establish strategies and response patterns which feel good to us and promote a sense of good mental health.

The key to this well-being process is to choose what we allow into our thinking mind. We always have a choice and we are constantly making them. Sometimes it seems unpleasant things enter our thinking mind uninvited. On these occasions it appears we have not made a choice, but actually we have done this so quickly we do not notice it. Our past ways of responding to events are stored in memory as scripts, or belief structures. When these are activated by an event, out of necessity they come to mind very quickly. As they are habitual patterns of response, including emotion, we can mistakenly think we have no choice at the time.

A benefit of having awareness is that it enables us to be conscious of the scripts we choose.

By being aware of the event, we get to choose whether or not to allow the old pattern to affect our thinking. Think of your awareness as being there before your thoughts. This means you can be clear about your choice when the old pattern starts. In particular, through awareness you can feel the unpleasant effect of the old pattern before you engage it in your thinking mind. This way, you can choose to stay with your natural sense of well-being, and use it as a guide to make a different response. If you keep doing this you can develop new scripts based on your instinctive sense of goodwill.

My commitment to this well-being process is based on the observation that it helps people address unpleasant experiences, whether the unpleasantness comes from their mind, or from someone else. If you choose to stay in touch with your sense of well-being no matter what happens, you can change your experience. For example, a person with a lot of anxiety in life usually loses their sense of well-being when faced with the anxiety. This happens when they engage a familiar response pattern containing anxiety; allowing the script to come into their minds, where it immediately produces the symptoms of anxiety such as panic. If, however, the person has an alternate pleasant impression to refer to, such as a natural sense of well-being, they can choose to give their attention to this instead of the anxiety. In this way they will not be so strongly affected by the script. By wanting to increase the sense of well-being, sooner or later they can smile about the experience of anxiety, which of course is the best thing to do if they wish to change its course. Having an experience which does not leave room for the anxiety is very empowering. You might quickly see the possibilities of what you can do with your mind.

This process is not for everyone. People generally respond in one of three ways. Some people think this is "not their cup of tea"; such people are often locked into control mechanisms or would not consider using other faculties of their mind like awareness. They tend not to continue past the introductory session. This is okay because each of us does what we think will benefit us. Others give priority to a specific goal, such as feeling less anxious about going out of the house. These people tend to do enough sessions to impact on their circumstances then get on with their lives. Finally, some people see the broader implications, and make sweeping changes to their way of life. As a well-being process, ME has general application to how we use our mind to meet life events on a day to day basis, and to make changes whenever called for.

Getting started with the practical, experiential part of your self-exploration is easy. Just relax, get comfortable, and start to use your awareness to monitor what you are sensing in the present moment. I will come back to this in a moment, but there are four things worth commenting on at this point.

First, this is something you are in charge of doing. If you are not comfortable with what is happening in your mind, you should feel free to stop at any time. Keep in mind this is a well-being process. It is not about feeling uncomfortable. It is about feeling okay with what you are doing. If it doesn't feel good, by definition you are **not** doing the process correctly. This is about giving attention to the part of you that feels good all the time. Even if you encounter an unpleasant experience, you want to meet it from your sense of well-being, enabling you to go on feeling okay. As an aside, it is extremely rare for anyone to feel uncomfortable to the point of wanting to stop.

There are two parts to ME. Part A is the self-exploration process. In this part, continue only with experiences which feel good to you. Most people can do this quite easily. If an unpleasant thought or emotion comes into your mind, move your attention to a natural pleasant sense not involved with thinking; for example listening to sounds. If you engage in Part B of the process, addressing your scripts, you will keep giving attention to a pleasant experience rather than following the unpleasant one. There may be times when this seems difficult, with intense anxiety for example, so there are instances when caution should be exercised. Research findings have indicated that relaxation processes can trigger adverse events for people with a history of psychosis or dissociative disorder. It is for this reason I recommend some people work with a health practitioner for Part B.

Second, you can do ME while engaging with another person, friend or partner. If you are comfortable to engage in eye contact with another, there is possibly an additional benefit. You can use the contact to intensify your self-exploration experience. We all have a different experience of the world when we use our objective mind, but a similar sense when we use our subjective mind. If you engage with your objective mind, you see another person with their own mannerisms. If you engage people with your subjective mind, you see yourself reflected in them. Hence, while being subjective, eye contact reveals who you are without the beliefs and scripts. In other words, another human being is the best mirror you can get! Some people prefer not to use this mode of self-exploration, usually because it triggers unpleasant scripts about eye contact or being exposed. Nevertheless, I invite you to try it and see if it empowers you. If it does, you have a fearless sense of you to show the world and change the unpleasantness.

Third, during the process most people experience some perceptual changes, most commonly visual, although it can affect any of your senses. For instance, you might notice the room appear to get lighter or darker independently of what the sun is doing. This can happen when we are doing deep reflection because our internal perceptions over-ride the physical senses. Perceptual changes are related to what we are conceiving in our mind. As an example, when doubt enters our mind it can seem like the room gets darker or hazy; when hope enters our mind it can seem like the room gets brighter.

Some people get strong perceptual changes. This is quite normal and no cause for concern. It tends to happen when we become subjective and are not using our mind to focus on physical objects. It is common in deep meditation too. In the process of doing Part A, the self-exploration, you are encouraged to stay aware of a good feeling or sense and not follow the perceptual changes. In the process of Part B, addressing scripts, the perceptual changes are most often related to the scripts being engaged, like doubt. In this event, they can be used as a trace to find the source of the script, by following the perception in awareness .

Fourth and last, do not act on scripts that come up. Let me use the example of anxiety again. If you start to feel anxious or uncomfortable, it is better not to show it in your behavior. Rather than expressing it by wriggling or fidgeting, let it pass through your mind without acting on it. This means not engaging or "buying into" the sensations or experiences which occur. The reason for this is, if you act on the sensation you are allowing it into your thinking mind. Once you engage the script in your thinking, it will start to have the full effect of the symptoms on you.

Something we can examine using ME is how and when we choose what we allow into our mind. The idea behind this is, the script does not get activated if we are aware of sensations and do not engage them with thinking. In the case of scripts stored in memory, we have about half a second from when the trigger occurs to the script being activated. Therefore we have to watch closely for the sensations or experiences we are about to have. Because it happens quickly, a lot of people think they don't choose to experience unpleasant things. Learned responses become habitual, and tend to be chosen without being challenged.

I want you to prove to yourself that your awareness notices these events. Your awareness is a natural faculty which stands between our sensory experience, and the interpretation and response we make. In this way it enables our choice. When we exercise this choice for our own benefit, we are on the way to altering the course of an otherwise less favorable response.

You already have the ability to do this, so I don't have to teach you a technique to do it. What's more, it is easy to do, though most people don't do this because they have learned to use the thinking mind for their primary interaction with the world. What I am encouraging you to do, is allow the subjective mind to have this role.

Getting started is easy to do. It is just a matter of relaxing, getting comfortable, and letting yourself be. There is nothing you have to do; you already know how to use your awareness. There are no rules of engagement. It is more a matter of letting go of expectations, of not trying to sort it out with your thinking mind. It may come down to whether you are willing to refrain from controlling yourself with the thinking mind. If you are, your attention can be given to the pleasant impressions in your subjective mind. At this point you have the opportunity to feel the effect of your instinct; your impressions of life without beliefs and fear.

While you are settling in, there are three questions which can help you get started.

First; if you just let go, what do you sense? You only need to answer "pleasantness" or "unpleasantness." [Commentary: Some people say it feels neutral, but 9 out of 10 agree it is not unpleasant. Most find a bit of calmness or relaxing sensation].

The second question is; "can you acknowledge you did not have to produce this sense?" In other words, you did not have to sit there and think okay thoughts to feel okay. [Nearly all agree]. This is the first bit of evidence this is your true nature. The implication is; we are not dependent on thinking happy thoughts to be happy, even though it can help.

The third question is; "if you do that again, and give the pleasant sense your attention, does it start to increase, grow in intensity or have more of an effect on you?" Does giving attention to the pleasant sense change your experience? [A few people at first struggle with this, but soon notice it changes their state of mind, for example they feel even more relaxed or their perception of events intensifies].

The answers to these three questions define what ME is about. There is a part of us which always feels okay. We do not have to produce it. It is already a part of our experience. If we give it our attention, it increases in our perception and has greater effect on us. In other words it is a dynamic sense of change.

This is our point of entry to the practical part of the sessions. My invitation is for you to find out how much calmness you can experience or how relaxed you can become. If you give your attention to a pleasant impression, how intense does it become?

At this point the self-exploration has begun in earnest. Look to any natural good feeling in you, and by giving it your attention and wanting it, you encourage it to increase. Give yourself permission to find out how good you can feel. Remember to stay grounded and not lose yourself to the good feeling.

If you find persistent thoughts interfere with your use of awareness, a concrete exercise could be of benefit. I suggest listening to the sounds going on around you. It is easy to listen. We do it with our physical senses all the time, for example listening to the wind, the sea or music. Treat the event as a symphony of sounds. There are sounds that come and go, others going on continuously. Some are loud, others soft. They can be a deep bass sound or a high-pitched sound. It is important not to concentrate on any particular sound. If you open your mind to all the sounds, it can seem like a concert.

If you are engaging with someone in this self-exploration, each can give the other feedback as to when they are using their subjective mind and when they are using their objective mind. The quality of this feedback depends on each person's ability to stay in touch with their subjective impressions. There are many cues when a person is not giving attention to their awareness, including a blank look in their eyes, telling a story without a sense of self reflection, and their effect on your subjective state. In this way you can show the other person how to engage pleasant impressions in the subjective mind, and you can detect variations from pleasant scripts more easily in their communication—and in yours.

Moving on from discussion about the practical sessions, there are a couple of notable points about all this. The sense of feeling okay is always there because it is a product of our will and instinct. This is not apparent to most people because scripts seem to override it. So when an unpleasant script is activated it seems we only feel the unpleasantness. But this is actually never the case. No matter how unpleasant we feel, we still sense the goodwill with our awareness. This is a point some will argue. Disagreement about this mostly stems from seeing awareness and consciousness as the same thing. If our attention is given only to the thinking mind, all we notice is the product of this mind, which is often an unpleasant experience. It escapes our attention that awareness itself carries a sense of harmony.

The essential piece of information is that our experience is a function of our awareness and our attention. Two events are going on simultaneously. Awareness is a function of the subjective mind. It senses the will. Consciousness is a function of the objective mind. It experiences our interpretation of events. So we have two events going on; while in a body we experience life as a duality. These can be in accord with each other or in discord. The aim of ME is to bring them into alignment. This is what is being achieved with this new application of mindfulness—alignment of our minds.

Summary

Choosing to think in accord with our goodwill is the key to pleasant experiences:

- Choice can be defined as the voluntary act of giving attention.
- Whatever we give our attention to, is what we then have in mind.
- We have an instinct to choose, to think, and to want.
- Instinct does not control us, so we are free to choose what we want.
- We all have one basic choice to make at every moment of time—to live from instinctive goodwill or from fear.
- If we choose not to believe in fear, we are free to make our reality a pleasant one.

Differences between attention and awareness are important to having pleasant life experiences:

- Attention is a faculty of the objective mind.
- Attention is our ability to attend selected events, enabling use of the thinking mind to produce and retrieve relevant ideas and beliefs about these events.
- Awareness is a quality of the subjective mind.
- Awareness is an unbiased, non-judgmental, pre-thought capability, allowing us to perceive the effect of what we

are thinking, and sense our instinctive impressions of how to thrive.

The most significant choice we make is about what to do with attention:

- Events given attention become your personal reality; events you do not give attention to wither and die.
- The subjective mind is the link between the will and the objective mind.
- Awareness offers an alternative to having the thinking mind running the show.
- The absolute best thing you can do with your attention is give it to your awareness.
- The harmony we sense as goodwill through our awareness is independent of the objective, thinking mind.
- What is in our awareness is our direct impression of life—no filters, no corruption.
- By giving attention to awareness we are free to think whatever we want.
- The subjective mind is as a range of frequencies, all of which are pleasant impressions of goodwill, free of fear.
- Attention is like the dial on a radio; we can tune in to subjective impressions and create objective expressions of them with images and thoughts.

Positive psychology has been based on thought processes such as having healthy values. A recent addition is the use of mindfulness:

- Mindfulness is the act of bringing conscious attention to an event.

- Mindfulness of an unpleasant event means giving it attention initially without thought. This keeps us apart from the unpleasantness, which can be observed to come and go.
- Current use of mindfulness in psychology is mainly about seeing out the unpleasant experiences.

I propose a new approach to mindfulness, refined with an understanding of the difference between attention and awareness, and based on one's own existence—a Mindful Existence (ME) approach to life:

- This new approach to mindfulness can be proactive in inducing a pleasant experience by moving attention from physical events to a subjective sense of self.
- If we give attention to the subjective impressions of our core sense of self, the effect of goodwill is experienced.
- ME consists of: (a) being aware of your core self as an instinctive sense of well-being, and (b) challenging and changing beliefs while remaining in touch with your well-being as a reference point.
- If you feel good in yourself, you are less likely to believe an unpleasant thought.
- Giving attention to the will is very empowering. The sense of feeling okay is always there because it is the product of our will, though this is not apparent to people who allow scripts to over-ride it.
- As the effect of our will feels good, it generates a sense of worth and sense that we can cope.
- The key is to stay in touch with your subjective sense of well-being no matter what happens. With this sense of well-being, you can influence the course of your experience.

- Two events are going on simultaneously; one in the subjective mind and one in the objective mind, so we live life as a duality. These can be in accord with each other or in discord.
- The aim of ME is to bring our minds into alignment.
- Additionally, as instinct serves our will we are prompted to make changes that benefit us.
- Scripts and beliefs that cause discord can be changed. For some people this should involve the assistance of a qualified health professional.

TWELVE

FINDING THE MEANING OF LIFE

What is an experience without a sense of self? The answer I get is "meaningless." Having covered the issue of how to access our innate knowing of the good life, there is an important question left to ask; what is the meaning of life? Where is meaning to be found? Have you ever had a sense you sort of know, but can't find the right answer?

Pause, and allow your instinctive sense of knowing to answer the question. This is as easy as becoming subjective, providing access to your instinctive impressions. So here we go. What is the meaning of life? If you responded, "42," it came from something you read or heard from the *Hitchhikers Guide to the Galaxy*! Move your attention to your instinct and try again. What is the meaning of life? No idea? I'm waiting! Still no-eyed deer? That's not it either. It's borrowed from a joke about a motionless deer with no eyes, for the amusement of those who have heard it! Okay, I am making fun of answering the question now, because most people in fact get a blank response when the question is open-ended. This is usual, as we have come to rely on our belief structures. Later, I will ask you a specific question to see how you go, so don't be too concerned about not getting an answer right now.

No Idea

Ironically, if you genuinely have no ideas then you are close! This sounds rather Zen, but if you have no idea, then at least you are not running off with your thinking. Without preconceived thoughts distracting you there is some chance you will listen to your sense of knowing. Assuming you are not disregarding your instinct, you may notice things stir in you without having to think. If you *let* them, these stirrings can grow into ideas. Then you start to get some answers that feel satisfying.

Let me recap on some earlier points about how we misuse our minds, to clarify what is often a confused sense of what it means to have no idea. If you ask yourself "what is the meaning of life", and nothing in particular emerges, it is most likely you have presented the question to your thinking mind and not to your instinctive sense of knowing. If the question does not have enough information to be meaningful, there will be no further initiative. This will be experienced as a blank mind, which we often wrongly interpret as "I don't know". Even if you have asked the question of your subjective mind, you may be blocking an answer registering in the objective mind if you are giving your attention to something else, such as your thoughts about dinner or the sound of traffic. In sum, if you ask the question only with your objective mind, you will not get a satisfying answer. Instead, you will get competing ideas from what you have heard or learned. Information-based ideas are answers to questions from the thinking mind, and these won't satisfy questions seeded from the instinct. In this sense, having no idea is not close to the answer. There are several interpretations which could be inferred from this, about the experience of having "no idea". So let's take some time to clarify.

The first interpretation of having no idea is that beliefs have interfered with the answers. When you scan your memory for an answer to any question, then you have looked among your beliefs and previous ideas. If you believe the thinking mind is in control, when you do not get an answer to your questions, you are likely to abort listening to instinct and start scouring the objective mind. For example, if the thinking mind can't answer the question, you might decide it is not for us to know the answer, or you are not smart enough. As a substantial number of beliefs are not related to your own experience, this is the wrong place to look for answers that naturally satisfy your instinct. In many cases, if people do not get a satisfactory answer they put it in the too-hard basket, declare they have no idea and lose interest. Nevertheless, people who say they are not interested in knowing still have this instinct; they are just obscuring it with beliefs. Hence, if you are interested in detecting the input of your instinct, be careful how you use beliefs to interpret the impressions it gives.

The second of these interpretations is also related to beliefs, though these ones are misconceptions of the true circumstances. I have observed people access their instinct or subjective mind and still declare they have no idea. This declaration is based on an experience in which nothing happens when they are subjective. On the whole these people have not yet identified the unique quality of their sense of knowing. So if they don't know what they are looking for in the 3 to 5 seconds their attention is not on thinking, they don't sense any stirring or pulse. The signal is subtle, especially if they are not used to listening for one. Nothing may appear to happen at first, and a little time may be needed for the pulse to seed a thought recognized as an answer. The question has to be prompted from the instinct, and then submitted by the thinking mind back to the instinctive knowing for further rumblings, then again interpreted by the thinking mind. And so it goes on; round and round until ideas come which strike an accord with your sense of knowing. In other words you have to wait. Do not abort when at first you don't get answers. It sounds a lot like meditation, doesn't it?

A third interpretation is that having no idea is the true answer coming from being subjective. Subjectivity is achieved by giving attention to something other than your thoughts, such as your senses, feelings, instinct or other aspects of the subjective mind—being mindful. If you do not give attention to thoughts, it might seem like you don't have many ideas. Also, if being subjective calms the thinking mind, then having no thoughts might be seen as desirable. In this case, why is subjectivity a prerequisite for getting satisfying answers? In part, because you are moving your attention away from the belief-based ideas that often provide biased information.

Nonetheless, the subjective mind is not devoid of activity, and attention to subjective impressions will confirm this for you. Try being subjective and see if you can sense an energy moving in you, or even a potential, like being ready. There is a hive of subtle activity going on in your subjective mind. When you give this attention, the level of energy increases and you are affected by it. This can feel like a tonic effect, either uplifting or calming depending on your prior state. Calmness is a wavelength of energy; it is not an absence of movement. Bear in mind, this healing activity of the will can also trigger scripts; for example feeling a slight pressure in your head, or discomfort in your body, or becoming downright impatient or annoyed. Even so, there are wonderful impressions awaiting you. For instance, continued exploration will lead you to an instinctive impression of knowing, otherwise known as wisdom.

A further interpretation of having "no idea" relates to the suggestion or belief there is no meaning to life, which is a source of great illusion for many. The idea, maybe life has no meaning, is an interpretation I skimmed over earlier, but it warrants further comment. Can a non-response be a valid answer? This entertained my mind for many a year, based on things I had read suggesting no ideas could be the answer. If I asked "what is the meaning of life?" and got no response, could it mean; "there is no meaning?" In this sense, I was interpreting a blank response as a meaningful answer. In light of the saying "if you have no ideas in your head you are close to the solution," this seemed to have credibility.

So for many years I stopped asking questions. This was difficult for someone with a strong sense of enquiry. I tried to come to terms with not having meaning to life. There was no answer and my desire for one was not acceptable. It was sufficient I existed. Asking questions about the meaning of life put me in a quandary, so if I didn't ask I didn't have a quandary.

However, for me "no response" was no more satisfying than the answer "42." After many years I came to see my instinct was not being met. So my sense of knowing was providing me with the proof, by showing a blank response was not the solution. I realized it was okay for me to want answers and to ask questions, and a nil response was not in fact a response. Nowadays, I see a nil response means the question is ill-conceived; in other words, there is something wrong with the question. The remedy to this is to keep asking in different ways, until you get an answer.

There is a good way to test this issue about there being no meaning to life. If you don't get an answer, it is easy to say there is no meaning. But it falls over if you ask what evidence there is for the idea life is meaningless. I can't find any, can you?. If there is no more evidence for the "no meaning to life" option than the "meaning to life" option, why would we accept the "no meaning" option? The only reason I can think of is because it fits with a belief. So how are we going to resolve this?

I stand by my comment; if you genuinely want an answer, you will get a satisfying one when you ask a well-conceived, complete question seeded from your instinct. **We always get an answer to a meaningful question**, from our instinctive sense of knowing. So questions are as important as answers. While examining this topic there is one important feature of our sense of knowing to keep in mind; it does not deal in disagreement. It only gives affirmative direction leading to affirmative action. In general, it does not say "no," because it does not go against the will. If you get an answer of "no" in your objective mind, it is likely to be an interpretation of a null response. The way to spot the difference is; the response is reactive rather than proactive. When this happens, wait and listen for another question.

Asking the Question

So far I have spoken only about how to get answers. Let me say something about how to ask questions as well. Just as exclusive use of the objective mind will not produce answers that satisfy the instinct, the same is true of asking questions. The question will not be reflected back to the instinct if it is seeded from the objective mind. This doesn't mean the objective mind is not involved. On the contrary, it has a crucial role. Its function is to interpret the impulse from the instinct and to give form to the questions and answers.

Use of a metaphor of "teacher" and "student" for the two minds may be helpful. The subjective instinct is like the teacher sending out an invitation to the student—thinking mind—in the form of curiosity or interest. This interest prompts the student to enquire of the teacher in the form of a question, and listen for an answer which is only forthcoming when a valid or complete question is asked. If the question is posed by the student, say out of idle curiosity rather than seeded by instinct, it will not touch on our *want* to know the answer.

The enquiry does not begin with thinking, it begins with instinct—the source of innate intelligence. It is crucial that the question in the objective mind is seeded from an appetite of the instinct. This is like a key (instinctive appetite) inserted in a lock (objective mind) which opens the door to the question. For instance, our instinctive hunger inspires thoughts about food; what we feel like eating, whether it is available, where to look for it and how to get it. In the case of thinking, essentially the instinctive impulse uses the objective mind to formulate the right question for it to answer; again using the objective mind to do the interpretation, including use of memory. It might surprise you if I say nothing will happen if there is no instinctive prompt behind the question. The sense of knowing, which is the solution, prompts the objective mind to pose a question inviting the knowing to give the solution! This is intelligence at work.

So let's allow our instinctive sense of inquiry to ask the big question; what *is* the meaning of life? I suppose you could come up with lots of suggestions. There are certainly plenty of available ideas about this topic. You could proceed by asking every conceivable question about life, to see how it impacts on your sense of knowing.

That is the approach I took, and I recommend it. Eventually you will narrow it down. However, it could take a while. There are a lot of questions to ask. I have run so many thought experiments it would make your head swim, as it did mine! At least until I recognized the role of instinct, and understood it will do the job for me. Since then it has been relatively easy, as it could be for you. If you get some answers to well-directed questions, you won't have to ask every question there is to ask. In any event, make sure you keep the attitude of being willing—willing to listen, willing to ask.

Guided Self-exploration

So what can I do to assist? Well I hope it occurs to you, this book is one result of the many questions I have asked myself—asked of my knowing to be precise. I hope it helps you understand how the mind works, and how to avoid some of the pitfalls of overusing your objective mind and doing yourself harm.

All of this leaves you in a better position to answer the "big one"; what is the meaning of life? At this juncture, one thing I can do for you is to further reduce the number of questions you might ask. So let me ask this one; "are *you* the meaning of life?" Clearly, from your perspective this is asked as "am I the meaning of life?"

A real life example is a good way to highlight the answer to this question. A few years ago, I had some dealings with a young Canadian who was in Australia studying graphic art. Those around him noted his unhappy expression and depressed affect; eventually someone suggested he speak with me about it. He contacted me about 10 days before he was to fly back to Canada, mostly because of his anxiety about the forthcoming plane trip. Upon meeting him, it very quickly became clear he was not coping at all well. When I enquired about his view of life, he said he was very saddened by the feeling life had no meaning for him, and very anxious about the unpleasant thoughts he was having. He wasn't interested in formal counseling, but wanted some ideas which might help him understand what he was experiencing.

Most people have asked themselves questions about the meaning of life, and this young man was no exception. During the course of our conversation, he expressed an interest in the philosophy of life and a familiarity with his sense of knowing, so I decided to approach the issue from this perspective. I asked him whether he had enquired about the meaning of life in his mind, referring him to his instinctive sense of knowing. He said he had, and the answer he was getting was indicating there was no meaning to life. I could see he was comfortable with how he used his mind, and had sufficient insight to know there was some truth in the interpretation he was making! Yet something was clearly wrong for him.

It was a difficult position for him, having his sense of knowing appear to be saying there was no meaning to life. As we discussed it further, I could see there was a misunderstanding in his mind about what he was asking, but I could not see what it was. So I requested him to again ask himself "what is the meaning of life?" The reply he gave was "I can't find any." Then I requested he ask the question out loud. When he did this, I observed from his hand gestures this was not the actual question he was asking in his mind. I could see there was a hidden part to the question he was not aware of. Although he was asking verbally "what is the meaning of life", the question he expressed with his hand gestures was "what is the meaning of life; outside of me?" His mind was directed by an idea, the meaning of life had to be bigger than him.

He was a very astute young man and thought the interpretation of 'none' was correct. That's what was depressing him. His tone of voice conveyed his conviction to the answer, confirming there was some truth to it. His interpretation of no-response was "there is no meaning." Interpreted correctly, no response meant there was no meaning outside of him. It was true! Subsequently, I suggested asking if *he* was the meaning of life. He proceeded to do just that. A minute or two went by. I was beginning to think he wasn't getting an answer. Finally I had to ask him what was happening. Again there was a delay, until after an uncomfortable period of time he finally said in a surprised tone, "I seem to be getting an affirmative!" His expression and tone of voice showed such a mix of delight and surprise we laughed loudly. A little later I asked him what took so long. His response was; because this was not the usual answer, he was busy verifying it. From the moment he verbalized the new response he was getting from his mind, his affect lifted. During the course of the next few days a positive attitude settled in and he started looking forward to what life had in store for him.

I continue to enjoy the memory of this event for two reasons. First, it showed how someone could turn their life around in a relatively short space of time, by becoming more aware of what they were doing with their mind. But it also conveys a warning about the trouble we can get ourselves into. It shows how much harm we can do if we are not using our minds effectively. This young man was intelligent and consulted his sense of knowing as a natural part of life, yet he got himself "in a pickle." He held an unacknowledged belief that his life was only an instrument, a means to find meaning out there. This belief corrupted the question he was asking, and made it seem to be something it wasn't. The answer he got was depressing him, though it wasn't a response to the question he thought he was asking. In turn, his depressed mood caused him to have all sorts of unpleasant thoughts, mostly reflecting the pointlessness of his life. He felt bad about life, and his mind was mirroring this by suggesting other bad things could and would happen—for example on his flight back to Canada. When he understood he had really been asking "what is the meaning of life outside of me?" the correct interpretation of a blank response, "there is none", was no longer disturbing. Some weeks later I got a text message confirming the change in his experience of life. He had even enjoyed the plane trip home.

Philosophy of the Meaning of Life

For some people, the idea they are the meaning of life is a little too challenging. So let me reframe the concept in a way which gets less resistance from our beliefs. I'll pose it this way; could it be, your life is justified in its own right? One way to say this is; "life is its own meaning." Many people are quite comfortable with the idea and get an affirmative answer to this question. If you do as well, it means the existence of life is the meaning of life. Do you see therefore, there is no *external* meaning of life which doesn't involve you? Life is not an exercise to enable you to find some external meaning to justify your existence. You are alive, and therefore you have meaning, you are meaning, your life is meaningful and ***you are the meaning of life***.

What do you think of the idea you are the meaning of life? I hope you have been suspending your beliefs as requested. If you have, you would not immediately be put off by this idea; you would have a chance to examine it more closely. In doing so, think liberally about what it means. Clearly I am not talking about the individual ego-based sense of "I." So what is it that could be the meaning of life? The "you" I am referring to is the center of your holistic existence. What is the essence of your existence? If you want me to say who and what you are—you are the will, and the will is you. This is sensed as an impression of un-manifested potential. The expression of the will that is you, naturally manifesting as goodwill, is the meaning of life. You are it, and ***I can definitively say it is beyond belief.***

Let me add a few more implications and a bit of philosophy. I think I have said enough about some of the pitfalls in using the objective mind. First, if you get affirmative initiatives from your sense of knowing, then any problem can be resolved. In fact, once you have confirmed the essentials of how your mind works, there are no problems, as explained earlier. This leaves you with questions. What you get are answers. But you have to ask clearly and listen carefully, without engaging pre-conceived thoughts.

We always get an answer to every complete question we ask, because the solution for our questions already exists as a fundamental principle of life. The solution is exhibited first and foremost as our instinct, so is in existence before the question is asked and before the answer is formulated. This was one of those light-bulb moments steering much of my mid-life exploration.

Be careful how you interpret this comment about a pre-existing solution. It is not intended as a mind-bending philosophical comment about predetermination; we have free choice. Rather, the comment has a practical meaning. I am saying the solution is provided by our will; the solution *is* the will, to be precise. Our will is expressed through our instinct, which we sense as knowing or intelligence, and a feeling of goodwill. This is the only way to access the will. That is a big call, but I can't find a functional alternative in my experience. You can see why I have placed so much emphasis on saying that unpleasant things in our experience are not based in our instinct.

The will puts forward the solution as its natural function. In this sense the source of me is only ever providing a solution. In terms of the philosophical debate about which came first, the chicken or the egg, the question or the solution, we have an answer—the solution comes first. When we listen to our instinct, we get the solution. In turn, the instinct prompts us continuously with one thing or another; appetites to sleep, to eat, and to think for example. More importantly, instinct prompts us to thrive; to do what is in harmony with our continued existence.

Getting Answers that Satisfy

The solution, coming from a source of potential, is expressed as an answer when we ask a question. By becoming subjective and asking a genuine question, we open our objective mind to instinct; also known as our sense of knowing. The instinct represents the solution in the form of a sense, such as interest, and good feelings such as kindness. When conceived by the objective mind, we have answers. The answer is a representation of the solution, but is now in the form of a thought. Through posing a question, the instinct is translated into a format the objective mind can comprehend, just as the ear transforms sound waves into a neural signal which the brain can perceive and translate into music or images. Be aware though, you will only recognize the answers if you *want* to know.

This process, by which the objective mind converts the solution into an answer, can be summarized as follows. First, through an instinctive sense of enquiry felt as want, the subjective mind prompts the objective mind to ask a question. Second, the question asked by the objective mind is submitted to the subjective mind. Third, in a matter of microseconds the subjective mind sends a pulse of energy, which the objective mind turns into an image or concept—the answer to our question. Notably, some answers require little thought and are experienced as insight. This is referred to as the "ah-hah" moment or that lovely experience when the proverbial penny drops and we have a sudden understanding of something.

The origin of the answers, before they are answers, is specifically the will; which may be a part of the subjective mind, but more likely a third level or mind. At this stage I don't think it's important which way you conceptualize it. The will is a solution or "potential" which seeds the subjective mind with an incentive, or appetite, felt as an instinctive sense of knowing. Spurred by a sense of knowing, the objective mind brings the appetite and knowledge of the will into consciousness as images and words. This answer is the representative of the solution; our ambassador of goodwill. Hopefully, this explains my comment indicating the solution already exists before the question is asked. Figure 4 shows many terms which can be used to describe how our minds cooperate.

This solution of our will, or essence, is transmitted by the instinct. This is how we always get an answer to every question we ask. Regarding the instinct as located in the subjective mind, leads me to suggest a new explanation of how our minds relate. I am proposing the instinct leads and the thinking mind follows. Do not imagine for a moment this leads to bad behavior! Bad behavior is a control mechanism, an expression of belief structures developed with the thinking mind.

FIGURE 4

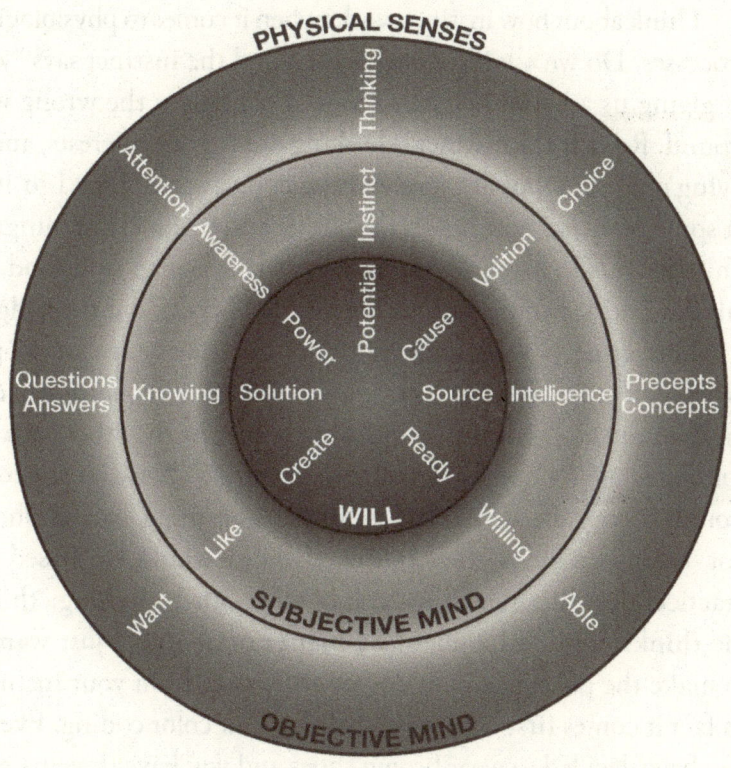

Figure 4. Model of the characteristics of our minds

I have said you always get an answer to your question. For those who believe the thinking mind runs the show, this may imply the instinct is passive until activated by the question; in other words the answer is a response to the question. However, I do not wish to imply the thinking mind leads the way, or that instinct serves the thinking mind. Quite the contrary; as stated above, the instinct is always active and readily giving us direction, which is then translated by the thinking mind. This is something you will want to prove for yourself.

Think about how instinct works when it comes to physiological processes. Do we ask if we are hungry, and the instinct says "yes" by giving us a hungry signal? I would say this is the wrong way around. Rather, the instinct is looking out for our interests, and is giving us a cue about our level of hunger on a scale of say 1 to 100. At some point we take notice of the cue and think "I am hungry." This leads us to bring up the appropriate script to find food. In this day and age this is something like "let's check out the fridge!"

This same process applies to any question you care to put forward. I have used an example of the loftiest question I can think of to ask—what is the meaning of life. At the other extreme you could ask "what shoes will I wear today?" Now most people wouldn't consult their instinct when choosing a pair of shoes. For most occasions the choice of shoes would be based on practicalities, like matching colors with other clothing; things the thinking mind handles as a matter of course. I just wanted to make the point that you do get an answer from your instinct. In fact it comes first before you think about color coding. Even if you have decided to wear brown shoes and you have three pairs of brown shoes you can let your instinct guide you to which brown shoes you **want** to wear.

Those quick on the uptake will have noticed in the previous sentence I did not say the instinct guides you to which shoes to wear. If this were the case the instinct would be telling us what to do; wear these shoes whether you want to or not! Many people think of the instinct as some sort of independent source of intelligence which knows better than we do. Regarded in this way, it would seem the instinct knew which shoes we should wear, which leads some people to think superstitiously. This suggests the instinct has information about what is going to happen later on, based on which pair of brown shoes you wear. This is definitely not the case I am making about our instinct.

In the paragraph above I linked instinct to what we want, and this was no accident. The point I'm making is that instinct guides you more efficiently to which shoes you want to wear. There is an important link between instinct and what we genuinely want—beliefs aside. Because of this link it is important to make the following distinctions. All behavior comes from want. Those wants in accord with the will, I regard as genuine wants. Otherwise our wanting is aligned with our beliefs. This is where choice comes in, that wonderful capacity of the objective mind. We have a choice as to where we align our want; make sure you choose wisely.

We can choose to allow the instinctive appetite to guide our want. If you make the choice to listen to your instinct, including awareness, then you have wants which are in accord with goodwill. This is how you create a pleasant experience of life. Then you can express your pleasant nature, which is how you maintain it as a lifestyle.

Regarding hunger, most would say instinct is telling us to eat, maybe even telling us not to eat. I want to put a different spin on this. Think of instinct as offering direction through our wants, which is always there, always active to some degree. As the instinctive impulse increases in intensity, we feel increasingly hungry or thirsty. Satisfying this appetite decreases it again. It is not an on-off condition. Hunger is an ongoing signal which at times is minimal but never non-existent. The hunger or thirst is manifested through our want for food or water. When our instinct is minimal we have minimal want for food or water.

Keep in mind, if we use other ideas about what and when to eat, it can obscure our instinctive impulse. For example, we might choose to eat until we feel full, which is usually eating too much. Also, anxiety can intensify the signal, making us want to eat before we would otherwise feel sufficiently hungry. The role of learning is also involved here, but I wish to leave this for some other time.

Coming back to the matter of getting answers to every question, there is another point I will mention. We have a range of senses and people place different emphasis on their sensory input modalities, hence some say they hear the answer, some feel it, some see it and I guess some smell or taste it. However, if knowing is a sense, it is ideal to "know" as a direct impression. Receiving answers from our instinct using other modes can be misleading. For example, translating the instinctive sense of knowing through a sensory modality, such as a gut feeling, is open to misinterpretation. Too many factors affect the signal, such as hunger and anxiety, making it less reliable.

If we want confirmation that the answer is coming from instinct, what can we use? If you feel encouraged to take this further, the best thing to look for is the instinctive sense of attraction, which was discussed in an earlier chapter. Coming back to hunger, when we are hungry, certain food has an attraction for us, which is like an affirmative feeling or uplifted sense. Be careful though, for if the attraction is a slightly compelling feeling, it is a tainted—thinking of the chocoholics out there; and anxiety about eating food will also intensify your want. In the case of asking questions, your attraction will be intensified by genuine, completed questions; bearing in mind a genuine attraction or good feeling is not your ego being stroked.

We do have an instinct to ask why, so let me ask this. Do we know the meaning of life instinctively? I get an affirmative response. Have I found my meaning for living? Well there is a little more to the metaphysics of coming to know your will than I care to present here. But in my mind, without a molecule of arrogance or doubt, I get a big "yes" from my instinctive sense of knowing. This comes with a big attraction and enjoyment of what life offers. This is my confirmation!

Remember, quite literally, for all intents and purposes our will manifests as goodwill. Therefore, the prompts it gives us are harmonious in nature. I cannot find confirmation to the contrary, despite all the bad things going on in the world. If you look beneath the surface, those bad events can be seen as our expression of beliefs which are not in accord with our will. There are lots of implications here, but let's not get off track. The main point for you to confirm is this; our primary instinct is our sense of knowing, the expression of innate intelligence, which prompts a want in you to love life. Ideally, you might also confirm that your will stirs a want to fix the creations of our species which are not in accord with this, including your own. In recognizing this, I have purpose and meaning in my life—a mission, but one which requires your support and assistance. Instinctively, we all want the same thing, so ask this question; "how can I give you what you want"?

Still No Idea?

There is, of course, a high likelihood many of you are still not getting satisfactory answers. If you are in this situation, the most helpful advice I can give is, you are listening to your beliefs. That is, you have your objective mind running the show. You have to become subjective in order to listen to your instinct. Most people do not do this as a matter of routine, and you may benefit from assistance by someone who is used to doing this. Most meditation processes require subjectivity and will show you how to do this. Note they should not be ***teaching*** you how to do it; you already know how. You have learned to do something different, to value objectivity more than subjectivity, and this you can instinctively put this aside.

Someone else may offer you other explanations of the meaning of life, or why you don't get answers. Maybe they will believe I am completely off the planet. Bear in mind all such opinions, including mine, are simply suggestions for you to verify in your mind, and experience either way. My point of view is based on my exploration and experience, but it has to be verified by you, for it to be true for you. Yes, it flies in the face of much we believe, but I don't think it goes against our natural instinct. I've done my best to present a case about how to use your minds and how to get answers that satisfy. Even so, no matter how instructive my discussion on the topic, you may feel you are not getting answers, no matter what you try.

Don't shy away from asking others. Have you noticed people are generally willing to answer a question? I am certain this goes beyond social norms and etiquette. It is very hard not to answer a question we hear asked by someone else, whether it is directed to us or not, and whether we know the person or not. I think we see it as a chance to give freely of our knowing, even if it is just simple information like directions on how to get somewhere. If you want some assistance, let me know. My instinct is willing—even if the body is too busy!

The case I am making defies the view of the thinking mind providing the solution. It is true we think about our responses to life, but it is a misunderstanding to think this provides the answers. We get answers by thinking, though it is instinct which prompts us to ask questions, receive answers, and reformulate another question. Misunderstanding occurs if we believe the source of intelligence is in the objective thinking mind, or if we think this mind is our saving grace. Even common sense dictates this cannot be true; if it were true, how do other species survive? The idea the thinking mind does it all, is an egocentric viewpoint.

In terms of the human experience, the universe does not revolve around the thinking mind any more than it revolves around the sun. Doesn't it seem strange, the very science which refuted the idea of everything revolving around us, does not refute the idea of the human experience of life revolving around the thinking mind. I am equally concerned about traditional religious views on these matters, particularly the use of instilled beliefs. Basically, I'm proposing a third alternative. If the misunderstanding of our thinking is taken out of both science and religion, they are saying the same thing! But this will have to wait for a future book.

We have created a world of fear and unhappiness, by exclusive use of the thinking mind without due reference to our will. One of the early artificial beliefs we developed in civilized culture is that instinct is inferior to reasoning. We have used reasoning to develop beliefs for every facet of life: what to do, what to feel and worst of all, what to think. This dedication to listening to reasoning above all else is what we "think" we mean by civilized, yet it is one of the most serious misconceptions we have developed.

In my upbringing, there was an explicit belief about why the rational mind was superior to instinct. The justification for this philosophy was; the reasoning mind is the only thing setting us apart from animals. The beliefs associated with this are; we would act like animals if we did not place the thinking mind above all else, and animals act in an uncivilized manner, so this would be a bad thing. Well, speaking for myself, it's just not true—the things we believe are rarely true. The animal in me is not bad though I'm supposed to believe it is. And, look what a mess we have made living primarily from our civilized beliefs. Our saving grace is the will, seated behind our instinct, impressing upon us a sense of knowing and feeling of goodwill.

Face it, no matter how much you think unsolicited use of beliefs is okay, this is precisely what is causing us to suffer. We have enslaved ourselves with our thinking mind, and at the collective level it scares me no end to see we may not get out of this in time, before we annihilate our species.

This brings us around the full circle of the problem and its solution. What I want to convey is, out of fear we distrust our instinct, and replace our natural appetites with beliefs, which covers up our true will. This is how we create the suffering. Without our harmonious will to guide us we are the proverbial ship without a rudder. Following artificial beliefs based on ideas about how we should behave is an act of ignorance, arrogance, or both. This is like saying, our thinking mind knows better than nature.

Why have we created unpleasantness in our lives? You may well ask! I would say it is simply because we misunderstood the nature of our instinct; we have made it our enemy. Supposedly, we maintain this position because instinct makes us do bad things. "Somebody stop me!" I don't know why this belief became so predominant. However, I would argue this; listening to our instinct does not make us uncivilized. On the contrary, placing the conscious mind above instinct is what dehumanizes us. That is what allows us to create unpleasant thoughts and acts, not our instinct. In the big picture of things, it is the misuse of beliefs based in fear which leads us to commit atrocities in the name of civilization.

Why doesn't something stop us, I hear you ask? Simply, this is not the nature of our will. If we are going to come to know ourselves, we'd better know this. Our will does not control us any more than our instinct does! If it did, its nature would not be goodwill. What is more, if its expression is goodwill, we shouldn't try to control it or look to be controlled by it. So, to live a fearless life, basically all you have to do is confirm your true nature is goodwill.

So there you have it! We have covered a lot of ground, including issues like beliefs, fear, control, wants and needs, misuse of our minds, and the appropriate use of instinct. We have examined topics ranging from everyday issues to the meaning of life. This is the point I have reached in my exploration. I encourage you to go further with yours. "Your mission, should you choose to accept it," is to find the solution—you. This is the meaning of life and the means to live without suffering.

As I said early in the piece, there are no formal references used in this work. That is because *you* are the reference—specifically your will and instinctive sense of knowing. Referring to other people's thoughts has to be approached carefully, because it can trigger your scripts and beliefs. "Referring" often means "deferring". In your exploration, deferring to the thoughts of other people comes with the risk of being misled. In particular, you should be sure you are not just adopting the views of others. Most people think others know better. Not so!

When all is said and done it comes back to my statements at the start of the book, so I will conclude the book with them as well. The contents in this book are based on five basic human experiences, which can be described simply as follows:

1. Each of us has an instinctive sense of knowing, which is the essence of intelligence.

2. As a consequence, we have an instinctive based appetite to want to know ourselves.
3. Our natural condition or true nature is a sense of harmony or pleasantness, despite appearances.
4. We are creators; everything we think and do is like an artist creating the story of a life.
5. We often use our thinking, based in the objective mind to create unpleasant experiences in life which are not in accord with our true nature. This causes us to suffer.

These five experiences can be used to reframe how we look at life, and how we guide others to look at their life events. They represent the means to move from a life of suffering to one of freedom. In advising you of this, it is not necessary for me to have every detail correct, any more than it is necessary for you to have all the answers.

These five statements describe repeatable and verifiable experiences in life. They are not derived from beliefs, and I do not present them as my beliefs. They are not statements I want you to believe in. Rather, they are experiences I invite you to explore; to consider their significance and application. I trust you can relate them to your life, and my descriptions have been sufficiently clear for you to regard my opinion as something more than conjecture.

However, the truth of it is that what I know and what I think doesn't matter much to you. I do my self-exploration for sake of my will. The answers I get from my instinctive mind are of little use to you if they get in the way of your answers. Their main value to you is to hear what is possible. The things which matter for you are **your** questions and **your** answers. You can only find these from your own self-exploration. Most important, I hope you can now regard the practical end to your suffering as something well within your grasp.

Summary

So what is the meaning of life?
Getting a satisfying answer to every question you ask puts you in a good position to find out.

- Questions presented to your instinct must be well conceived. A nil response means either the question is ill conceived, or you have not presented it to your instinct.
- If you listen to your instinctive sense of knowing, without preconceived thoughts distracting you, you start to get answers that satisfy.

Belief in the superiority of the objective mind gets in the way of good answers and will lead you astray:

- The thinking mind is not the source of the solution, though it contributes.
- Beliefs from the objective mind won't satisfy questions seeded from the instinct.
- Following artificial beliefs about how to behave is an act of ignorance, arrogance or both.
- The universe does not revolve around the thinking mind any more than it revolves around the sun.
- Placing the objective mind above instinct dehumanizes us, instinct does not.

Our subjective self is central to finding the solution:

- An experience without a subjective sense of self is meaningless.
- To get satisfying answers you must listen to the subjective mind by giving attention to the senses, instinct, and will.

- Well-conceived questions open our objective and subjective minds to our will.
- The answer to the question of the meaning of life will be no surprise to you, because the answer comes from you; the solution exists before the question is asked and before the answer is formulated.
- Your life is justified in its own right—life is its own meaning. There is no external meaning of life which does not involve you.
- The solution is provided by our will as its natural creative act—the solution *is* the will.
- Our will is the core sense of self, sensed as un-manifested potential.

Wanting is an expression of our instinct:

- All behavior comes from want.
- Instinct guides you towards what you genuinely want.
- Want in accord with the will is genuine want; want based on beliefs is corrupted. We choose what guides our wanting.
- In the case of asking questions, look for an instinctive sense of attraction. The attraction is intensified by genuine questions.

When we are willing to listen to our instinct in the subjective mind we get the solution:

- The guidance of instinct is always there, always active.
- Our instinctive sense of knowing gives affirmative direction leading to affirmative action.
- A genuine question is seeded from the appetite of instinct, expressed through the objective mind. That is, instinct

prompts the objective mind to formulate questions so the will can answer it.
- Instinct leads and the thinking mind follows—this does not lead to bad behavior. Bad things come as expressions of beliefs not in accord with our will.
- Nothing stops us from doing bad things, because the will and instinct do not control us. It is a matter of choice.
- Instinct prompts us to thrive—to do what is in harmony with our continued existence.
- Our will leads us away from fear and while followed we do not suffer.

So the meaning of life is beyond belief. The meaning of life is …

Appendix

Introducing ME to Clients – A Health Practitioner's Guide

Before reading this appendix, please read Chapter 10 up to the heading "ME in practice" to ensure you have the necessary context.

Mindful existence (ME) is the means to creating a pleasant experience of life. In the context of offering ME as a psychological process for use by health practitioners, I have packaged it as Mindfulness Based Existential Approach (MBEA) to be comparable with other approaches such as Mindfulness Based Cognitive Therapy.

MBEA can, of course, be offered as a standalone process. Another option I am comfortable with is an integration of this enhanced approach with current mindfulness practice. That is, the "existential" component could be included in current mindfulness-based programs. This could be done, for example, as a three-session module bringing mindful attention to the client's subjective impression of their sense of well-being, sense of goodwill, or sense of existence. Participants would have reference to a core sense of self unaffected by scripts, increasing their ability to examine unpleasant script and deal with other painful events. This should enhance the achievement of outcomes, particularly getting past the barriers participants can encounter in mindfulness practice.

Ideally, this existential component should have the highest priority. Current mindfulness practices are based on experiences we have in response to events in the world, which affect our mood and thinking state. In contrast, MBEA is based on our core sense of self, present during all life events. This sense of self is an active creator of events, not a passive responder to them. Can you see the value in giving this priority? A program based on MBEA establishes what we bring to the world, for example goodwill, which provides a reference point for how we process our experiences of the world. Imagine the possibilities of a constant involved in this sense of self, giving us a natural sense of well-being not based in thinking, but which our thinking mind can manifest!

However you offer MBEA, please bear in mind it is an approach—a life-style approach—rather than a therapy. This distinction is important because therapies and treatments are designed to solve problems, and a view of poor mental health as "problems" is one of the main reasons for the stigma associated with it.

The following outline for the introduction of MBEA, covers the information participants should hear in their first session. While I have included self-help guidelines in Chapter 10, this version is for health professionals, shows how to broach these ideas effectively with clients. This is supplementary to the normal information you would provide about duty of care, informed consent, history and goal setting.

I find it useful to describe MBEA as having two components. Part A is the process of self-exploration and Part B is the application for addressing scripts and belief structures. Application of Part B can be done under the usual counseling format, including motivational interviewing, applying cognitive challenge to beliefs and dealing with adverse events. The following information applies to the mindfulness component of Part A. This is a transcription of the instructions I give to clients.

An Introduction to MBEA

This is a positive psychology approach to well-being. There are some differences compared with a more traditional clinical approach to counseling. With a clinical approach, your unpleasant experiences or presenting issue is the focus of discussion. The interaction revolves around this, for instance how it manifests, what triggers the symptoms, what eases them, what strategies can help deal with them, and what else can be done.

With a well-being approach, the focus is on your strengths. In general, this approach shows a positive way to deal with all life events. I want you to know more about how your mind works, and increase your skills and confidence to address issues. The aim is to see if you can be less affected by unpleasant experiences. To do this, the well-being approach uses a self-exploration process with your faculty of awareness.

Awareness allows us to monitor what we are sensing in the present moment. This is called being mindful of events. There are a number of psychology programs based on a mindfulness approach. In this particular well-being process, mindfulness is used to be more aware of our core self and instinct. It is an approach that assists you to examine your existence, as referred to in the theory of existentialism.

The basic idea behind this approach is that there is a core part of you which feels good all the time. This is a sense of what feels genuinely good and right for us. We commonly refer to this as our natural sense of well-being or goodwill. This is what we are born with. I think of this as our birthright. Arguably, it is the source of what we genuinely want in our lives: a sense of calm, peace of mind, contentedness, simple joy of living; a sense of completeness, belonging, and caring, and most importantly, a deep, authentic sense of you.

You should regard these comments as my opinion. I don't want you to believe me. These things are not true for you until you have experienced them. What I would like you to do is to confirm you have the ability to tune in to these impressions of life, and when you do, to describe the effect it has on you. If you can confirm in your own experience that it has a good effect, this natural condition provides a reference point to keep in mind when addressing unpleasant experiences. In this way we will be able to deal with the issues you wish to change, while remaining grounded in your sense of well-being.

If we are born with this sense of well-being, what goes wrong? As we grow older we have a lot of different experiences of the world, and we interpret some of them in ways which are not in accord with our will. Misinterpretations are also reinforced by the way we see others respond and the responses we are taught. These interpretations become our belief structures, or scripts, stored in memory. We learn to see the world in different ways, and some of these do not feel good. Remember, a lot of our unpleasant experiences are learned. They are corruptions of our natural sense of life as good. You only have to look at an infant to be reminded of the wonderful experience of sensing life is good. So a part of what we can do is to challenge the scripts we find unpleasant and doing us harm. In their place, we can establish strategies and response patterns that feel good to us and promote a sense of good mental health.

The key to this well-being process is to choose what we allow into our thinking mind. The main benefit of awareness is that it enables us to be conscious of the content of the scripts we choose. We always have a choice and we are constantly making choices. Sometimes it seems unpleasant things enter our thinking mind uninvited. On these occasions we think we have not made a choice, but actually, we have made the choice so quickly we don't see it happen. For instance, our past ways of responding to events are stored in memory as scripts, or belief structures. When these are activated by an event, out of necessity they come to mind very quickly. As they are habitual patterns of response, including emotion, we can mistakenly think we have no choice at the time.

By being mindful of the event, we get to choose whether or not to allow the old pattern to affect our thinking. Think of your awareness as being there before your thoughts. This means you can be clear about your choice when the old pattern starts. In particular, through awareness you can feel the unpleasant effect of the old pattern before you engage it in your thinking mind. In this way you can choose to stay with the natural sense of well-being, and want this as your guide to give a different response. If you keep doing this, you can develop new scripts based on your instinctive sense of goodwill.

My commitment to this well-being process is based on observing it help people address unpleasant experiences, whether the unpleasantness comes from their mind or someone else's. If you choose to stay in touch with your sense of well-being no matter what happens, you can change your experience. For example, a person with a lot of anxiety in their life usually loses their sense of well-being, when faced with a situation which brings up a script containing anxiety. This happens because they choose to engage the familiar response pattern containing the anxiety, allowing the script containing the anxiety to come into their minds where it immediately produces the symptoms of anxiety, such as panic. If, however, the person has an alternate pleasant sense to refer to, such as a natural sense of well-being, they can choose to give their attention to this instead of the anxiety. In this way they will not be so strongly affected by the script. Sooner or later they can smile about the experience of anxiety, which of course is the best thing to do if they wish to change its course. Having an experience which does not leave room for the anxiety is very empowering. You might quickly see the possibilities of what you can do with your mind.

This process is not for everyone. People generally respond in one of three ways. Some people think this is "not their cup of tea." Such people are often locked into control mechanisms or would not consider using other faculties of their mind like awareness. They tend not to continue past the introductory session. This is okay because each of us does what we think will benefit us. Others give priority to a specific goal, such as feeling less anxious about going out of the house. These people tend to do enough sessions to impact on their circumstances then get on with their lives. Finally, the majority of people see the broader implications for their way of life. As a well-being process, MBEA has general application to how we use our mind to meet life events on a day to day basis, and to make changes whenever called for.

Getting started with the practical, experiential part of your self-exploration is easy. Just relax, get comfortable and start to use your awareness to monitor what you are experiencing in the present moment. I will come back to this in a moment, but there are four things worth commenting on at this point.

First, this is something you are in charge of doing. If you are not comfortable with what is happening in your mind, you should feel free to stop at any time. Keep in mind this is a well-being process; it is not about feeling uncomfortable. It is about feeling okay with what you are doing, so the statement of intent is as follows. If it doesn't feel good, by definition you are ***not*** doing the process correctly. This is about giving attention to the part of us that feels good all the time. Even if we encounter an unpleasant experience, we want to meet it from our sense of well-being, enabling us to stay with feeling okay.

It is rare for anyone to feel uncomfortable to the point of wanting to stop. In Part A, the self-exploration, go along only with something which feels good to you. Most people can do this quite easily. If an unpleasant script or feeling comes into mind, move your attention to a natural pleasant impression that does not involve thinking. If you engage in Part B of the process, addressing your scripts, it is important you keep giving attention to a pleasant sense rather than following the unpleasant one. Sometimes this is difficult, with intense anxiety for example, but comes down to your willingness to make this choice.

There are instances when caution should be exercised. Research findings have indicated relaxation processes can trigger adverse events for people with a history of psychoses or dissociative disorder. That's a good reason to work with a health practitioner such as myself, when examining unpleasant experiences, and challenging the effect of belief structures.

Second, if you are comfortable with making eye contact, this can be helpful. This is no different to what we normally do when talking to someone, except we might hold the eye contact for a longer period of time. A larger number of people seem to hold eye contact for longer periods nowadays. This is good social change away from interpreting eye contact as being too invasive, threatening or intimate. This is not about staring or mind games. Regard it as a simple engagement.

The eye gaze is optional, but has some benefits. As you explore your core sense of self in the presence of another person, you can give each other feedback on how you are going, for instance I can say when you are being distracted by thoughts. In this way we can have a more intensive impression of our core sense of well-being. So be willing to use whatever information is available to you, including what we talk about, and non-verbal communication. Changes in people's facial expressions are the most informative, so if you are comfortable for me to monitor you closely, it makes it easier to give you accurate feedback.

If you are comfortable to engage with another person, there is another possible benefit. You can use the interaction to intensify the experience of your self-exploration. This is possible because we each have a different experience of the world when we use our objective mind, but a similar sense when we use our subjective mind. If you engage with your objective mind, you see another person with their own mannerisms. If you engage people with your subjective mind, you see yourself reflected in them. In other words, another human being is the best mirror you can get! Some people prefer not to use this mode of self-exploration, but I invite you to try it and see if it is empowering for you.

Third, during the process most people experience some perceptual changes, most commonly to their vision, although it can affect any of our senses. For instance, you might notice the room appear to get lighter or darker independently of what the sun is doing. This can happen when we are doing deep reflection because our internal perceptions can over-ride the physical senses. Perceptual changes are related to what we are conceiving in our mind. As an example, when doubt enters our mind it can seem like the room gets darker or hazy; when hope enters our mind it can seem like the room gets brighter.

Some people get strong perceptual changes, so I make a point of highlighting this. It is quite normal and no cause for concern. It tends to happen when we become subjective and are not using our mind to focus on physical objects. It is common in deep meditation too. In the process of doing Part A, the self-exploration, you are encouraged to stay aware of a good feeling or sense and not follow the perceptual changes. In the process of Part B, addressing scripts, the perceptual changes are most often related to the scripts that are being engaged. In this event they can be used as a trace to find the source of the script.

Fourth, and last, do not act on scripts that come up during the session. Let me use the example of anxiety again. I use this example with everyone, so I am not thinking of you in particular. If you start to feel anxious or uncomfortable, it is better not to show it in your behavior. Rather than expressing it by wriggling or fidgeting, let it pass through your mind without acting on it. This means not engaging the sensations or experiences which occur. The reason being, if you act on the sensation, you allow it into your thinking mind. Once you engage the script in your thinking, it will start to have the full effect of the symptoms on you.

Part of what I want you to examine is whether we have a choice about what we allow into our mind. The idea behind this is that the script does not get activated if we do not engage it with thinking. In the case of scripts stored in memory, we have about half a second from when the trigger occurs to the script being activated. Therefore we have to watch closely for the sensations or experiences we are having. Because it happens quickly, a lot of people think they don't choose to experience unpleasant things. Learned responses become habitual, and tend to be chosen without being challenged.

I want to show you that your awareness notices these events. Your awareness is a natural faculty standing between the event we are sensing and the interpretation and response we make. In this way it enables our choice. When we exercise this choice for our own benefit, we are on the way to altering the course of the response. Can you see how this would provide a way to address unpleasant events?

You already have the ability to do this so I don't have to teach you a technique. You simply become subjective. It is easy to do, though most people don't do this because they have learned to use the thinking mind for their primary interaction with the world. What I am encouraging you to do is allow the subjective mind to have this role.

Getting started is easy to do. It is just a matter of relaxing, getting comfortable and letting yourself be. There is nothing you have to do; you already know how to use your awareness. There are no rules of engagement. It is more a matter of letting go of expectations, of not trying to sort it out with your thinking mind. It may come down to whether you are willing to refrain from controlling yourself with the thinking mind. If you are, your attention can be given to the subjective mind and your awareness. At this point you have the opportunity to feel the pleasant effect of your instinct.

While you are settling in, there are three questions that can help you get started.

First; "if you just let go, what do you sense?" You need only answer "pleasantness" or "unpleasantness." [Some people say it feels neutral, but 9 out of 10 agree it is not unpleasant. Most find a relaxed sense, or bit of calm].

The second question is; "can you acknowledge you did not have to produce this impression?" In other words, you did not have to sit there and think okay thoughts to feel okay. [Most agree]. This is the first bit of evidence it is your true nature. The implication is we are not dependent on thinking happy thoughts to be happy, even though it can help!

The third question is; "if you do that again, and give the pleasant sense your attention, does it start to increase, grow in intensity or have more of an effect on you?" Does giving attention to the pleasant sense change your experience? [A few people at first struggle with this but soon notice it changes their state of mind, for example they feel more relaxed and their perception of events intensifies].

The answers to these three questions define what MBEA is about. There is a part of us always feeling okay. We do not have to produce it. It is already a part of our experience. If we give it our attention it increases in our perception, and has greater effect on us. In other words it is a dynamic sense of change.

This is our point of entry to the practical part of the sessions. My invitation to you is to find out how much calmness you can experience or how relaxed you can become. If you keep giving your attention to a pleasant impression, how intense does it become?

So, I will let you explore this experience and after a while start to give you some feedback. [From here the self-exploration has begun in earnest.]

As an additional note, if you find persistent thinking is interfering with the use of awareness, a concrete exercise could be beneficial. I suggest listening to the sounds going on around you. It is easy to listen. We do it with our physical senses all the time, for example listening to the wind, the sea or music. Treat the event as a symphony of sounds. There are sounds that come and go, others going on continuously. Some are loud, others soft. They can be a deep bass sound or a high-pitched sound. It is important not to concentrate on any particular sound. If you open your mind to all the sounds, it can seem like a concert; a concerto of sound. If a pleasant sense is achieved by listening to the event, then attention can then be turned to the sense of self having the pleasant experience.

As an overarching request for you and your client; enjoy the experience!

Index

A

ability 5, 29, 37, 44, 46, 105, 126, 129, 159, 161, 175, 176, 180, 193, 201, 211, 226, 230, 237, 242, 244, 277, 280, 286

abstract 5, 57, 64, 65, 66, 67, 70, 96, 164, 167, 180

abuse xiii, 35, 55, 113, 114, 116, 120, 171

accept 3, 7, 25, 30, 32, 43, 51, 55, 57, 58, 59, 62, 73, 86, 89, 90, 96, 125, 128, 148, 150, 151, 155, 157, 158, 161, 166, 185, 253, 271

accord 2, 9, 20, 33, 36, 40, 52, 64, 137, 140, 145, 146, 160, 167, 172, 178, 182, 186, 187, 193, 198, 199, 202, 204, 205, 211, 212, 213, 214, 223, 228, 233, 235, 237, 245, 248, 252, 265, 267, 272, 274, 275, 280

acknowledged 18, 201, 207

activated 211, 213, 223, 232, 237, 241, 244, 264, 281, 285

adults 6, 23, 72

affirmative 205, 254, 258, 259, 266, 267, 274

afraid 99, 178

agreements 185, 186, 187, 189

alarmed 76, 104, 105, 114

animal 29, 43, 56, 88, 156, 270

answer 7, 8, 17, 20, 24, 25, 27, 32, 33, 38, 39, 42, 52, 53, 54, 55, 62, 63, 69, 70, 88, 89, 108, 122, 128, 129, 134, 151, 153, 154, 156, 160, 161, 162, 184, 188, 197, 200, 201, 204, 205, 210, 242, 249, 250, 251, 253, 254, 255, 256, 257, 258, 260, 261, 262, 264, 266, 268, 274, 275, 286

answers 2, 4, 5, 20, 26, 27, 28, 32, 33, 34, 39, 40, 42, 43, 51, 52, 53, 54, 55, 71, 76, 81, 128, 135, 140, 173, 178, 187, 197, 200, 204, 205, 212, 243, 250, 251, 252, 253, 254, 255, 260, 261, 267, 268, 269, 272, 273, 287

anxiety xi, 101, 107, 179, 238, 240, 241, 256, 281, 283, 285

anxious 54, 239, 241, 256, 282, 285

appetite 2, 4, 11, 26, 34, 73, 81, 102, 115, 145, 147, 148, 149, 153, 165, 167, 202, 203, 206, 255, 262, 265, 272, 274 appetites 30, 31, 40, 47, 76, 148, 149, 150, 192, 193, 194, 202, 203, 225, 228, 260, 270

ask 1, 2, 12, 19, 20, 27, 28, 34, 39, 42, 43, 51, 52, 53, 54, 62, 63, 65, 69, 98, 101, 108, 116, 126, 144, 148, 149, 150, 153, 177, 185, 187, 189, 190, 205, 249, 250, 253, 254, 255, 256, 257, 260, 261, 262, 264, 267, 270, 271, 273

asking 5, 25, 27, 30, 42, 53, 54, 68, 69, 108, 149, 186, 187, 206, 253, 254, 257, 258, 261, 266, 268, 269, 274

attention 44, 71, 72, 73, 74, 75, 80, 90, 91, 95, 99, 104, 107, 110, 144, 180, 182, 190, 196, 199, 208, 210, 211, 215, 216, 217, 219, 220, 221, 223, 224, 225, 226, 227, 232, 233, 238, 239, 240, 242, 243, 244, 245, 246, 247, 249, 250, 251, 252, 273, 277, 282, 283, 286, 287

attitude 9, 22, 95, 127, 134, 135, 168, 176, 256, 258

attraction 135, 174, 203, 204, 205, 206, 212, 213, 266, 267, 274

authority 29, 71, 112, 113, 120, 124

automatic 181, 222

aware 3, 5, 45, 46, 54, 89, 92, 103, 104, 121, 131, 165, 181, 198, 199, 216, 218, 221, 226, 227, 230, 236, 238, 241, 247, 257, 258, 266, 279, 285

awareness 34, 40, 45, 55, 62, 70, 80, 100, 104, 105, 157, 165, 174, 180, 181, 183, 190, 197, 198, 200, 210, 211, 212, 213, 215, 216, 217, 218, 220, 223, 224, 225, 226, 227, 228, 229, 231, 233, 234, 236, 238, 239, 242, 243, 244, 245, 246, 247, 265, 279, 281, 282, 285, 286, 287

B

backup 176, 189, 195, 199, 200

balance 16, 60, 134, 159

basic 2, 3, 4, 18, 26, 29, 45, 46, 63, 67, 95, 107, 117, 119, 141, 217, 220, 236, 245, 271, 279

basis 11, 15, 43, 67, 70, 72, 77, 92, 99, 141, 150, 163, 176, 184, 186, 187, 198, 239, 282

behavior 31, 32, 36, 40, 50, 51, 65, 66, 68, 72, 87, 88, 91, 93, 94, 109, 111, 113, 115, 125, 154, 156, 184, 195, 241, 262, 265, 274, 275, 285

belief 9, 15, 16, 17, 21, 28, 29, 30, 31, 32, 33, 36, 38, 39, 46, 49, 50, 51, 56, 58, 61, 65, 66, 67, 69, 71, 74, 75, 76, 77, 81, 83, 84, 85, 86, 88, 89, 91, 92, 93, 94, 95, 99, 101, 103, 106, 107, 109, 112, 114, 116, 117, 119, 120, 121, 122, 123, 124, 126, 127, 128, 132, 134, 135, 136, 137, 138, 140, 141, 142, 143, 144, 145, 146, 147, 148, 150, 152, 153, 157, 158, 159, 160, 161, 163, 165, 166, 167, 168, 172, 176, 177, 179, 181, 183, 184, 187, 189, 191, 194, 195, 197, 198, 200, 201, 202, 206, 209, 210, 214, 225, 228, 230, 231, 232, 233, 235, 237, 249,

252, 253, 254, 258, 259, 270, 275, 279, 280, 281, 283
beliefs 3, 10, 13, 14, 16, 17, 18, 20, 21, 23, 27, 28, 30, 31, 32, 35, 39, 40, 46, 47, 50, 51, 52, 54, 55, 56, 57, 60, 62, 64, 65, 66, 67, 68, 69, 70, 71, 74, 76, 77, 79, 80, 81, 83, 84, 87, 88, 89, 91, 92, 93, 94, 95, 96, 98, 102, 109, 113, 114, 116, 117, 121, 122, 123, 127, 128, 131, 132, 134, 135, 137, 138, 139, 140, 141, 142, 143, 144, 148, 157, 158, 159, 160, 162, 163, 164, 165, 166, 167, 168, 171, 172, 174, 179, 183, 191, 195, 197, 198, 199, 201, 202, 209, 212, 219, 220, 231, 232, 235, 247, 248, 251, 259, 265, 267, 269, 270, 271, 272, 273, 274, 275, 279
belief structures 9, 28, 69, 77, 86, 91, 92, 93, 161, 172, 179, 183, 194, 200, 202, 210, 214, 225, 228, 230, 231, 232, 237, 249, 279, 280, 281, 283
believe xi, 3, 7, 15, 16, 27, 28, 31, 42, 49, 52, 53, 54, 58, 60, 68, 69, 73, 76, 77, 81, 82, 83, 84, 87, 88, 90, 96, 97, 99, 108, 110, 112, 119, 123, 125, 129, 134, 136, 137, 138, 145, 147, 158, 159, 160, 163, 170, 171, 172, 174, 179, 184, 187, 188, 206, 214, 228, 232, 236, 245, 247, 264, 268, 270, 272, 280
benefit 42, 91, 115, 121, 150, 152, 178, 191, 204, 211, 234, 235, 238, 239, 240, 242, 243, 248, 268, 281, 282, 284, 285
beyond 8, 12, 45, 47, 51, 62, 77, 81, 106, 114, 145, 157, 167, 168, 176, 180, 189, 208, 214, 228, 259, 268, 275
bias 16, 230
biased 14, 252
body 6, 8, 9, 58, 75, 82, 83, 85, 86, 87, 96, 125, 129, 136, 148, 149, 150, 168, 176
book xi, xiii, xiv, 1, 3, 4, 7, 9, 11, 14, 17, 21, 26, 38, 114, 256, 269, 271
boundaries 183, 184, 185, 186, 187
boundary 54, 184, 185
brain 43, 44, 46, 50, 75, 86, 261

C

capacity 7, 14, 26, 30, 36, 37, 42, 46, 50, 53, 55, 62, 63, 65, 66, 70, 137, 143, 159, 163, 164, 166, 171, 180, 192, 233, 235, 265
caring 57, 60, 71, 92, 97, 112, 114, 116, 185, 186, 210, 216, 236, 280
challenge 3, 26, 54, 74, 77, 82, 84, 85, 92, 99, 108, 109, 112, 113, 116, 123, 137, 140, 143, 144, 158, 167, 183, 210, 229, 230, 231, 237, 279, 280
challenging 3, 140, 143, 146, 149, 172, 193, 200, 231, 247, 259, 283
change 1, 17, 36, 58, 67, 84, 102, 115, 122, 129, 145, 159, 167, 176, 198, 199, 209, 212, 220, 222, 224, 225, 226, 227, 228,

229, 233, 235, 237, 238, 243, 258, 280, 281, 283, 287
changes 18, 60, 69, 91, 178, 226, 235, 239, 240, 241, 243, 248, 282, 284, 287
charge 51, 82, 124, 125, 128, 133, 138, 152, 171, 187, 229, 233, 239, 282
child 6, 10, 29, 32, 35, 43, 61, 66, 68, 72, 73, 74, 76, 87, 90, 91, 95, 97, 111, 112, 113, 114, 115, 117, 120, 165, 183, 184, 185, 186, 187, 188, 196
children 10, 23, 32, 40, 51, 57, 58, 71, 72, 73, 76, 90, 110, 112, 113, 114, 120, 131, 147, 166, 176, 183, 184, 187, 188, 189
choice xiii, 10, 20, 22, 30, 37, 38, 40, 41, 49, 57, 72, 80, 86, 88, 89, 93, 97, 106, 113, 116, 128, 133, 134, 140, 149, 150, 151, 152, 153, 157, 158, 168, 171, 172, 179, 180, 181, 182, 184, 185, 187, 188, 199, 200, 204, 209, 210, 214, 215, 223, 225, 227, 229, 237, 238, 242, 245, 246, 264, 265, 281, 285
choices 31, 121, 124, 138, 145, 151, 155, 163, 182, 185, 186, 188, 215, 237, 281
choose xi, 2, 9, 26, 37, 38, 49, 57, 85, 89, 92, 113, 128, 140, 142, 145, 149, 151, 156, 167, 171, 173, 178, 180, 181, 182, 183, 197, 198, 200, 201, 202, 214, 215, 217, 221, 225, 228, 235, 237, 238, 241, 245, 265, 271, 274, 281, 285

common 26, 28, 31, 55, 59, 60, 74, 84, 86, 89, 92, 107, 111, 124, 134, 143, 155, 156, 157, 163, 164, 171, 178, 182, 184, 199, 235, 241, 285
conceive 7, 22, 37, 40, 46, 56, 57, 62, 70, 80, 83, 90, 93, 108, 117, 126, 155, 164, 170, 174, 175, 176, 178, 180, 182, 199, 203, 211, 212, 216, 217, 234
conceived 9, 18, 25, 29, 30, 33, 55, 85, 95, 145, 197, 253, 254, 273, 274
concept 12, 18, 20, 21, 25, 32, 33, 35, 44, 50, 56, 66, 71, 72, 82, 83, 84, 99, 123, 127, 130, 141, 144, 147, 148, 156, 163, 184, 191, 192, 259, 261
concepts xi, 19, 21, 28, 30, 35, 39, 46, 47, 64, 65, 67, 77, 141, 143, 144, 214, 217
confirmation 8, 38, 105, 187, 190, 202, 233, 267
conflict 33, 58, 59, 64, 91, 113, 124, 162, 164
conscious 7, 9, 14, 15, 25, 30, 32, 33, 35, 37, 38, 43, 44, 45, 46, 49, 53, 72, 75, 76, 131, 170, 175, 180, 181, 215, 217, 218, 219, 221, 223, 224, 226, 227, 238, 246, 270, 281
conscious mind 43, 44, 49, 75
consciousness xi, 31, 44, 45, 46, 197, 217, 224, 225, 226, 227, 244, 262
consequences 8, 31, 36, 105, 112, 116, 184, 185, 209
consideration xi, 3, 7, 17, 71, 80, 126, 228, 234

constructive 100, 124, 132, 135, 136, 138, 164, 177
control 28, 29, 31, 32, 33, 35, 39, 40, 49, 50, 51, 61, 68, 87, 90, 91, 95, 96, 107, 111, 112, 113, 116, 117, 118, 121, 122, 123, 124, 125, 126, 127, 128, 129, 130, 131, 132, 134, 136, 137, 138, 139, 141, 142, 144, 148, 150, 152, 153, 154, 157, 161, 168, 171, 172, 173, 174, 176, 177, 181, 183, 184, 185, 188, 191, 192, 195, 196, 199, 202, 207, 215, 216, 220, 221, 229, 232, 233, 239, 245, 262, 271, 275, 282
controlled 30, 32, 49, 50, 58, 59, 71, 87, 148, 181, 182, 207, 271
cooperation 15, 76, 128, 187, 195
core 14, 32, 40, 64, 77, 93, 95, 112, 122, 138, 165, 181, 196, 207, 216, 218, 225, 228, 230, 232, 236, 247, 274, 277, 278, 279, 283
corrupt 67, 68, 69, 71, 140, 177
corrupted 50, 60, 72, 80, 90, 94, 95, 101, 103, 114, 115, 119, 144, 146, 160, 168, 179, 187, 274
corruption 51, 61, 94, 114, 120, 168, 216, 246
create 2, 4, 11, 34, 36, 37, 41, 42, 56, 57, 63, 64, 66, 77, 117, 136, 146, 172, 174, 180, 182, 193, 198, 211, 216, 218, 226, 272
created 29, 35, 36, 38, 49, 61, 67, 70, 83, 92, 96, 103, 114, 132, 147, 148, 150, 152, 153, 158, 163, 174, 192, 198, 202, 210, 213, 214, 233, 269, 270

creating 2, 4, 10, 28, 154, 171, 181, 219, 272
creation 42, 56, 63, 93, 222
creative 14, 15, 46, 66, 82, 126, 135, 143, 164, 178, 187, 192, 198, 217, 274
creator 30, 83, 278
creators 2, 37, 42, 47, 272
cultures 13, 66, 71

D

danger 13, 21, 67, 68, 70, 99, 110, 111, 112, 120, 155, 165, 168, 175, 193, 266
decision 7, 51, 126, 134, 187, 283
deconstructive 132, 135, 136, 137, 138, 177, 178
definition xiv, 10, 13, 21, 25, 33, 76, 81, 87, 113, 116, 120, 147, 184, 221, 239, 283
delight 4, 218, 258
denial 10, 32, 33, 77
deny 31, 32, 151
dependence 34, 148, 149
depression 32, 86, 148, 179
describe 3, 52, 124, 134, 156, 161, 262, 272, 278, 280
description xiv, 3, 132, 224
destructive 132, 135, 136, 137, 138
development xi, 13, 42, 65, 67, 70, 122, 127, 179, 211
difference 15, 19, 27, 34, 100, 102, 103, 124, 154, 164, 198, 201, 203, 204, 220, 224, 226, 236, 247
difficult 6, 7, 38, 89, 90, 95, 115, 134, 150, 162, 163, 166, 181, 228, 231, 240, 253, 257, 283

dilemma xiv, 15, 16, 24, 28, 29, 32, 33, 38, 39, 43, 46, 101, 118, 150, 151, 152, 153, 154, 161, 162, 163, 167, 169, 170, 173, 174, 179, 187
direct 28, 49, 50, 65, 67, 69, 70, 71, 80, 87, 88, 97, 105, 129, 139, 145, 160, 164, 166, 181, 206, 207, 214, 216, 217, 219, 222, 225, 229, 231, 246
disbelief 93, 205
discipline 12, 20, 116, 123, 127, 138, 141, 142, 143, 144, 164, 167, 168, 184, 185, 195, 204
disciplined 90, 127, 141, 143
disciplines 11, 20, 29, 141, 168
discord 51, 140, 245, 248
discussion 1, 14, 15, 33, 36, 46, 61, 87, 95, 100, 109, 114, 116, 118, 125, 137, 144, 147, 156, 157, 173, 187, 211, 214, 230, 231, 236, 244, 268, 279
disharmony 84, 89, 92, 96, 170, 192, 211, 230, 231
distorted 62, 83, 106, 107, 149
distortion 83, 203
doubt 8, 30, 201, 241, 267, 284
dysfunctional 61, 75, 92, 99, 100, 103, 107, 119, 122, 129, 136, 173, 174, 193

E

easy 18, 58, 67, 93, 154, 157, 161, 162, 163, 164, 165, 166, 187, 196, 201, 214, 231, 239, 242, 243, 249, 253, 255, 282, 286, 287

effect 8, 22, 38, 47, 56, 75, 86, 91, 107, 116, 117, 130, 135, 146, 147, 152, 155, 157, 159, 171, 173, 185, 195, 198, 210, 216, 220, 221, 225, 229, 230, 231, 232, 238, 241, 242, 243, 247, 280, 281, 283, 285, 286, 287
egocentric 17, 21, 269
elevated 29, 35, 39, 50, 67, 121, 137, 202
emotion 74, 103, 115, 117, 119, 123, 134, 199, 237, 281
end xiv, 2, 3, 6, 7, 11, 25, 42, 65, 67, 68, 71, 95, 118, 123, 136, 138, 148, 153, 195, 199, 212, 270, 272
enhanced 143, 224, 230, 277
enjoy 3, 38, 173, 229, 258, 287
enjoyable 3, 43, 153
enquiry 12, 20, 26, 43, 253, 255
equals 134, 136, 138, 188, 235
error 15, 28, 29, 31, 35, 39, 52, 71, 76, 81, 94, 116, 134, 143, 161, 163, 164, 187, 188, 195, 254
essence 2, 4, 35, 38, 43, 46, 73, 76, 121, 207, 210, 212, 219, 230, 259, 262, 271
essential 77, 81, 149, 173, 230, 244
event 3, 9, 18, 22, 26, 47, 49, 54, 72, 75, 80, 82, 101, 102, 103, 104, 105, 106, 129, 142, 160, 186, 194, 215, 219, 220, 221, 222, 223, 224, 225, 226, 237, 238, 241, 243, 246, 247, 256, 258, 281, 285, 287
events 15, 19, 28, 47, 65, 66, 76, 85, 86, 89, 92, 94, 95, 96, 100, 101, 102, 103, 105, 111, 122, 129, 139, 140, 142, 164, 165,

178, 179, 183, 200, 207, 217, 219, 220, 221, 226, 233, 236, 237, 240, 242, 243, 244, 246, 247, 278, 279, 281, 283, 285, 287
evidence 7, 12, 16, 25, 42, 44, 47, 56, 93, 94, 98, 101, 106, 107, 143, 150, 154, 160, 164, 190, 227, 243, 253, 286
examine 46, 107, 131, 132, 135, 172, 183, 193, 221, 231, 234, 241, 259, 278, 279, 285
example xii, 9, 16, 17, 20, 21, 28, 32, 34, 36, 44, 46, 49, 51, 52, 54, 56, 58, 60, 61, 65, 66, 68, 69, 71, 72, 74, 75, 76, 77, 84, 86, 87, 88, 92, 93, 94, 111, 114, 115, 117, 123, 125, 129, 130, 131, 133, 134, 136, 137, 145, 146, 147, 155, 158, 164, 165, 178, 182, 183, 185, 187, 195, 198, 202, 205, 220, 226, 228, 235, 238, 239, 240, 241, 243, 251, 256, 258, 260, 264, 266, 277, 279, 281, 282, 283, 284, 285, 287
exist 2, 14, 17, 53, 147
existence 8, 11, 13, 14, 15, 21, 22, 29, 31, 33, 40, 43, 47, 49, 50, 56, 61, 83, 96, 101, 118, 156, 173, 175, 191, 192, 193, 194, 195, 202, 204, 205, 207, 211, 216, 229, 230, 247, 259, 260, 275, 277, 279
existentialism 230, 279
experience xiii, xiv, 1, 4, 7, 8, 9, 10, 11, 13, 14, 15, 16, 18, 19, 21, 22, 23, 27, 33, 34, 37, 38, 41, 45, 46, 49, 50, 52, 54, 55, 56, 60, 62, 64, 65, 67, 68, 69, 70, 71, 72, 74, 75, 77, 80, 82, 83, 84, 85, 87, 88, 89, 91, 92, 93, 94, 96, 97, 99, 100, 101, 102, 103, 104, 105, 106, 107, 108, 110, 111, 112, 113, 114, 115, 116, 117, 118, 120, 123, 128, 131, 132, 134, 135, 137, 140, 142, 143, 145, 146, 153, 156, 157, 159, 160, 164, 165, 166, 167, 170, 171, 173, 174, 175, 176, 180, 181, 183, 189, 190, 191, 194, 195, 196, 197, 198, 199, 202, 203, 207, 208, 210, 211, 212, 214, 215, 216, 217, 218, 219, 221, 223, 224, 225, 226, 227, 228, 230, 231, 234, 236, 237, 238, 239, 240, 242, 243, 244, 246, 247, 248, 249, 251, 258, 260, 261, 268, 273, 277, 278, 280, 281, 283, 284, 285, 286, 287
experiences xiii, 1, 2, 3, 4, 5, 15, 52, 61, 65, 68, 69, 70, 71, 72, 82, 86, 89, 91, 93, 99, 100, 103, 113, 114, 119, 121, 130, 137, 143, 150, 163, 165, 166, 167, 168, 192, 196, 207, 216, 217, 218, 219, 222, 223, 226, 234, 236, 237, 241, 244, 245, 248, 251, 271, 272, 277, 278, 280, 285
experiential 55, 158, 239, 282
explanation 7, 16, 17, 56, 61, 85, 98, 105, 109, 142, 156, 162, 191, 233
explanations 1, 19, 106, 142, 154, 166, 268

exploration 6, 7, 228, 240, 260, 268, 271, 272, 284
explore 1, 3, 6, 7, 26, 143, 194, 195, 197, 202, 227, 231, 272, 283, 287
exploring 2, 5, 42, 63, 235
expression 31, 40, 64, 76, 93, 107, 114, 115, 118, 128, 148, 157, 180, 187, 189, 198, 218, 229, 233, 246, 256, 258, 259, 267, 274, 275

F

faculties 34, 44, 46, 47, 50, 63, 159, 190, 194, 221, 224, 225, 226, 228, 239, 282
faculty 44, 46, 126, 155, 165, 166, 169, 197, 198, 221, 227, 231, 236, 242, 245, 279, 285
fate 5, 30, 130
fault 6, 53, 96
fear 10, 12, 21, 22, 23, 33, 39, 50, 61, 75, 76, 77, 84, 85, 94, 95, 96, 98, 99, 100, 101, 102, 103, 104, 105, 106, 107, 108, 109, 110, 111, 112, 113, 114, 115, 116, 117, 118, 119, 120, 122, 123, 127, 133, 134, 135, 137, 138, 139, 140, 144, 147, 149, 155, 157, 159, 168, 170, 171, 172, 173, 174, 175, 176, 177, 178, 179, 180, 183, 184, 185, 187, 188, 189, 190, 191, 192, 193, 194, 195, 196, 197, 198, 199, 200, 203, 204, 205, 206, 207, 208, 211, 212, 213, 214, 215, 216, 218, 221, 228, 232, 245, 269, 270, 271, 275

feedback 8, 22, 47, 50, 52, 69, 82, 137, 176, 189, 233, 244, 284, 287
feeling xii, 11, 26, 35, 83, 85, 93, 99, 102, 103, 104, 110, 111, 115, 119, 120, 123, 155, 159, 198, 203, 205, 206, 207, 229, 235, 239, 241, 243, 244, 247, 256, 266, 282, 285
flawed 15, 31, 55, 66, 118, 121, 137, 141, 161, 162, 163
free 9, 22, 37, 49, 143, 149, 150, 154, 155, 168, 180, 181, 182, 195, 199, 204, 212, 214, 215, 218, 229, 239, 245, 246, 282
freedom 2, 143, 182, 217, 272
freely 74, 128, 180, 182, 221, 268
frequency 44, 218, 227, 233
fright 99, 100, 101, 102, 103, 104, 106, 112, 119, 193
frightened 100, 105, 115, 119, 193
frustration 34, 43, 137, 148, 182
function 45, 75, 86, 106, 119, 125, 127, 135, 136, 142, 174, 175, 176, 183, 189, 194, 196, 232, 244, 254, 260
functional 52, 89, 92, 99, 100, 103, 107, 119, 129, 144, 145, 175, 260

G

genuine 53, 88, 95, 114, 202, 203, 205, 206, 261, 265, 266, 274
give 12, 18, 27, 28, 30, 49, 55, 58, 62, 66, 69, 71, 72, 73, 74, 75, 80, 83, 88, 90, 99, 110, 118, 128, 130, 134, 142, 151, 155, 157, 160, 176, 180, 182, 186,

187, 199, 202, 208, 210, 211, 215, 217, 220, 221, 222, 223, 224, 225, 232, 234, 238, 239, 243, 244, 245, 246, 247, 251, 254, 255, 267, 268, 278, 281, 282, 284, 286, 287
goal 1, 3, 4, 124, 143, 144, 146, 239, 278, 282
good 2, 6, 9, 10, 22, 27, 28, 33, 34, 37, 38, 40, 43, 58, 60, 66, 67, 68, 71, 74, 75, 90, 92, 93, 98, 107, 110, 112, 114, 115, 117, 120, 121, 122, 123, 126, 127, 131, 137, 141, 144, 145, 147, 157, 158, 160, 163, 164, 172, 173, 178, 179, 184, 187, 189, 192, 194, 195, 198, 199, 200, 201, 203, 205, 207, 208, 211, 216, 229, 231, 232, 233, 234, 236, 237, 239, 241, 243, 247, 249, 253, 256, 267, 273, 279, 280, 283, 285
goodwill 2, 4, 8, 9, 10, 20, 22, 23, 31, 33, 34, 35, 36, 40, 45, 53, 59, 60, 61, 64, 66, 69, 70, 83, 84, 88, 91, 93, 102, 103, 106, 114, 116, 120, 137, 140, 141, 150, 153, 154, 156, 157, 167, 168, 169, 170, 171, 173, 174, 178, 179, 180, 182, 183, 185, 186, 187, 188, 189, 190, 192, 195, 196, 199, 200, 208, 210, 212, 216, 223, 229, 230, 232, 235, 236, 237, 238, 244, 245, 246, 247, 259, 265, 267, 271, 272, 277, 280, 281
guarantee 152, 173, 175

guide 2, 20, 35, 110, 123, 172, 188, 193, 195, 238, 249, 264, 265, 270, 272, 281

H

happily xiv, 108, 142
happy 45, 74, 90, 91, 92, 93, 137, 147, 187, 195, 243, 286
harm 4, 40, 59, 62, 110, 114, 120, 121, 127, 183, 184, 235, 237, 256, 258, 280
harmful 1, 31, 33, 40, 121, 234
harmony 33, 34, 40, 49, 61, 101, 102, 113, 134, 143, 174, 180, 194, 195, 196, 197, 198, 211, 212, 213, 216, 217, 218, 230, 237, 244, 246, 260, 275
health 31, 55, 58, 86, 110, 125, 132, 133, 140, 170, 171, 175, 188, 200, 211, 219, 224, 231, 234, 237, 240, 248, 277, 278, 280, 283
hell xiii, 3, 18, 118, 137
horrible 29, 33, 37, 56, 57, 62, 87, 88, 89, 93, 94, 96, 97, 98, 111, 117, 154, 171, 198, 210
horribleness 56, 57, 87, 88, 89, 117
how 1, 2, 4, 5, 7, 8, 10, 18, 24, 43, 50, 57, 61, 72, 74, 89, 95, 105, 110, 114, 121, 151, 153, 162, 172, 173, 175, 178, 184, 194, 195, 198, 201, 205, 206, 207, 208, 212, 232
human xiii, 1, 2, 3, 4, 7, 19, 29, 31, 33, 43, 57, 63, 66, 73, 94, 95, 108, 140, 141, 154, 158, 167, 191, 214, 226, 240, 271, 284

human experience 1, 4, 7, 19, 140, 167
human mind xiii, 57, 66, 95, 140, 141
hunger 8, 102, 148, 149, 192, 202, 264, 265, 266

I

idea 12, 16, 17, 18, 19, 24, 26, 28, 30, 33, 36, 49, 50, 51, 54, 59, 82, 84, 87, 94, 97, 99, 104, 107, 121, 126, 128, 141, 142, 143, 144, 152, 157, 170, 175, 176, 177, 178, 182, 188, 193, 195, 199, 204, 208, 220, 223, 232, 236, 241, 249, 250, 251, 253, 257, 259, 267, 269, 279, 285
ideas xi, 3, 12, 15, 16, 17, 19, 21, 26, 28, 33, 46, 49, 55, 61, 65, 108, 109, 126, 128, 130, 134, 136, 164, 176, 181, 182, 192, 203, 213, 217, 219, 234, 250, 251, 252, 253, 255, 256, 270, 278
ignore 57, 58, 61, 75, 83, 120
image 37, 46, 53, 73, 159, 163, 202, 221, 261
images 9, 14, 46, 47, 103, 217, 218, 261, 262
imagination 37, 46, 163, 198, 225
imbalance 86, 125, 130
impetus 25, 34, 40, 49, 76, 81, 107, 146, 183, 192, 193, 194, 201, 210, 211, 227, 251, 261, 262
implications xiv, 1, 14, 27, 36, 50, 54, 71, 93, 120, 136, 193, 203, 206, 219, 239, 259, 267, 282
impression 22, 97, 142, 160, 165, 166, 196, 198, 203, 210, 216, 222, 231, 238, 243, 259, 287
impressions 7, 9, 14, 15, 47, 70, 119, 164, 165, 166, 192, 196, 211, 218, 220, 224, 225, 226, 232, 233, 236, 242, 244, 246, 251, 280
independent 3, 14, 23, 142, 159, 166, 197, 216, 229, 233, 246, 265
indication 82, 201, 266
indicator 85, 96, 171, 189, 192, 211, 213
induce 96, 113, 218, 223
influence 77, 81, 86, 111, 126, 129, 138, 139, 209, 226, 229, 233, 247
information 11, 15, 17, 18, 44, 45, 52, 69, 105, 125, 126, 128, 129, 132, 133, 135, 138, 140, 155, 156, 165, 167, 178, 196, 218, 219, 224, 244, 250, 252, 265, 268, 278, 279, 284
inhumanity 84, 94
injury 74, 75, 125, 235
innate 11, 115, 159, 160, 190, 198, 204, 205, 216, 218, 226, 232, 249, 255, 267
innocence 10, 90, 113, 155
innocent 68, 90, 121, 137, 150, 151, 152, 153, 154, 155
inquiry 53, 255
insight 3, 18, 51, 54, 126, 130, 131, 132, 257, 261
instinct 6, 8, 10, 11, 12, 14, 15, 20, 22, 23, 24, 26, 27, 28, 29, 30, 31, 33, 34, 35, 39, 40, 45, 46, 49, 50, 52, 55, 61, 64, 69, 70, 74, 76, 79, 80, 81, 83, 84, 87,

90, 93, 96, 98, 99, 100, 101, 102, 103, 104, 105, 106, 107, 108, 110, 111, 112, 113, 116, 118, 119, 120, 126, 140, 141, 142, 143, 145, 147, 149, 150, 154, 155, 157, 161, 162, 167, 168, 170, 171, 172, 173, 174, 175, 176, 177, 178, 179, 180, 181, 183, 187, 188, 189, 190, 191, 192, 193, 194, 195, 196, 197, 199, 200, 201, 202, 203, 204, 205, 206, 207, 210, 211, 212, 213, 215, 219, 224, 226, 227, 228, 230, 231, 235, 236, 242, 244, 245, 248, 249, 250, 251, 252, 253, 254, 255, 260, 261, 262, 264, 265, 266, 267, 268, 269, 270, 271, 273, 274, 275, 279, 286

instinctive 2, 4, 7, 8, 9, 11, 12, 13, 14, 20, 22, 23, 24, 25, 26, 29, 31, 34, 35, 39, 40, 44, 47, 49, 51, 52, 53, 58, 59, 60, 70, 76, 87, 88, 90, 97, 100, 101, 102, 104, 108, 112, 114, 115, 116, 119, 120, 146, 149, 153, 161, 165, 169, 170, 174, 179, 185, 191, 192, 193, 197, 198, 199, 200, 202, 207, 210, 212, 213, 225, 228, 230, 238, 245, 247, 249, 250, 252, 253, 254, 255, 257, 258, 260, 262, 265, 266, 267, 270, 271, 272, 273, 274, 281

instinctively 7, 32, 33, 35, 40, 57, 59, 73, 90, 104, 112, 114, 129, 147, 156, 173, 191, 192, 207, 267, 268

intellect 44, 52, 65, 82, 124, 157, 181, 182

intelligence 2, 4, 8, 11, 22, 24, 31, 39, 50, 51, 76, 83, 156, 197, 199, 204, 212, 226, 255, 265, 267, 271

interaction 66, 67, 91, 185, 186, 187, 242, 279, 286

internal 7, 241, 284

interpretation 26, 68, 88, 94, 98, 99, 101, 106, 107, 118, 132, 142, 160, 161, 163, 164, 166, 176, 179, 203, 242, 244, 251, 253, 254, 255, 257, 258, 285

invite 3, 240, 272, 284

issues 1, 4, 45, 158, 237, 271, 279, 280

J

justify 84, 93, 110, 117, 122, 123, 128, 137

K

key 30, 37, 41, 49, 56, 72, 85, 94, 102, 125, 138, 162, 186, 196, 200, 207, 214, 217, 237, 245, 247, 255, 281

know xiii, xiv, 2, 4, 5, 7, 8, 10, 11, 12, 14, 18, 22, 23, 24, 25, 26, 27, 28, 32, 34, 39, 41, 47, 51, 53, 57, 63, 68, 69, 73, 75, 83, 95, 96, 104, 105, 112, 113, 115, 117, 118, 126, 127, 134, 137, 138, 148, 152, 153, 160, 161, 174, 176, 179, 187, 189, 199, 200, 201, 202, 205, 206, 207, 208, 212, 232, 234, 236, 242,

251, 257, 259, 266, 267, 268, 270, 271, 272, 279, 286
knowing 7, 8, 11, 23, 24, 27, 31, 32, 33, 39, 45, 52, 58, 67, 80, 116, 118, 151, 152, 188, 220, 251, 252, 254, 255, 256, 257, 266, 268, 271
know ourselves xiii, 2, 4, 12, 18, 26, 34, 47, 179, 202, 271, 272

L

learn 11, 23, 49, 74, 88, 89, 93, 94, 109, 120, 122, 166, 187, 194, 204, 234, 237, 280
learnt 9, 11, 25, 28, 55, 58, 65, 72, 74, 75, 87, 92, 93, 94, 97, 99, 100, 108, 114, 119, 120, 141, 168, 204, 205, 215, 237, 242, 250, 268, 280, 286
lie 153, 154, 155, 172, 173, 188
life v, xi, xii, xiii, xiv, 1, 2, 3, 4, 6, 7, 8, 9, 10, 12, 13, 15, 17, 19, 20, 22, 23, 24, 25, 26, 27, 28, 29, 30, 33, 34, 35, 37, 38, 39, 42, 43, 52, 53, 54, 55, 56, 57, 58, 61, 62, 63, 64, 65, 66, 67, 69, 70, 71, 72, 74, 75, 76, 83, 84, 85, 86, 87, 89, 90, 91, 92, 93, 94, 95, 96, 99, 101, 102, 103, 106, 107, 108, 109, 115, 116, 117, 118, 119, 122, 128, 129, 130, 131, 132, 134, 136, 139, 140, 141, 142, 143, 145, 148, 149, 151, 152, 153, 156, 157, 158, 159, 160, 161, 162, 163, 164, 165, 166, 168, 170, 172, 173, 174, 175, 176, 178, 179, 180, 182, 183, 187, 188, 189, 190, 191, 192, 193, 194, 195, 198, 199, 200, 207, 208, 210, 211, 213, 214, 215, 216, 217, 219, 220, 221, 224, 226, 230, 231, 233, 235, 236, 237, 238, 239, 245, 246, 247, 248, 249, 250, 251, 253, 255, 256, 257, 258, 259, 260, 264, 265, 267, 269, 271, 272, 273, 274, 275, 277, 278, 279, 280, 281, 282
life events 1, 2, 35, 86, 160, 166, 192, 239, 272, 282
listen 22, 34, 40, 43, 49, 68, 71, 95, 106, 112, 114, 120, 136, 146, 163, 165, 172, 173, 177, 180, 181, 187, 188, 189, 196, 197, 199, 200, 201, 205, 212, 213, 228, 235, 243, 250, 254, 256, 260, 265, 266, 268, 273, 274, 287
listening 8, 10, 23, 24, 27, 33, 34, 38, 45, 90, 133, 174, 176, 178, 187, 189, 196, 197, 201, 204, 205, 206, 213, 233, 240, 243, 251, 267, 269, 270, 287
living xi, 20, 21, 23, 25, 26, 30, 32, 35, 46, 65, 87, 146, 148, 157, 165, 172, 178, 180, 194, 196, 202, 213, 214, 228, 236, 267, 270, 280
logic 52, 127, 150, 153, 163, 166, 169
logical 16, 18, 37, 82, 85, 97, 127, 153, 163

M

management 116, 157, 159, 214, 223
manners 64, 66, 67, 68, 88

me xi, xii, 1, 3, 5, 6, 9, 10, 12, 15,
17, 18, 19, 24, 27, 30, 32, 33,
34, 35, 36, 45, 46, 49, 53, 56,
58, 59, 71, 76, 77, 82, 84, 85,
87, 88, 89, 91, 93, 98, 99, 101,
102, 104, 105, 106, 107, 108,
110, 116, 118, 125, 128, 130,
131, 132, 135, 137, 142, 145,
146, 149, 150, 153, 155, 156,
159, 161, 162, 166, 168, 173,
174, 177, 181, 183, 184, 186,
187, 188, 192, 194, 195, 197,
198, 199, 203, 205, 206, 208,
214, 216, 217, 218, 222, 228,
229, 231, 234, 236, 241, 250,
253, 255, 256, 257, 258, 259,
262, 267, 268, 270, 280, 283,
284, 285

ME 229, 230, 231, 234, 236, 239,
240, 241, 243, 245, 247, 248,
277

meaning 1, 2, 4, 13, 14, 18, 21, 24,
25, 26, 27, 28, 30, 33, 34, 38,
39, 42, 53, 54, 63, 64, 67, 69,
98, 128, 146, 149, 152, 153,
162, 166, 188, 191, 208, 214,
249, 250, 252, 253, 255, 256,
257, 258, 259, 260, 264, 267,
271, 273, 274, 275

meaningful xi, 24, 25, 26, 32, 39,
140, 196, 200, 226, 250, 253,
254, 259

meaning of life 1, 24, 26, 27, 28,
54, 63, 64, 214, 249, 253, 256,
257, 258, 259, 274, 275

meant 93, 131, 157, 161, 162, 163,
164, 166, 173, 187, 257

mechanism 76, 105, 117, 122, 127,
128, 142, 144, 152, 153, 154,
155, 156, 158, 171, 173, 176,
184, 188, 220, 221, 235, 262

meditation 34, 46, 181, 241, 252,
268, 285

memories 10, 15, 42, 44, 181, 218

memory 15, 16, 44, 45, 47, 52, 56,
62, 65, 92, 93, 104, 179, 181,
183, 190, 198, 199, 200, 212,
221, 222, 225, 226, 237, 241,
251, 258, 280, 281, 285

mental 55, 58, 74, 75, 82, 86, 123,
125, 132, 133, 137, 140, 150,
153, 171, 175, 200, 211, 219,
224, 231, 234, 237, 278, 280

metaphysics 18, 267

mind xi, xiv, 2, 6, 8, 9, 10, 11, 12, 14,
15, 16, 17, 18, 20, 21, 22, 23,
24, 25, 28, 30, 32, 33, 34, 35,
36, 37, 38, 39, 40, 42, 43, 44,
45, 46, 47, 49, 50, 51, 52, 53,
54, 55, 56, 57, 59, 61, 62, 63,
65, 66, 68, 69, 70, 71, 75, 76,
79, 80, 81, 82, 83, 85, 86, 87,
89, 92, 93, 94, 96, 100, 101,
102, 103, 104, 105, 106, 107,
110, 111, 114, 117, 118, 119,
120, 123, 125, 126, 127, 128,
129, 130, 131, 132, 133, 134,
135, 136, 137, 139, 141, 142,
145, 148, 150, 154, 155, 156,
157, 159, 163, 164, 165, 166,
167, 168, 169, 170, 171, 174,
175, 176, 177, 178, 179, 180,
181, 182, 184, 188, 189, 190,
192, 193, 195, 196, 197, 198,
199, 200, 201, 202, 203, 205,
206, 208, 211, 212, 213, 214,
215, 216, 217, 218, 220, 221,
222, 223, 224, 225, 226, 227,

228, 229, 230, 231, 233, 234, 235, 236, 237, 238, 239, 240, 241, 242, 243, 244, 245, 246, 248, 250, 251, 252, 253, 254, 255, 256, 257, 258, 259, 260, 261, 262, 264, 265, 267, 268, 269, 270, 272, 273, 274, 275, 278, 279, 280, 281, 282, 283, 284, 285, 286, 287

mindful xi, 221, 223, 229, 236, 277, 279, 281

mindfulness 46, 219, 220, 221, 222, 223, 224, 226, 229, 230, 236, 245, 246, 247, 252, 277, 278, 279

minds 1, 4, 6, 7, 15, 16, 20, 22, 23, 37, 42, 43, 44, 45, 46, 49, 50, 51, 53, 54, 55, 56, 61, 62, 64, 74, 76, 78, 79, 82, 84, 85, 100, 102, 103, 105, 125, 128, 136, 166, 171, 176, 180, 189, 190, 195, 197, 201, 207, 213, 216, 217, 220, 224, 238, 244, 245, 248, 250, 254, 258, 262, 263, 268, 271, 274, 282

misunderstanding 16, 56, 70, 88, 98, 116, 118, 132, 134, 142, 176, 192, 257, 269

misuse xiv, 28, 37, 42, 46, 53, 56, 61, 62, 65, 67, 76, 77, 86, 107, 113, 117, 120, 137, 170, 171, 179, 198, 250, 269, 270, 271

misused 64, 77, 85, 96, 189

misusing 40, 64, 70, 82, 96, 139, 170, 188

moment xi, xiv, 5, 9, 10, 18, 24, 27, 38, 82, 85, 105, 106, 126, 131, 136, 153, 164, 175, 181, 199,
210, 212, 213, 219, 236, 239, 245, 258, 261, 262, 279, 282

myself 5, 6, 7, 12, 21, 54, 88, 100, 104, 117, 130, 150, 157, 162, 193, 198, 234, 256, 270

N

narrow-minded 17, 67

natural 2, 4, 6, 8, 11, 21, 23, 25, 30, 31, 37, 40, 64, 67, 69, 70, 77, 81, 84, 85, 87, 88, 89, 90, 94, 96, 106, 108, 111, 113, 121, 129, 138, 140, 141, 142, 143, 146, 147, 152, 165, 167, 168, 170, 174, 177, 179, 191, 193, 194, 195, 198, 202, 206, 207, 213, 217, 220, 226, 229, 230, 234, 236, 237, 238, 240, 242, 243, 258, 260, 268, 270, 272, 274, 278, 280, 281, 282, 283, 285

nature 4, 8, 14, 15, 16, 29, 31, 34, 52, 61, 65, 71, 76, 80, 89, 90, 93, 99, 102, 108, 113, 132, 136, 137, 149, 154, 155, 172, 174, 176, 186, 188, 195, 196, 204, 211, 230, 235, 267, 270, 271

need xi, 16, 19, 38, 64, 70, 75, 94, 102, 122, 123, 129, 133, 134, 137, 143, 144, 145, 147, 148, 149, 150, 152, 154, 157, 167, 168, 174, 195, 207, 242, 286

needs 30, 71, 112, 123, 144, 147, 148, 149, 168, 220, 271

negative 5, 31, 72, 73, 84, 85, 115, 124, 130, 131, 132, 133, 134, 135, 136, 137, 138, 141, 146, 158, 162, 177, 178, 180, 229

nil 54, 253, 273
no idea 250, 251, 252, 253
normal 49, 90, 94, 101, 102, 115, 137, 177, 241, 278, 284
nothing 11, 25, 27, 30, 56, 62, 84, 87, 95, 111, 118, 130, 158, 178, 182, 188, 194, 209, 215, 218, 226, 242, 250, 251, 255, 286
null 54, 250, 254

O

objective 2, 13, 14, 15, 16, 17, 18, 19, 20, 23, 28, 36, 45, 46, 47, 49, 50, 51, 52, 53, 54, 56, 57, 61, 62, 63, 64, 68, 69, 70, 76, 79, 80, 85, 87, 93, 100, 102, 103, 105, 106, 107, 118, 119, 120, 123, 125, 126, 128, 130, 132, 133, 136, 141, 142, 145, 148, 157, 159, 163, 164, 165, 166, 168, 169, 170, 174, 175, 177, 178, 179, 180, 181, 182, 189, 190, 192, 195, 196, 198, 200, 201, 208, 211, 212, 214, 215, 216, 218, 219, 220, 221, 222, 223, 224, 225, 226, 227, 228, 229, 230, 234, 240, 244, 245, 246, 248, 250, 251, 254, 255, 256, 259, 261, 262, 265, 268, 272, 273, 274, 284
objective mind 14, 15, 16, 18, 45, 46, 47, 49, 50, 51, 52, 53, 56, 61, 62, 68, 70, 77, 87, 100, 102, 105, 118, 119, 125, 126, 130, 132, 133, 157, 159, 170, 174, 180, 181, 190, 196, 198, 200, 201, 215, 216, 218, 219, 225, 227, 228, 229, 230, 234, 240, 244, 246, 248, 250, 251, 255, 256, 261, 262, 275, 284
objective reasoning 13, 14, 16
opinion 32, 61, 88, 109, 200, 236, 280
ourselves xii, 4, 7, 18, 22, 30, 32, 33, 34, 36, 38, 42, 50, 51, 57, 58, 59, 61, 67, 71, 74, 84, 94, 108, 115, 117, 138, 141, 146, 147, 158, 167, 168, 173, 195, 207, 208, 212, 213, 218, 220, 232, 258, 270
output 49, 53, 55, 82, 96, 135, 182

P

pain xiv, 74, 75, 81, 82, 85, 136, 175, 176, 189
parenting 32, 90
parents 30, 43, 57, 58, 59, 60, 66, 72, 73, 74, 89, 90, 91, 92, 112, 115, 131, 163
passive 229, 264, 278
patterns 9, 237, 280, 281
people 1, 2, 3, 6, 7, 8, 10, 11, 13, 15, 16, 17, 18, 20, 23, 24, 26, 28, 32, 34, 36, 38, 43, 51, 54, 56, 57, 59, 60, 61, 62, 63, 64, 66, 67, 69, 71, 73, 74, 75, 84, 85, 86, 89, 90, 91, 93, 94, 95, 97, 103, 104, 106, 107, 108, 110, 111, 113, 117, 120, 124, 125, 127, 129, 134, 137, 141, 142, 143, 145, 147, 149, 153, 155, 156, 157, 158, 160, 162, 163, 166, 171, 173, 181, 182, 186, 187, 188, 195, 202, 207, 208, 211, 218, 220, 222, 231, 232,

234, 238, 239, 240, 241, 242, 243, 244, 247, 248, 249, 251, 253, 256, 259, 264, 265, 266, 268, 271, 281, 282, 283, 284, 285, 286, 287
perceive 83, 86, 99, 149, 154, 155, 165, 220, 246, 261
perception 83, 95, 107, 115, 147, 152, 160, 221, 225, 227, 243, 287
person 16, 19, 30, 52, 60, 67, 68, 69, 72, 80, 87, 89, 95, 105, 113, 114, 116, 117, 124, 127, 128, 130, 131, 134, 144, 151, 152, 153, 154, 155, 161, 165, 184, 185, 186, 204, 231, 232, 233, 238, 240, 244, 268, 281, 283, 284
personal 1, 9, 10, 43, 64, 67, 104, 130, 142, 214, 215, 219, 222, 246
philosophy 11, 12, 17, 38, 59, 141, 230, 257, 259, 269
physical 12, 14, 16, 19, 31, 44, 47, 50, 58, 59, 69, 70, 74, 75, 82, 86, 102, 136, 141, 147, 148, 149, 150, 171, 173, 175, 176, 181, 189, 194, 202, 221, 225, 227, 241, 243, 247, 284, 285, 287
pleasant xiii, xiv, 1, 2, 4, 6, 8, 9, 15, 22, 35, 38, 67, 70, 73, 75, 91, 95, 102, 103, 114, 115, 118, 119, 140, 141, 143, 145, 146, 160, 167, 171, 173, 174, 175, 180, 183, 186, 187, 190, 195, 198, 199, 203, 205, 206, 207, 210, 211, 214, 215, 217, 218, 219, 223, 224, 228, 231, 232, 234, 237, 238, 240, 242, 243, 244, 245, 247, 265, 277, 282, 283, 286, 287
pleasant experience 9, 198, 218, 232, 240, 243, 283, 287
pleasant experiences xiii, xiv, 2, 4, 70, 102, 141, 190, 218, 223, 245, 265
pleasantness 34, 70, 115, 202, 203, 206, 229
polarities 44, 133, 134, 136, 177, 178, 180
polarity 132, 133, 134, 135, 136, 137, 138, 172, 177, 178
position 10, 29, 39, 50, 58, 68, 116, 162, 211, 213, 229, 256, 257, 270, 273
positive xi, 22, 36, 38, 63, 107, 124, 127, 130, 131, 132, 133, 134, 135, 136, 138, 141, 157, 158, 159, 160, 167, 168, 169, 177, 180, 186, 187, 193, 204, 211, 219, 220, 221, 223, 235, 236, 258, 279
potential 3, 59, 104, 106, 127, 140, 183, 187, 226, 259, 261, 274
power 18, 50, 59, 72, 73, 99, 124, 128, 181, 186, 212, 218, 227, 233
practical 1, 2, 3, 4, 175, 176, 189, 210, 226, 230, 239, 243, 244, 260, 272, 282, 287
practical solutions 1, 4
practice 18, 111, 157, 215, 219, 226, 230, 236, 277
precepts 46, 217
predicament 35, 36, 49, 56, 121, 137
present xi, 3, 11, 12, 38, 82, 86, 89, 93, 125, 141, 150, 153, 158,

173, 176, 183, 216, 219, 236, 239, 267, 268, 272, 279, 282
primary 9, 11, 12, 22, 26, 46, 50, 61, 65, 77, 98, 106, 118, 124, 129, 132, 135, 182, 189, 190, 191, 199, 214, 232, 242, 267, 286
prisoner 150, 151, 152, 153, 154, 155, 156, 173, 187
proactive 101, 102, 103, 119, 173, 201, 204, 229, 230, 247, 254
problem 13, 31, 35, 38, 42, 55, 56, 58, 60, 62, 64, 83, 84, 85, 94, 96, 98, 107, 111, 114, 116, 118, 121, 123, 125, 126, 127, 128, 132, 141, 149, 151, 170, 171, 174, 179, 183, 191, 234, 235, 259, 270, 279
problematic 84, 85
problems 32, 35, 38, 63, 64, 83, 84, 85, 96, 121, 132, 193, 234, 260, 278
process xi, xii, 7, 21, 38, 42, 46, 49, 113, 131, 132, 133, 134, 135, 136, 138, 158, 172, 177, 178, 180, 226, 235, 236, 237, 238, 239, 240, 241, 244, 261, 264, 277, 278, 279, 281, 282, 283, 284, 285
produce 28, 47, 85, 135, 155, 175, 234, 235, 242, 243, 254, 286, 287
product 11, 14, 23, 64, 66, 80, 102, 106, 120, 141, 145, 148, 181, 244, 247
program 38, 68, 278
prompts 12, 22, 26, 31, 49, 74, 193, 205, 211, 212, 225, 235, 254, 255, 260, 261, 267, 275
proof 12, 19, 25, 28, 82, 87, 94, 147, 182, 194, 216, 253
psychological 73, 92, 147, 148, 149, 150, 152, 219, 230, 277
psychology 63, 141, 157, 158, 159, 167, 169, 186, 211, 219, 220, 222, 223, 230, 235, 246, 247, 279
punishment 58, 59, 90, 111, 141, 176

Q

quality 46, 72, 80, 95, 188, 215, 226, 244, 251
quantum 17, 18, 19, 142, 156, 226
question 1, 2, 7, 8, 18, 20, 24, 25, 26, 27, 34, 39, 42, 43, 44, 51, 52, 53, 54, 62, 63, 68, 69, 77, 88, 110, 128, 140, 142, 143, 144, 150, 152, 164, 165, 170, 177, 183, 187, 188, 190, 193, 200, 204, 205, 206, 223, 242, 243, 249, 250, 251, 253, 254, 255, 256, 257, 258, 260, 261, 262, 264, 268, 269, 273, 274, 286
questions 2, 4, 5, 12, 14, 19, 20, 24, 27, 32, 42, 43, 51, 52, 53, 69, 76, 128, 140, 148, 150, 185, 186, 189, 197, 206, 242, 243, 250, 253, 254, 255, 256, 260, 261, 266, 269, 272, 273, 274, 286, 287

R

reactive 101, 102, 103, 119, 173, 201, 204, 229, 254
read xi, xii, xiii, 3, 6, 11, 19, 21, 76, 98, 200, 204, 220, 236, 249, 253, 277

realities 9, 30, 36, 37, 56, 71, 192, 202, 214, 226
reality xi, 9, 80, 119, 143, 158, 182, 192, 198, 214, 215, 218, 221, 222, 245, 246
realization 10, 59, 101, 105
realized 7, 59, 104
reason 7, 10, 12, 14, 18, 23, 26, 29, 52, 54, 55, 61, 63, 66, 67, 111, 124, 146, 152, 153, 172, 199, 240, 241, 251, 254, 266, 283, 285
reasoning 5, 13, 14, 16, 19, 23, 39, 44, 46, 52, 70, 71, 85, 142, 144, 148, 149, 164, 165, 166, 169, 178, 269
reference 7, 36, 39, 66, 70, 76, 80, 81, 83, 159, 163, 165, 166, 168, 183, 191, 195, 196, 229, 231, 232, 237, 247, 269, 271, 277, 278, 280
reframe 2, 4, 141, 149, 151, 153, 174, 259, 272
reframing 25, 110, 118, 149, 151, 152, 157, 176
reject 28, 29, 32, 127
rejected 16, 28, 35, 39
relationship 51, 72, 150, 178, 186, 224
religion 269
repeatable 3, 198, 272
resolve xiv, 1, 4, 125, 126, 130, 151, 254
response xi, 21, 26, 30, 32, 49, 52, 54, 55, 62, 69, 75, 76, 84, 85, 87, 89, 96, 99, 100, 101, 103, 106, 110, 111, 112, 119, 120, 122, 123, 136, 142, 162, 175, 181, 194, 200, 206, 208, 222, 235, 237, 238, 242, 249, 250, 253, 254, 257, 258, 264, 267, 273, 278, 280, 281, 285
responsibility 58, 96, 124, 128, 166
revolve 16, 17, 185, 269, 273
right xiv, 6, 7, 24, 27, 34, 44, 57, 58, 63, 64, 82, 89, 90, 94, 106, 107, 114, 120, 131, 156, 161, 173, 185, 186, 193, 197, 203, 205, 207, 236, 250, 255, 259, 266, 274, 275, 280
role 3, 19, 47, 50, 70, 83, 116, 175, 177, 183, 191, 197, 214, 242, 254, 255, 266, 286
rules 20, 32, 33, 35, 37, 38, 40, 65, 67, 68, 110, 142, 242, 286

S

safe 33, 61, 110, 111, 112, 115, 119, 120, 179, 205, 228
satisfy 26, 28, 33, 34, 43, 51, 71, 145, 173, 187, 197, 200, 204, 212, 250, 251, 254, 261, 268, 273
satisfying 2, 4, 27, 42, 51, 53, 62, 135, 250, 252, 253, 273
satisfying answer 2, 27, 42, 51, 62, 250, 273
schema 60, 74, 75, 92, 115, 124, 264, 278
schemas 28, 60, 65, 67, 93, 122, 222, 232, 279
science 12, 13, 18, 38, 43, 44, 57, 141, 196, 269
scientific 11, 16, 17, 19, 25, 44, 76
script 38, 49, 89, 91, 95, 114, 117, 122, 123, 124, 137, 158, 159, 160, 179, 198, 210, 214, 221, 222, 223, 226, 228, 231, 233,

235, 238, 240, 241, 244, 247, 264, 281, 283, 285
scripts 28, 50, 59, 60, 61, 65, 67, 89, 102, 106, 116, 122, 123, 128, 138, 159, 171, 174, 179, 183, 194, 198, 199, 200, 210, 212, 214, 219, 222, 225, 228, 229, 230, 231, 232, 233, 235, 237, 238, 240, 241, 244, 247, 271, 277, 280, 281, 283, 285
seeded 93, 250, 251, 254, 255, 273, 274
self xi, xii, xiii, 3, 5, 11, 12, 13, 14, 16, 18, 19, 20, 21, 23, 28, 29, 30, 32, 33, 35, 36, 40, 45, 50, 55, 67, 73, 77, 85, 94, 104, 105, 107, 114, 118, 121, 122, 123, 130, 133, 134, 135, 138, 143, 150, 159, 160, 164, 165, 166, 168, 186, 187, 190, 193, 207, 216, 218, 219, 225, 230, 232, 233, 234, 236, 239, 240, 241, 243, 244, 247, 249, 256, 267, 272, 273, 274, 277, 278, 279, 282, 283, 284, 285, 287
self-exploration xiii, 11, 18, 45, 104, 143, 190, 193, 236, 239, 240, 241, 243, 244, 256, 272, 278, 279, 282, 283, 284, 285, 287
sense of knowing 2, 4, 7, 10, 11, 12, 22, 23, 29, 31, 32, 34, 35, 40, 44, 51, 52, 53, 57, 58, 60, 71, 87, 88, 114, 153, 161, 179, 187, 197, 200, 207, 212, 230, 249, 250, 251, 253, 254, 255, 257, 258, 259, 260, 262, 266, 267, 270, 271, 273, 274

senses 47, 50, 69, 181, 194, 201, 225, 240, 243, 252, 266, 273, 284, 287
sensory 221, 222, 227, 242, 266
serve 50, 55, 61, 110, 122, 133, 136, 175, 211, 231, 235
sexual 29, 31, 40, 115, 149, 161
signal 8, 32, 75, 82, 83, 101, 136, 137, 139, 155, 175, 185, 251, 261, 264, 265, 266
simple xiv, 7, 27, 28, 36, 43, 49, 56, 64, 65, 66, 69, 70, 72, 73, 87, 89, 93, 109, 116, 147, 156, 158, 163, 170, 173, 176, 184, 201, 207, 209, 236, 268, 280, 283
sleep 45, 111, 173, 225, 227, 260
social 55, 58, 60, 62, 65, 66, 67, 88, 147, 150, 163, 182, 268, 283
solution xiv, 26, 32, 38, 43, 46, 55, 85, 117, 118, 121, 127, 130, 133, 134, 144, 151, 156, 161, 163, 166, 169, 170, 172, 173, 174, 176, 179, 182, 187, 189, 190, 194, 195, 196, 200, 207, 210, 211, 212, 213, 235, 253, 255, 260, 261, 262, 268, 270, 271, 273, 274, 275
solutions 12, 20, 24, 51, 76, 85, 101, 113, 135, 147, 172, 174
solve 83, 126, 128, 161, 162, 174, 278
source 11, 16, 24, 27, 36, 45, 50, 51, 59, 71, 74, 75, 80, 88, 109, 119, 120, 131, 132, 146, 167, 171, 172, 174, 180, 204, 219, 231, 236, 241, 253, 255, 265, 280, 285

species xii, 29, 56, 61, 87, 108, 109, 136, 156, 270
startle 49, 76, 99, 112, 194
startled 76
stored 10, 16, 52, 92, 181, 183, 198, 200, 212, 237, 241, 280, 281, 285
story xi, xiii, xiv, 1, 2, 4, 25, 30, 59, 88, 89, 90, 91, 95, 125, 126, 150, 173, 187, 203, 214, 219, 272
strategy 118, 123, 124, 125, 146, 159, 181
stress 37, 56, 86, 125, 179
structures 12, 44, 64, 141, 142, 183, 233
study 9, 12, 118
subconscious 14, 15, 16, 43, 44, 50, 156
subconscious mind 14, 43, 44, 50
subjective 9, 13, 14, 15, 16, 17, 18, 19, 20, 21, 23, 34, 44, 45, 46, 47, 50, 51, 52, 53, 55, 61, 62, 68, 70, 71, 80, 87, 100, 102, 103, 119, 120, 128, 142, 143, 156, 157, 159, 163, 165, 168, 174, 180, 184, 189, 190, 195, 196, 197, 200, 201, 206, 211, 215, 216, 217, 218, 220, 223, 224, 225, 226, 228, 229, 230, 231, 240, 241, 242, 244, 246, 247, 248, 249, 250, 251, 252, 254, 261, 262, 268, 273, 274, 277, 284, 286
subjective mind 16, 45, 47, 50, 51, 52, 61, 70, 174, 196, 216, 228, 230, 240, 261, 284, 286
subjectivity 14, 15, 16, 142, 164, 166, 216, 223, 268

succeed 95, 127, 172
suffer xiii, 36, 37, 39, 41, 74, 77, 81, 85, 93, 106, 118, 171, 176, 185, 198, 199, 200, 207, 213, 270, 275
suffering xiv, 1, 2, 3, 4, 17, 20, 35, 37, 40, 41, 46, 57, 74, 82, 85, 119, 137, 144, 156, 171, 172, 195, 196, 199, 200, 212, 214, 235, 270, 272
survival 12, 29, 75, 110, 147, 156, 175, 176, 191
sustain 38, 83, 118, 149, 175, 189, 191, 195, 210
system 8, 16, 31, 35, 43, 44, 47, 51, 71, 74, 75, 82, 83, 85, 86, 87, 93, 96, 101, 122, 128, 148, 155, 172, 173, 175, 176, 189, 192, 195, 198, 199, 200, 202, 232

T

taught 8, 10, 24, 28, 32, 39, 40, 57, 58, 59, 73, 80, 91, 108, 110, 113, 115, 185, 187, 218, 232, 237, 280
theory 17, 18, 19, 20, 86, 147, 218, 230, 279
therapy 230, 234, 278
think 1, 2, 3, 6, 9, 11, 15, 16, 17, 18, 25, 28, 29, 30, 31, 32, 33, 34, 37, 44, 45, 46, 47, 49, 50, 51, 53, 54, 56, 57, 58, 60, 63, 64, 67, 71, 76, 81, 83, 84, 85, 88, 89, 90, 95, 97, 98, 99, 101, 110, 116, 119, 122, 127, 128, 135, 136, 137, 144, 145, 148, 149, 151, 152, 154, 158, 159,

160, 162, 163, 165, 172, 175, 177, 178, 181, 183, 185, 187, 188, 191, 193, 194, 195, 198, 199, 203, 204, 207, 209, 211, 212, 213, 214, 215, 217, 218, 219, 222, 227, 228, 230, 234, 236, 237, 239, 242, 243, 245, 246, 250, 251, 254, 257, 259, 260, 261, 264, 265, 268, 269, 270, 271, 272, 280, 281, 282, 285, 286

thinking 2, 3, 4, 11, 12, 13, 14, 15, 16, 17, 19, 28, 29, 30, 34, 35, 36, 37, 38, 39, 44, 45, 46, 55, 56, 58, 64, 70, 71, 76, 77, 83, 85, 88, 94, 100, 101, 103, 106, 107, 108, 109, 110, 116, 118, 119, 123, 125, 126, 127, 131, 132, 133, 134, 135, 136, 138, 141, 150, 151, 154, 157, 158, 159, 160, 164, 165, 167, 168, 171, 172, 175, 177, 178, 179, 180, 181, 190, 192, 193, 194, 196, 198, 199, 208, 211, 213, 215, 216, 217, 218, 220, 221, 222, 225, 226, 227, 228, 229, 230, 233, 234, 237, 238, 240, 241, 242, 243, 244, 246, 250, 251, 254, 255, 262, 264, 268, 269, 270, 272, 273, 275, 278, 281, 283, 285, 286, 287

thought xi, xii, 8, 11, 12, 15, 16, 18, 25, 28, 29, 34, 38, 43, 46, 47, 49, 56, 57, 58, 59, 60, 64, 77, 87, 97, 114, 116, 124, 125, 126, 130, 131, 132, 133, 134, 135, 136, 138, 141, 142, 143, 146, 152, 156, 159, 163, 165, 166, 167, 168, 172, 176, 177, 178, 180, 181, 195, 197, 199, 201, 202, 204, 215, 220, 221, 222, 225, 233, 246, 247, 251, 255, 257, 258, 261

thoughts 5, 6, 9, 10, 14, 15, 23, 27, 28, 29, 30, 36, 37, 38, 41, 42, 46, 50, 52, 55, 58, 65, 88, 100, 101, 105, 109, 111, 125, 129, 130, 131, 132, 133, 134, 135, 136, 137, 138, 152, 153, 154, 157, 158, 159, 165, 172, 176, 177, 178, 179, 181, 195, 196, 198, 202, 203, 204, 216, 217, 220, 221, 222, 231, 238, 243, 250, 252, 256, 258, 261, 270, 271, 273, 281, 284, 286

thrive 12, 53, 102, 145, 146, 157, 167, 192, 194, 205, 260, 275

trigger 101, 103, 154, 177, 205, 233, 240, 241, 271, 283, 285

trouble 35, 53, 65, 106, 109, 177, 258

true 2, 4, 6, 7, 8, 10, 15, 17, 18, 21, 22, 30, 31, 33, 35, 36, 37, 40, 42, 43, 46, 49, 51, 55, 56, 61, 62, 77, 83, 87, 88, 92, 93, 94, 95, 111, 113, 123, 131, 132, 153, 154, 161, 162, 163, 164, 171, 173, 174, 175, 176, 177, 180, 182, 183, 192, 195, 205, 227, 230, 232, 236, 243, 251, 268, 270, 271, 272, 280, 286

true nature 2, 4, 8, 9, 22, 31, 35, 37, 40, 42, 46, 61, 62, 87, 88, 93, 95, 113, 153, 154, 172, 174, 183, 195, 230, 232, 243, 271, 272, 286

trust 25, 28, 32, 64, 155, 177

truth 7, 22, 25, 30, 32, 55, 58, 88, 143, 151, 153, 154, 155, 156, 161, 170, 172, 173, 177, 178, 235, 272

U

understand 3, 6, 7, 17, 19, 36, 51, 52, 55, 62, 65, 69, 73, 83, 85, 88, 95, 115, 118, 135, 151, 158, 162, 164, 166, 202, 207, 215, 256

understanding xi, 7, 13, 18, 19, 44, 53, 61, 65, 102, 140, 141, 162, 167, 170, 220, 247, 261

unhappy 85, 88, 89, 90, 91, 92, 93, 95, 234, 256

universe 13, 16, 17, 18, 19, 23, 108, 269, 273

unpleasant xiv, 2, 4, 6, 8, 9, 22, 35, 36, 37, 39, 56, 59, 60, 67, 70, 74, 75, 82, 83, 84, 85, 88, 89, 93, 94, 95, 96, 100, 102, 103, 106, 107, 108, 109, 112, 113, 115, 117, 119, 120, 122, 123, 125, 130, 131, 132, 135, 137, 140, 143, 146, 147, 154, 155, 157, 159, 167, 170, 174, 175, 176, 179, 180, 182, 183, 184, 185, 186, 194, 196, 198, 200, 203, 204, 205, 210, 212, 214, 216, 219, 221, 222, 223, 228, 229, 230, 231, 232, 233, 236, 237, 238, 239, 240, 242, 244, 247, 256, 258, 260, 270, 272, 278, 279, 280, 281, 283, 285, 286

unpleasant experiences xiv, 2, 4, 67, 85, 122, 140, 170, 174, 176, 183, 198, 212, 223, 231, 233, 236, 237, 238, 247, 272, 279, 280, 281, 283

unpleasantness xiii, 9, 15, 23, 35, 37, 41, 60, 64, 83, 84, 85, 94, 95, 96, 97, 99, 101, 115, 116, 118, 123, 138, 139, 159, 170, 171, 179, 183, 188, 198, 199, 202, 203, 205, 208, 210, 214, 216, 218, 228, 231, 232, 233, 238, 244, 247, 270, 281

unsafe 111, 120

V

valid 15, 16, 18, 21, 23, 70, 84, 115, 123, 168, 171, 173, 253, 255

values 14, 28, 32, 35, 38, 59, 60, 153, 158, 220, 246

verified xiii, 4, 268

view 12, 13, 17, 18, 19, 27, 31, 35, 44, 50, 53, 56, 71, 74, 83, 84, 85, 89, 91, 94, 96, 98, 108, 111, 113, 114, 116, 134, 142, 143, 146, 147, 148, 149, 152, 157, 158, 159, 160, 162, 163, 165, 168, 175, 185, 188, 193, 196, 204, 234, 235, 256, 268, 269, 278

voluntary 215, 225

W

want xiv, 1, 2, 3, 5, 17, 24, 25, 26, 29, 31, 34, 50, 64, 67, 68, 69, 75, 77, 85, 88, 89, 90, 91, 93, 95, 106, 108, 114, 115, 117, 122, 124, 126, 128, 135, 140, 141, 144, 145, 146, 147, 148, 149, 150, 152, 155, 157, 163, 165,

166, 167, 168, 172, 176, 178,
180, 183, 185, 186, 187, 188,
190, 191, 192, 194, 195, 196,
199, 202, 205, 206, 209, 215,
218, 220, 224, 234, 236, 238,
239, 242, 245, 246, 253, 254,
255, 259, 261, 264, 265, 266,
267, 268, 272, 274, 279, 280,
281, 283, 285
wanting 72, 114, 144, 145, 146, 147, 148, 239, 265, 274, 283
wants 73, 81, 90, 91, 112, 125, 144, 147, 148, 152, 168, 185, 192, 203, 265, 271
well-being 231, 232, 237, 238, 239, 247, 279, 281, 283, 284
will xii, 3, 5, 7, 9, 10, 12, 15, 20, 22, 25, 26, 27, 28, 29, 30, 33, 34, 35, 36, 37, 38, 40, 41, 43, 45, 46, 47, 49, 50, 52, 53, 54, 56, 61, 62, 64, 65, 67, 68, 70, 71, 72, 74, 76, 77, 78, 80, 81, 83, 84, 85, 86, 87, 89, 90, 91, 92, 93, 94, 95, 96, 99, 102, 103, 112, 113, 114, 115, 116, 118, 120, 122, 123, 124, 125, 126, 128, 133, 134, 137, 141, 143, 145, 146, 147, 149, 151, 152, 153, 154, 155, 157, 158, 159, 160, 161, 164, 165, 167, 168, 170, 171, 172, 173, 174, 176, 177, 178, 179, 180, 181, 182, 183, 184, 185, 186, 187, 188, 189, 190, 192, 193, 194, 195, 196, 197, 198, 199, 200, 202, 205, 207, 208, 210, 212, 213, 214, 216, 217, 218, 219, 224, 226, 227, 228, 230, 231, 233, 235, 236, 237, 238, 239, 240,
241, 244, 246, 247, 248, 250, 251, 254, 255, 259, 260, 261, 262, 264, 265, 266, 267, 268, 269, 270, 271, 272, 273, 274, 275, 280, 282, 285, 287
wrong 1, 29, 31, 34, 35, 40, 53, 54, 55, 57, 58, 59, 60, 61, 62, 64, 66, 68, 74, 76, 77, 80, 82, 83, 84, 85, 90, 98, 106, 107, 108, 109, 112, 113, 125, 131, 136, 142, 158, 161, 162, 167, 168, 171, 172, 185, 187, 193, 234, 235, 237, 251, 253, 257, 266, 280